The Legend of Joseph Nokato

This novel dramatizes black confrontation and the struggle
for power in the new African nations. The stakes are the
economic wealth and the control of the people of those
countries, but the game is played in America and Europe and
ends in the legend of Joseph Nokato. The plan to set up
a Pan-African Movement that will end the exploitation and
wars in the Central African States is abruptly ended by the
hi-jacking and imprisonment of the charismatic President
Joseph Nokato. While being brutally interrogated, Ben Clancy,
the young American international lawyer, learns that he was
the unwitting decoy that placed the president on the hi-jacked
plane. Determined to release Joseph Nokato and equally
determined to discover who used him so cunningly and why,
Ben Clancy retraces through the maze of international finance
the steps that led to the abduction of the African leader. He
is helped by Archie Smith, former All American and Olympic
competitor, who opted out of the Black Movement because he
abhorred violence and because he was certain that the future
of his people lay with Joseph Nokato and the unification of
the emerging African countries. Every step the American
lawyer takes is met with opposition. At the centre of the web
is the mysterious Mr Johnson, the American Mr Five Percent
for Africa, who can arrange and switch oil leases, mineral
rights and economic concessions for the highest bidders. Told
through the eyes of Ben Clancy this story explains certain
key factors in the power struggle for Africa.

Lawrence P. Bachmann

The Legend
of Joseph Nokato

Collins
St James's Place, London, 1971

William Collins Sons & Co Ltd
London · Glasgow · Sydney · Auckland
Toronto · Johannesburg

For Betty Hart Bachmann

First published 1971
© Lawrence P. Bachmann 1971

ISBN 0 00 221477 6

Set in Monotype Baskerville
Made and Printed in Great Britain by
William Collins Sons & Co Ltd Glasgow

Chapter One

We were hi-jacked after taking off from Ibiza heading back to Majorca. Suddenly Maurice Richard had a gun in his hand. One of the Spanish policemen moved and Richard shot him in the leg. The only calm one was President Nokato. His face registered shock and then resignation: this was what he had feared and guarded against. The five of us sat frozen as the sun sank into the Mediterranean and the Algerian coast approached.

I ignite with difficulty but once lit I burn with a steady heat. The fuel was the cell in which I could not stand upright or lay outstretched; the nonsensical questions of the interrogators; the sudden bright lights punctuated by the hammering on the inverted metal bucket held over my head. Even in my fury I recognized that the machinations to make me the decoy who would lure Nokato onto the private aircraft had begun a year and a half ago.

Two months later I was cleaned up and brought from prison to the office of a cabinet minister. He not only apologized but he invited me to return to Algiers as the guest of his government. "I'm afraid you may have formed the wrong impression of my country, Mr Clancy," he concluded. It was the understatement of the year.

I was too dazed to ask if he was joking. I wanted to know what had happened to Françoise.

"She was released a month ago, at the same time as the British pilots. I was told, you knew that."

I nodded. There was no point in telling him that Polly,

my interrogator, had tormented me by saying that she was still being held. I was not certain this interview too wasn't another trick to break me down, like Polly's had been.

"President Nokato? Has he been released?" I asked.

"No, he has not." A frown crossed the dark, terrier-like face of the Minister. "It is a very delicate political situation."

"And Maurice Richard?"

"He is being held. Richard has committed a criminal act."

A gangling man in his mid-thirties with a heavy moustache was shown into the office and introduced as the American Vice-Consul. We left the government building and drove along the wide boulevards. The intense sunlight after my months of confinement made the colors overly brilliant: the red-tiled roofs, the green of the grass and trees, the blocks of white concrete buildings, the brown onion-domed minarets of the mosques, the men in western dress, the women in white gowns covering them from head to ankles. My eyes absorbed it all, especially the bay and the sapphire sea.

"They wouldn't let me visit you, Mr Clancy," the Vice-Consul said. "The Algerians kept assuring me you were all right and would be freed as soon as they were satisfied you had nothing to do with the hi-jacking."

"And the longer they held me the more it proved that I had something to do with it!"

"I didn't mean that, Mr Clancy."

The fact that I was finally free should have made me happy, but it didn't. I got a grip on myself. There was no point in antagonizing the first ally I had. I squeezed out an apology, explaining that I was worried about Françoise and of course President Nokato. The Vice-Consul brought out a packet of letters. The writing was

6

Françoise's, the postmark was Paris, the first arrondissement. They were addressed to me, care of the American Consulate.

"Did you get back all your things?"

"I only had what I was wearing. They returned my wrist watch and wallet." I pulled out my wallet. "All the money seems to be here."

"That's good."

I felt in the small compartment and then searched the billfold before saying: "One thing is missing. It's a small gold pin, a girl's hair-clip with a name engraved on it. It's my good luck charm." I added bitterly: "It didn't do me much good."

"I'll inform the authorities," he said.

In front of the building on the top of the flagpole was the Stars and Stripes. The polished brass plaque on the front door gave the hours the Consulate was open. There was a cheerful sound of typewriters. My host led me up the stairs. He left me in a corner room where the lowered shutters let in a diffused green glow. I pushed open the shutters; I'd been closed in too long.

The diplomatic licence plates allowed us to drive onto the airfield. I recognized the twin jet executive airplane parked at the end in a bay. The British pilots had been returned but the aircraft was still being held. It made as little sense as everything else. We pulled up in front of the metal steps leading into the Caravelle. I thanked the Vice-Consul and said goodbye.

I was in the first class compartment. There were two other men in first class. One seated in the same row across the aisle, the other a row behind. Probably they too were guests of the government. I felt them watching me during the flight. Forty-five minutes out of Paris the steward brought me a radio message. It was from Ralph, telling me to remain on board when the plane landed.

Over Paris I confirmed the landmarks: I had been making this landing in my imagination the past two months. We stopped in front of the long glass building of Orly. The door slid up. The passengers disembarked. There was a clatter on the steps and Ralph was in front of me his hand in mine.

"You've lost some weight," he said. "Still you don't look too bad except that you're pale."

"They forgot to turn on the sun-lamp in my cell. How are Mildred and Junior?"

"He's now called *Troisième*. I'm Junior but only you can call me that."

We grinned at this joke that went back to the days when we were room-mates at college. Ralph Roberts had a triangular face that gave the impression of sloping backwards from a pointed chin, broadening at the cheeks. He had slanting green eyes and closely cropped red hair. He looked like a fox. We made an odd combination. He was a head taller than I. He was thin, always cheerful. I was stocky, brusque. In our senior year Ralph was elected head of the student body; I ran his campaign. He had gone to Georgetown to the Institute of Foreign Relations and then into the State Department. I'd gone to law school. Whenever we met we always picked up the dialogue.

"Françoise is okay. She's waiting at our place," he said. "Let's go."

Ralph held my arm. "The newspaper and television people are waiting outside."

"I don't want to talk to anyone until I get my bearings."

"That's understandable. The newspapers were alerted from Algiers that you were on this plane. The British pilots' story has been running in the newspapers for the past three Sundays. The hi-jacking is still news."

Two cleaning men dressed in gray coveralls were

standing in the opening between the two passenger compartments. One turned on the vacuum cleaner while the other passed us and made his way to the flight deck.

"I think you should talk to them, Ben." Ralph's face creased. "They'll hound you until you do. Better to get it over with. Then they'll leave you alone."

"What am I supposed to tell them?" I snapped. "That I'm glad I'm back and sorry it happened?"

Ralph followed me out onto the top of the movable staircase, talking to me over my shoulder as we went down the steps. My thoughts were as black as the tarmac below.

"Something like that," Ralph agreed. "They're going to throw a lot of rough questions at you. Don't answer them."

"Why not?"

"Because they're convinced you're a CIA agent. That you and Maurice Richard were in cahoots in the hijacking of President Nokato's plane."

A few hours later I got to view my arrival and the press conference on television at Ralph's and Mildred's. At first I didn't recognize myself but then I hadn't seen much of myself lately. I was snarling at the newspapermen surrounding me. My fists were clenched as though I were about to hit them. My hair was long and untrimmed. The open shirt with rolled up sleeves, bloused above the tight belt holding up my too large pants. I needed a shave. There must have been a shortage of news that night: my return ran five minutes. As I watched myself I marveled that I had held my temper. When Ralph turned off the set I was drenched with sweat and became aware that Françoise's arm was about me. I drained the martini in one gulp and gagged on it.

It was an elaborate dinner served on the Swedish modern table I knew so well. A year and a half ago, on arriving in Paris I had spent my first week in this two-room apartment, sleeping on the couch until I'd moved into a small hotel on the Left Bank. Our hosts chatted away as though they'd seen us just a few nights before. Françoise's blue eyes were round as she stared at me with the sad expression of a beautiful clown.

"What are you going to do, darling?" Françoise asked the question that had been hanging over the table.

It was on the tip of my tongue to say that after being away from her for two months she knew damned well what I was going to do but I didn't. Instead I said: "I'm going back to work. God knows what's happened to my practice. At the same time I'm going to do everything I can to get Nokato freed." I pushed the plate away from me and sat up straight. "And I'm going to find out who framed me."

"Why not leave well enough alone?" Mildred asked. Her black bangs, plump cheeks and small rounded chin gave her the appearance of an old-fashioned doll. But appearances are deceptive: there was nothing doll-like about her.

"Because someone didn't leave me alone. Because I was the fall-guy for this setup."

"I'm sure things are being done about getting President Nokato released," Ralph said.

"I'm going to make absolutely certain they are."

When we left, Ralph gave me a large government envelope with the newspaper clippings of the hi-jacking as well as the pilots' three-part story. "Just read them quietly and don't blow your top. Come in and see me tomorrow afternoon at the Embassy. I'll try to answer some of the questions then."

Françoise moaned in her sleep. As my arms went about her she woke with a scream. She cried without effort, with no distortion of her features. After I'd turned out the light she sobbed gently, then her breath became deeper and she was asleep although she still clung to me. In the darkness of the bedroom I was comforted by her, too. The courtyard on which the windows of the bedroom faced was quiet. Through the closed door leading to the studio I could hear the sound of traffic. It was a soothing mixture of familiar noises recalling happy times. It acted like music lulling the top layers of my conscious mind; the fury was there but I could think rationally about what I had learned in the past hours.

Eventually the curtains at the windows became lighter gray blocks. I slipped out of bed and padded into the studio, gently closing the door behind me. The sky behind the church across the square was clear and bright. I pulled open the windows and breathed deeply. Turning I glanced at the canvas on the easel. It was masses of thick paint laid on with a pallet knife. I backed away and got the impression that it might be a portrait. It was different from Françoise's kinetic figurative landscapes. I was pleased that she was working.

Three nights after I had first arrived in Paris, Ralph and Mildred went to a diplomatic dinner. They suggested I try the oldest and most historic restaurant in Paris, the Café Procope. Sitting at the small table beside me on the rose banquette which ran the length of the narrow room was an attractive auburn-haired girl. She watched me struggle with the handwritten menu. She took it away from me, told the waitress to come back in a few minutes and poured me a glass of wine from her carafe. She translated the menu, explaining how the dishes were prepared. We ate, drank and talked while the long oval portraits of eighteenth-century actors of the Comédie française looked down on us. She did not argue when I picked up her check and followed her out into the narrow street.

"Everyone knows that all Americans are wealthy," she explained later, "And besides, if I had acted too independent you might not have asked to see me home."

We didn't take a taxi. When she learned I'd just arrived in Paris, she walked me about the Left Bank pointing out places I'd read about, and across the Pont des Artistes which I hadn't. We stood in the middle of the pedestrian bridge watching the lights dance on the Seine, along with some other couples who had known each other longer and were checking to make certain. We walked through the courtyards of the Louvre, past the police station hidden in the arch, along the arcades of the Rue de Rivoli where some of the shop windows were lit, through the empty space where Les Halles had been and where I could still smell vegetables and fruit in the remaining produce shops.

Her name was Françoise Moran. She came from Aix-en-Provence where her father practiced medicine. A few years ago she had spent two periods of six months in London as an au pair girl, taking care of some children while studying English and the habits of the natives.

She would have preferred the Left Bank but she could not find a studio as good as this one for the price. She had a mischievous gleam in her blue eyes when I struggled to regain my breath after winding up six flights of wooden steps.

"The air is fine up this high," she said, "and there is a fine view. And it does discourage visitors."

I wasn't easily discouraged: I ceased being a visitor. I got so I could go up the steps two at a time and carry on a conversation, even if it was in Braille, when she opened the door. Ralph and Mildred approved of Françoise; so did everyone else who met her. She never completely filled in her recent background. It stopped worrying me when one evening a few months after we had met, while waiting for her to change, I noticed a thick bundle of charred letters in the fireplace. I knew that she had exorcized the relationship she had been having with an older married man. We would never have met but for Ralph's suggestion of that particular restaurant.

Chapter Two

The early morning light filled Françoise's living room. I stretched out on the curved settee that ran under the windows and ended beside the fireplace. I read the three articles written for the British Sunday newspaper. There was little that was new; still some of it bothered me. The pilots explained that they knew nothing about Maurice Richard and his activities. During the past year they had picked him up in the jet plane at various places on the Continent and flown him to others. He appeared to be an industrialist – a European synonym that covered virtually every business activity. He was quiet, reserved and considerate. The pilots had been put up at the best hotels.

The pilots in the articles described me as an American lawyer based in Paris working with Maurice Richard. They had flown me to Geneva and Zurich and with Richard to Madrid, before the disastrous hop to Ibiza for lunch and a swim. I was trying to recall certain things which the pilots did not mention and to which I wanted answers.

As usual after staying the night at Françoise's I walked across to Ile de la Cité. André, the concierge in my apartment house, welcomed me. He was a thin man with a sallow, oblong face. He assured me that he didn't believe what he had been reading about me. He told me that he was at my service at any time. I thanked him and we shook hands again. We had hit it off from the day I had moved in. His cousin, Marie, took care of my apartment.

The apartment had been done by an interior decorator who was in his Louis Seize époque. There were too many small tables with delicate legs holding china too good to be used for ash-trays. After the first week I got used to it, although every time I had a visitor I saw the apartment freshly through his or her eyes and winced. It was a far cry from the sort of places in which I had lived. It was an even farther cry from the kind in which I wanted to live.

The apartment was clean with a slightly musty odour of not having been occupied. I changed my clothing. The suit was too big but I'd grow back into it. I made a few telephone calls. There was a hollowness, bordering on an echo in the connections, revealing that the wire-tapping equipment was old. It gave me a bit more to think about as I walked to my office. When I was late and the traffic was too heavy for a taxi I generally took the Metro, but I was not happy about going underground into a dark confined space.

The coffin shaped elevator carried me up to the familiar door. Coquette, the switchboard operator, jumped up and kissed me on both cheeks. All the secretaries and clerks welcomed me. They had been expecting me: those who hadn't caught my performance last evening on television had read about it in this morning's newspapers. Jean Reinach's elderly secretary started to put out her hand and then leaned over and kissed me on both cheeks. Bringing out a handkerchief she wiped off all the lipstick from my cheeks. I assured her I was fine and that I'd like to see her boss when he was free.

In my office everything was as usual except for the large stack of letters and the dozen white carnations in a vase someone had put on the desk. I sat in the battered high-backed swivel chair which Françoise and I had found at the Flea Market. I glanced at the letters but did not open them. On the side of the desk were foolscap-size heavy folders filled with correspondence, documents, figures, estimates, surveys which I had made for Maurice Richard and his Swiss and American colleagues.

I shook myself and glanced at my watch. I'd been sitting for twenty minutes. Thinking could become a bad habit: I'd done nothing but that for two months. It was time for action. Stopping by Jean Reinach's office I cut off his secretary's apologies that he was still busy, by asking if he was free for lunch. She glanced at her diary and said he did have an appointment today for lunch but she was quite certain tomorrow would be all right, at Émile's at one o'clock.

Walking to the American Embassy I took a long route. On the Champs Elysées I glanced unseeingly into the plate glass windows of the cafés, airline offices, movie theatres and auto showrooms. I knew that the meeting with Ralph would be constructive if for no other reason than it would give me an opportunity to talk out loud. I was weary debating with my other selves. Ralph and I had thrashed out our problems, hopes, plans and expectations during the four years we were at university.

Ethel Holden, his American secretary, kissed and hugged me. She was a tall girl with a solid figure curved at the right places. She stood and sat vertical like the Greek female figures used as pillars. I knew that she was really a little girl in a woman's frame.

"You sure had us worried, pal," she said.

"I had me worried too, pal," I replied. "Don't say it. I'm too thin. I need mother's apple pie."

"Not my mother's," she said. "It was always better at the local bakery."

She pushed down the button of the intercom and when she heard the answering click said: "Mr Roberts, the prodigal son is here." She listened and hung up. "He said for me to amuse you while he finishes with his visitor. They forgot to send up the fattened calf today. What would you like: the can-can or my Hawaiian hulu?" Gracefully she moved her hands.

"I lost my ukulele," I said.

"If that's all you've lost you're okay."

"I haven't gone through the full inventory yet. I'm going to run through the check-list with Ralph."

"He's the boy who can help you." She patted my hand. "We'll soon put you together as good as new. Since you won't let me entertain you, perhaps you'll settle for something as mundane as a Coke or coffee? Or would you like tea?"

"Tea will be fine."

She opened one of the dark brown paneled doors and stepped into a cupboard where she plugged in an electric kettle. Over the rattle of cups and saucers she said that she'd join me. She reappeared with Ralph's black homburg on her head. She was telling me about a Frenchman she'd met who lived in Turkey when Ralph pushed open his door and looked at us quizzically.

"I thought only Jewish gentlemen of orthodox persuasion wore hats when eating," he said.

"We're starting a new sect," Ethel replied. "How about a cup of tea?"

"All right, so long as I don't have to eat that hat. I've got a *yomuika* of my own."

Ethel put the tray on the low oblong coffee table in front of the worn leather couch and armchair. "I'm not talking to anyone. Pick up the intercom too." In answer to her questioning glance Ralph went on: "That goes for everyone, including the Ambassador."

"Sure you don't want to use the secure room to talk?" she asked.

"We'll be all right here."

"Let's take it from the beginning," I said. "Somewhere, somehow, someone put the finger on me."

"I'm not so sure that's the best way to take it. The main question here is, 'why was President Nokato kidnaped?'"

"To turn him over to his enemy, General Moki."

"Then why didn't the plane fly there?"

"It was too far."

The air hissed out of the leather cushion when Ralph sat on the couch. I felt better on my feet, walking about. I still had not gotten used to the idea that I was free to do this.

"That plane could have made the trip. Or it could have flown to a country that would have been more sympathetic to having him extradited to General Moki." Ralph shook his head. "Maybe Maurice Richard was doing it solely for ransom and something went wrong."

"I find that hard to believe," I said. "Still, I'm willing to examine everything. I agree that a man gets kidnaped for ransom. But he wasn't going to be held for ransom and he wasn't going to be flown to the country that wanted to execute him. Why was he abducted?"

"To get him out of the way. To stop him from doing something. It was an open secret that President Nokato was preparing a revolution in his country. Abducting him put an end to that."

"If I go along with that premise – I'm not saying it isn't a good one – it means that someone had the foresight a year ago to start setting me up as the bait."

"You're convinced that your part in this isn't accidental, a coincidence?" Ralph asked.

"I'm convinced. And you know it too. You know more about how these things are arranged and operate than I do."

"You're saying that the CIA or the Deuxième Bureau, were the ones who engineered this."

"It's their function to do things of this nature. I'm willing to bet they were encouraging Nokato to plan his revolt. Maybe even gave him money. Then it was decided that things were all right in his country: that they wanted to maintain the status quo. They had to abruptly turn off Nokato and his revolt. They were gentlemanly enough not to kill him. They just neutralized him by hi-jacking him to Algiers."

Sliding down in the couch Ralph placed his feet on the table and stared at me over the top of his black shoes. "I think you're giving the CIA and the Deuxième Bureau more credit than they deserve."

"They did it. I want to know who selected me and why."

"You're wrong. Neither the CIA nor the Deuxième Bureau arranged the hi-jacking."

"How do you know?" I demanded.

"Just take my word that I know. That I checked the correct sources. I did it the moment I learned you'd been hi-jacked and were being held in Algiers. The boys in the CIA are as mystified as you are and so are the French."

"I don't believe Richard was acting by himself or for himself."

Sitting on the broad arm of the black leather couch I stared down at Ralph. His eyes were partly closed in concentration. He said quietly: "Is that what Richard claimed?"

"We were interrogated together twice by the Algerians. We were blindfolded. At least they had me blindfolded and I assume he was, because he didn't say anything until he heard me talk. I accused him of doing it for General Moki and his government. Richard insisted he was working alone."

"Was he clever enough to have done all this?"

I hesitated. "No, I don't think he was. He always claimed in my dealings with him that he was merely the representative of a group."

Ralph pushed himself a bit higher so he was half sitting, half reclining. "Why did these people want to get rid of Nokato? And why at that exact moment? Couldn't they have done it sooner?"

"I don't believe so. It was the only time he'd ever set foot in that private airplane."

"If your supposition is correct, it's an organization with money."

"A lot of money. Richard spent it as though he were running a one man Marshall Plan."

"All right, a lot of money decided some time ago they wanted to neutralize Nokato. And, apparently, to neutralize him just as he was about to attempt to regain control of his country. Why? And who are they?"

"General Moki, the president of the country, his deadly rival," I said. "The scheme went wrong when the plane landed at Algiers."

"But, according to the pilots, when Richard drew the gun he ordered them to fly to Algiers. He didn't tell them to fly into Africa to Nokato's country."

"Yes," I admitted. "Right from the start Richard was screaming that he was taking us to Algiers. Richard thought he was going to be well treated. I was watching his face when that Algerian Army captain took the gun from him."

"So something went wrong for him too," Ralph reminded me.

"I don't know." I searched my memory to recall

19

certain things. "Occasionally I saw Richard in the exercise yard. He didn't appear too despondent. Still, he was genuinely shocked when he was arrested after we landed."

"Sit down a minute, Ben. I'm getting dizzy watching you circle." Ralph waited until I dropped into a chair. "The primary thing it accomplished was to prevent Nokato from leading a revolt to regain power. Well, that's a good motive. I suggest you concentrate on Maurice Richard. He's the one who can lead you back to his masters, if he has any."

"I agree. I've been trying to recall every detail of every meeting."

"Who and what is Maurice Richard?" Ralph asked.

"He's my height. He's about forty-six. He's French."

"Are you certain?"

I hesitated. "No, I'm not. I'd say that French is his native language although I've heard him speak Italian and it didn't seem to me that he had an accent. He's also fluent in Spanish, German and of course English. Until the hi-jacking I'd have said he was a solid, hard-working, clever, sophisticated front man."

"The change was dramatic?"

"It was quicker and more startling that Dr Jekyll turning into Mr Hyde. He wasn't the same man. This was a murderous killer." I shook my head at the remembrance. "It wouldn't have bothered him to have killed all of us. The Spanish bodyguard was lucky he only got it in the leg."

"And yet he hid that side of himself?"

"He sure did. He was introduced to me by Jean Reinach, the head of my law firm. He had come for advice in setting up a series of companies in various European countries. There were complications regarding controls, taxes and the like. At first Jean Reinach called me in for advice about American law. The things he had in mind were substantial. A great deal of money was involved. I was brought more and more into handling his affairs."

"Well, he couldn't have picked a better lawyer," Ralph said.

"Or a bigger sucker," I added.

"That's debatable." Slowly Ralph got to his feet. I watched him walk to the window and stare out. Absent-mindedly he ran his forefinger along the ledge and glanced at the dirt it gathered. Pulling open a desk drawer he drew out a tissue, wiped his hand and threw the paper into the wastepaper basket. He glanced about the dark paneled room as though wondering if the walls were as dirty as the window ledge. I knew that something important was coming.

"Ben, I know you pretty well. About as well as I know myself," Ralph said. "You're not going to like what I suggest. I also know that you won't do it."

"Then why not skip it?"

"Because in good conscience I can't. Take my advice. Forget the whole thing." He held his hands out. The gold mesh cuff links showed below the sleeve of the blue suit. "Maybe you were put into a pipe-line. Maybe you weren't. Maybe there's an international gang behind Richard. Maybe he is a lone wolf. The point is you've had a lousy experience. Think of it as though you had an auto accident, went into the hospital for two months and now you're out. You wouldn't try to track down the people who were in the taxi that hit your car?"

"Why should I forget it? What do you know about this that you're not telling me?" Ralph's head jerked back as though I'd hit him. He saw the apology on my face.

"It's all right," he said. "Forget I told you to forget it."

"I won't," I hastened to assure him. "I would like to

slip back into my old life and pretend this happened to someone else. Only it didn't. And President Nokato is still being held in Algiers."

"I have my sources and contacts, Ben. I'm trying to give you everything I've learned. They can't understand why Nokato is still there. They think he'll be released any day."

"Then that'll be the day I'll consider accepting your suggestion."

"There's no stopping you is there?"

"Not until I find the truth." I looked at him intently. "I need help, Ralph."

He nodded slowly and I was comforted. I waited as he walked to his desk. "I guess we don't change," he said as much to himself as to me. I didn't reply for he knew the answer. "I suggest you go to this address." Picking up a piece of paper wedged into the side of the desk blotter he handed it to me. "Ask for Albert Giraud. He's expecting you. He'll be able to fill you in on Maurice Richard."

I glanced at the address on the paper. I knew the street and approximately where this number was, but I could not associate it with any particular building. "What is the place?" I asked.

"It's the World Headquarters of Interpol."

Chapter Three

It was a nondescript building which could have been anything from a factory to a hospital; I had passed it many times. I told the attendant at the information desk that I wanted to see Monsieur Albert Giraud. He didn't ask if I had an appointment: he wrote down my name, showed me into a small room and closed the door. The bare walls were dark green, the one window was frosted: it had just a little more charm and a lot more space than the cell I had occupied. I realized I'd become accustomed to waiting: a surprising trait to develop after twenty-eight years of being impatient.

A quarter of an hour later a dapper man about five feet ten opened the door. He introduced himself as Inspector Giraud and invited me into his office. It was four times the size of the waiting room and twice as charming. Loose-leaf file binders filled the book shelves that took up one wall. The floor was almost covered by a worn beige carpet. Inspector Giraud was in his early forties. He had a long block of a face, a wide forehead with three quarters of a crop of waving sandy hair. His eyes were deep gray. He had no stomach and looked as though he did a half hour of callisthenics every morning. His movements, speech and attitude had the efficiency of a man who'd had a time-study check run on him and had accepted all the suggestions.

"You know who I am, Inspector?" I asked after I'd taken the chair he indicated, across from the desk.

"Yes. What may I do for you Mr Clancy?"

I could see him sizing me up. I could have helped him with the inventory but our totals would have been different: five feet seven inches; weight, one hundred and thirty five pounds; black eyes; light brown hair; light complexion; straight nose, strong jaw, causing a slightly grim expression; wide mouth, even teeth; no visible scars. How he put it all together was his department.

"As I understand it Interpol is a clearing house of information on criminal activities throughout the world," I said.

"There are a number of countries which do not belong."

"The countries concerned in my hi-jacking do, don't they?"

"Spain, France, the United States, Great Britain, Algiers belong, but President Nokato's country does not," he said. "As you can well understand, the hi-jacking of aircraft is an Interpol problem. We are having meetings about this with IATA, the international airline organization."

"Then you have a file on the plane I was on."

"Of course. If this was simply a political occurrence, such as a man taking refuge in another country, then it would not fall within our scope. Interpol is non-political. The hi-jacking of an aircraft is most certainly an international crime."

"What are you going to do to Maurice Richard?" I asked.

"Nothing. We are not a police force. We are essentially a central filing system and communication network servicing all the police forces belonging to our organization. We can and do investigate but we have no power to arrest. The individual police forces apprehend criminals."

"Then who prosecutes Maurice Richard?" I asked.

"The Spanish government would like to. So would the British because it was a British aircraft. I do not know what the Algerian policy is."

The scarred top of the desk held a fan of colored ball-point pens. On one side of the desk was a long, lined, yellow pad, on the other an open, large, loose-leaf, black folder, similar to the ones on the shelves.

"Then you can tell me who Maurice Richard is."

Inspector Giraud nodded. "I assumed that is what you were seeking. Of course you're aware of his immediate past." He spoke easily, knowledgeably as between two men of the same profession. I didn't know what story Ralph or his contact had given Giraud but it was

24

apparent from his attitude that he believed I was from one of the American security organizations. I was not going to disillusion him.

Putting his hand on the loose-leaf book he moved it towards me and turned it around so I could read it. "This color tab at the corner of the page means the man is wanted by the police. Another color tab is for a man who is a criminal but not wanted. It's a warning to the police to beware if he shows up. Until the hi-jacking Maurice Richard had a tab of warning. He was released two years ago after serving nine years of a fifteen-year sentence."

My arm reached out for the book. "What was he sentenced for?"

An expression of incredulity came over the Inspector's face. "You don't know?"

"No."

Slowly Inspector Giraud pulled the book away from me. He glanced down at it and then slowly looked up at me. "Either your organization is not careful or they did not want you to know about Maurice Richard. In view of who he is and what happened I would say it was the latter."

I was shaking with anxiety and irritation. I wanted to know the facts. I did not want a lesson in espionage. Yet I knew that I must play along. I forced a smile on my lips. "What had he done?"

"You hire a kidnaper to do a kidnaping, don't you?"

I gasped as though he'd thrown the book into my solar plexus.

"Maurice Richard, and that is his correct name, kidnaped an important industrialist in Lyons and held him for a huge ransom. He collected it. Six months later, inadvertently, he got caught. It was a skilful kidnaping. The victim was held captive within walking distance of his

25

own house and business. Richard had been dealing with the firm for the previous year. He was never suspected."

I thanked Inspector Giraud and left. The sidewalks were a flowing stream of people on their way home after work. I tried to move more swiftly than the current, darting in and out of the gutter dodging the traffic. After a while I slowed my pace. I had not done much walking during the past months. By the time I reached the end of Rue St Honoré the sidewalks were emptier. I cut across into the peculiarly deserted area of Les Halles. The porters, merchants, butchers, truckers had been banished to a huge characterless area near Orly Airport. I stopped at a small flower shop.

Turning into the familiar street I looked up at the top floor. The very top and the sides of the building had a facing of larger bricks. The lights were on in the windows. I pushed the button, the street door clicked. At the same time I heard the bell ring in the concierge's apartment. I made my way through the low, dark burrow which ended in the courtyard in front of the concierge's flat. The staircases to the apartments facing the street were here. The other staircases for the back apartments were across the courtyard. A hand was holding back the lower part of the window curtain. It dropped into place when Madame Albert recognized me. I pushed the button at the foot of the wooden spiral staircase and tried to get as far up as possible before the time-switch turned off the lights. I was caught between the third and fourth landing. Formerly I was able to get to Françoise's by then. I groped my way up. The walls gave off more than a hundred years of collected cooking odors. I found the light switch. I stood gasping for air in front of the familiar aubergine-painted door, before taking the keys from my pocket.

The key did not go into the lock. It had been so long

I'd forgotten which key to use. I tried them all: none fitted. The staircase lights went out. I pressed the button and they went on again. I pressed another button and heard the bell dimly ring in the kitchen. There was no sound. I rang again. I knocked on the door. I was fumbling with my hand trying to find the light switch when suddenly a different light went on. It came from above the top of the door and was dazzlingly bright.

There was a slight sound. I noticed the peep hole newly inserted in the door. A guard-chain rattled. Two bolts clicked. The handle turned and the door opened. Françoise stood there wearing paint-stained jeans and shirt.

"What gives?" I asked.

She motioned me in, then closed the door, turned the locks and flicked off the new switch to the outside light over the door. I stopped her from putting on the guard-chain. She leaned forward to kiss me.

"Thank you for the lovely flowers, my dear." She took them from my hand. "Daisies are my favourites."

I followed her into the narrow kitchen, the window at the end of the kitchen was on the courtyard with a view of the roofs and chimney pots. "Sorry, I forgot to give you the new keys." She took a vase from the top shelf opposite the stove. "I had the locks changed."

"What brought that on?" I asked. "And the peephole and the new lights?"

She told me what had brought that on. A week after her return from Algiers she had come home after being out less than an hour. Taking off her coat she entered the bedroom. The cupboard door stuck. It had a tendency to stick so she dropped the coat on the bed and walked into the studio. Something had changed but she could not pin it down. In the living room everything appeared to be as she had left it. She pulled back the large windows which opened inward and looked down onto the street from the sixth floor.

She heard a squeak. She spun around. She stood frozen waiting for someone to appear. There was a quiet click. The front door had closed. She screamed.

When she got control of herself she rushed to the front door. The landing and staircase were dark. She could hear the clatter of footsteps going down the steps. She pressed the switch, the dim lights went on at each landing. Leaning over the railing she could only see the gloved hand and brown cloth arm of a coat on the banister below, then that was gone. There was the echo of footsteps along the cement passageway and the slam of the street door.

In the bedroom the cupboard door was open, clothing pushed back. Even now it took courage for her to open that door. She couldn't sleep that night although she had barricaded the front door. Next day she had the lock changed, put in an additional one, installed the peephole and the light, which she could switch on from the inside.

A week later she realized what was missing from the studio when Ralph and Mildred showed her the first of the newspaper articles written by the British pilots: it was the photograph taken of the two of us on a picnic at Montfort-L'Amaury. It had been on the bulletin board in her studio amid notices, reminders, bills and letters to be answered. I did not tell her now that the snapshot must have been taken during the month she was held in Algiers. And that the visitor must have been after something else. I leaned across the flowers she was arranging and kissed her.

"Don't get too close, darling. You'll get dirty with paint." Avoiding my grasp she thrust the vase of flowers into my hands. "Here, put these in the living room while I wash and change."

After placing the flowers on the mantel of the fireplace

I took off my jacket and tie. I stood in the door of the bathroom watching her bend over the wash basin. I always liked Bonnard's paintings of nudes in the bathroom and felt a brief regret that he would never paint this. Françoise's hands were groping. I gave her the blue towel. She rubbed her face and her eyes opened wider in mock surprise.

"Just what are you doing, Monsieur?"

My shoes were off. I was unbuttoning my shirt with one hand and unzipping my trousers with the other. "If you don't know, I'm not going to tell you. And then it can all come as a horrible surprise."

We were hungry when we left the apartment but it was too late for the local restaurants. We walked across the bridge and into the maze of the Left Bank.

"Where are we going?" Françoise asked.

"To a place where we can get hot food, music and entertainment."

"I could have given you all that at my place," she said. "You did not like my entertainment, no?"

"That wasn't entertainment. That was heaven."

She slipped her arm through mine, pressing it against her side. I could feel the swelling of her breast. When it is good, as it always was with Françoise, it washes away tension, bringing a communion, so that later I could not recall if we talked or simply read each other's mind.

Le Town House was the right place for us tonight. We pushed past the crowd about the bar. I nodded back to some people who recognized me but kept moving, holding Françoise's hand. A new band was making as much noise as the last group. All the tables were filled and so was the minute dance floor. The maître d'hôtel appeared at my elbow, his mouth set in a big smile which his hard eyes contradicted. He put on an act of being pleased to see us. After telling him we were fine, I asked for Archie.

"He'll be along about one o'clock."

"We'll wait," I said. "Do you have any of those special steaks left, Stan? We're hungry."

He led us to Archie's table in the corner alcove. We had the steaks and the special potatoes and some wine. Françoise was physically relaxed but I could see the worry seeping back into her face.

The dance floor was filled with soloists who didn't seem to be having a good time, at least not by their expressions. The music finished in a crescendo that went through the sound barrier. The floor cleared, a phonograph record of a Strauss waltz came through the hidden loudspeakers. No one here was going to dance to that.

Three weeks after I first got to Paris a letter came for me at the Roberts's. It was the only address I had to give when I left New York. But the letter was postmarked Paris. It was from someone named Archie Smith who wrote that he'd heard I was here and he'd be happy to be of any service. He would like to meet and thank me for everything I'd done for his Aunt Margaret. He suggested I stop by his discotheque, Le Town House. He apologized for writing but had not been able to get my telephone number from information.

"Le Town House is a swinging place," Mildred said when I read them the note. She waddled back into the kitchen; she was eight months pregnant.

"How about all of us going there after dinner?" I suggested.

"I take up too much room."

When Ralph got home from the Embassy I repeated the invitation. He agreed with Mildred that it would not be advisable. He too had heard of Le Town House.

"Who's Aunt Margaret and what did you do for her?"

Mildred asked after Ralph had given us each a glass of wine.

"Search me," I replied. "Where is this place?"

"On the Left Bank, just off St Germain des Près," Ralph said. "Not far from Lipp's and Aux Deux Magots."

Off Boulevard Saint-Germain I took a turn down a narrow street and found myself in front of a polished wooden door with a red neon light over it, "Le Town House." I pushed open the door and entered a small lobby with a checkroom to the left. A few steps led down into the bar where there were the usual stools in front of the high curved stretch of deeply polished wood, a brass railing along the bottom and a lot of bottles behind it reflected in a large mirror. A big man with the beefy flat face of a prize fighter out of training, looked up with a frown while dumping a bucket of chopped ice into a metal cupboard. He was wearing an undershirt with a crop of hair curling over the top and a faded blue apron.

"We're not open yet," he said.

"Sorry. I'm looking for Archie Smith. What time will he be here?"

"After midnight. Come back then."

"That's a bit too late for me tonight. Tell him Ben Clancy dropped by."

A voice from around the corner of the bar called: "I'm here. Come on in, Mr Clancy, and join me."

I walked past the bar, down a couple of steps and into the main room. A few bare bulbs in the ceiling lit the nightclub giving it the atmosphere of an empty theatre. Three waiters wearing faded blue aprons were setting the tables. One of the waiters jerked a thumb in the direction of the corner of the other side of the minute dance floor. I stumbled over some chairs to where a shaded bulb illuminated an oblong table in an alcove. A man was getting to his feet to welcome me.

31

"It's very nice of you to come, Mr Clancy," he said in a Down East American accent. "Welcome to Paris."

"Thank you."

"Please join me."

I slid in and sat on the comfortable bench alongside him. "I take it you're Mr Archie Smith?" I asked.

"You take it right," he grinned. "I got your address some time ago but I didn't want to impose on you. I figured you'd be busy getting settled."

"I'm not sure I'm staying," I said. "I can't find a place to live. Apartments are murder to get here."

"They're difficult but not impossible. Where are you staying now? At the address where I wrote you?"

"No, I'm at a little hotel not too far from here." I gave him the name of it and he nodded.

"Please forgive me." He gestured to the plates in front of him. "I'm having my breakfast. Won't you join me?"

I thanked him and said it was a bit early, or rather a bit late, for my breakfast. At his urging I had a drink. I watched him while he ate and talked. He had the powerful solid physique of a man whose age, height and weight matched the tables on public scales: mid-thirties; six feet two inches; one hundred and eighty-five pounds. His face was oval, hewed in straight lines, under curly black hair cropped close to the scalp so that it fitted like a cap. A small roman nose, broad mouth with full lips, strong chin with a dimple in the middle. His whole manner was that of honest outspokenness and determination. Only his eyes were out of character. They were deep set under heavy eyebrows as though seeking shelter. They were those of a dreamer or poet: they did not match the strength of his face and figure. He was sharply dressed in the latest Italian style and it suited him admirably.

He chatted amusingly about Paris as contrasted to New York. His leisurely breakfast was interrupted by members of the staff. He had quick answers for all, ranging from the chef to the cashier. It was evident that he knew his business. When I complimented him he explained that he'd learned saloon keeping the hard way: from the bottom up.

"Old soldiers may fade away but old athletes are a dime a dozen. So I decided during my university days to have an occupation where I did not have to train all the time and where I didn't have to get up early. I hate getting up early. I guess that's because I was raised in Maine on a farm where I had to be up at dawn."

"Don't you miss America?" I asked.

"No. Do you?"

"I don't know yet. I haven't been gone that long."

"Well, I can tell you they miss you in Harlem. I hear that from my aunt and from others."

I nodded. Now I had it placed although I could not remember his aunt. "The clinic is continuing without me. It even got a grant from a foundation just before I left."

"But you were the sparkplug. You virtually started the Legal Aid Clinic. My aunt wrote and told me how you battled for her. She was going to be evicted."

That still didn't place her for me: there'd been a lot of eviction cases. Archie went on: "You wouldn't take any money for helping her."

"It's free," I said. "Same as a medical clinic."

"When she wrote me that you were coming here I wanted to meet you so that I could thank you."

"I'm delighted," I said with sincerity.

"I'd be pleased if you came here with your friends at any time as my guests." I knew he meant it. I assured him I would.

"Please consider this your local." He explained that in Britain the pub which one frequented was called that: it was the equivalent of a club. "We don't have darts here but the chow is good, better than in England, although that wouldn't be difficult. The beer is cold and we don't have closing hours."

When I asked where he got the name for the night club Archie explained it was called this when he bought the place. "Besides I always wanted to own a town house."

I came back the next night with Françoise. We made a habit of dropping in a couple of nights a week. After the first evening when Archie insisted on picking up the tab, I told him I would not return unless I paid. Archie replied that I had not been paid by his aunt in Harlem. I flatly told him that was different: besides I hadn't been putting out money for salaries, rent, musicians, food and drink; I'd only been donating my services.

Archie suggested a compromise: I'd pay fifty percent of the usual charges; that was the best he would do; any more than that and he wouldn't let me in. Le Town House became my Paris local.

Françoise enjoyed meeting at Archie's table people about whom she had heard and read. It was like being elected to a club and getting to know the other members. The qualifications for admission seemed to be that you were interesting and well known; still that didn't apply to me. I realized that the only criterion was that you'd been approved by Archie.

Chapter Four

A month after arriving in Paris, a fortnight after meeting Archie, he introduced me to a huge black man. In the roar of Le Town House music I did not catch his name although I knew I had seen his photograph. He squeezed in on the other side of Françoise. At the same time several other men joined the table and I began talking to them. It was always musical chairs at the club table. From time to time I caught Françoise's eyes and she would smile happily and then turn back to the man beside her. I could see that there was something about him that made her open up and want to talk and also to listen.

Walking back later, not long before dawn, taking the same route through the Louvre courtyard, Françoise told me that the newcomer to the table was President Joseph Nokato. No wonder he looked familiar. He was the George Washington of his country. He had the distinction of having been taken out of prison by his captors and asked to form a government: the colony was about to become an independent nation.

Under his leadership the country was described as the best run democracy of the newly formed African states. There was a minimum amount of corruption and a major amount of co-operation with America, and other major powers, especially with the former governing country. Schools, hospitals, docks and roads were built. Agriculture, increased exploration and exploitation of its rich mineral wealth were encouraged. A national airline was formed of two Boeings under charter. There were protests and agitation from former colleagues of Nokato's at renewing franchises and honoring agreements with the big American and European companies.

With his charisma and integrity, President Joseph Nokato was able to quell these hot heads. He explained that theirs was an emerging nation that needed all the assistance it could get. When the country had developed technicians, managers, teachers, scientists and professional men and women, they would take over and run everything. Right now the country was taking the giant step from tribal life into the twentieth century. Although he did not encourage a rival political party, still President Nokato was not harsh to those differing from him and his policies. When his second term of office ended, he stepped aside in accordance with the terms of the country's constitution which he had helped to write. General Moki, the chief of staff of the army, was elected president.

President Joseph Nokato brought his wife and six children to Europe to put them into school and to have a holiday. He went on to New York where he was his country's representative and one of the leading African delegates at the United Nations. Less than a year later a military junta overthrew the government but General Moki remained as president: he had engineered the revolt. Nokato's men were either killed, jailed or fled the country. Nokato was declared a traitor, an enemy of his people, accused of corruption, of having drained the treasury of a staggering amount which was now deposited abroad. The constitution was in abeyance under the dictatorship of General Moki. It did Joseph Nokato little good to protest his innocence to his people: nothing was published in the newspapers or broadcast over the radio in his country favorable to him. He joined the growing list of former rulers in exile in Europe.

Unlike most of the others, Nokato did not take these accusations calmly. He remained in the public eye. He was an imposing figure of six feet, three inches, as broad as an overweight football linesman. There was an enduring determined set of his head on a strong short neck. The nose was too broad for the cartilage and moved when he talked. He had marvelous teeth that showed with his infectious laugh. He was difficult to describe: essentially he radiated personality and charm along with a sharp intelligence and a high amount of tolerance. He had the charisma of all great popular leaders.

President Nokato gave press conferences and appeared on television panels discussing the political and economic situations not only of his country but of neighboring states. He invited Françoise and me to accompany him one night when he was interviewed for an American network news program about Africa. Françoise and I were placed in the monitoring booth where we could watch the screens on the mixing panel and also look through the window to the studio. Even seated, President Nokato dwarfed the three men facing him.

"You've proved to be a male Cassandra, Mr President," the *New York Times* correspondent said after the introduction.

The smile faded from Nokato's face. "I would be happier if I had been wrong."

"Many people thought it was just sour grapes on your part when you made such dire prophecies after the new government seized power in your country."

"You're giving me more credit than I deserve. I believe I qualified my remarks. You should know that politicians never go out on a limb."

The three questioners smiled at his frankness. The network commentator picked up a paper. "You didn't qualify them very much. I have your statement here: 'If these men reverse the direction towards which I led my country the economy will deteriorate. There will be rioting in the major cities. The military will be used to put down demonstrations. Violence and disorder will follow.'" He stopped reading. "This and a lot more has occurred just as you predicted."

Nokato waved his hand in protest. "Any well-read schoolboy would rationalize that this would happen given the same set of circumstances."

"But you foresaw the circumstances that would lead to it," the third man, an economist, said. "You also said there would be a food shortage. That relief food shipments would have to be made from other countries. That a black market would spring up."

"There's always a black market when food is scarce," Nokato replied.

"Has this ever happened before in your country?"

"No. We are a very rich and fertile land. There's never been a famine or a shortage of food. In fact we've been able to build up a surplus. The farmers and the cattle raisers were able to trade with the nearest towns and thus improve their standard of living. Gradually this was building to the point where we were exporting and starting to reach a favorable balance of trade."

"It was at this point in your country's progress that you gave up the presidency and went abroad, was it not?" asked the newspaper man.

"My term of office had ended. We were set on a course of fair wind and prosperous trade. When I heard that agreements were abruptly annulled with foreign companies I knew that the wrong tack had been taken. The economy was thrown out of gear. Work stopped. The result can verge on anarchy."

Françoise was more interested in the mechanics of the television studio than in what was being said. I was intent on watching President Nokato as he explained, while apologizing for, what was happening in his now un-fortunate country. Deftly he side-stepped responsibility for the recent breakaway of the most important territory from the republic. Without it being stated it was evident that what had been a model new country in Africa was now like the worst of them.

After the interview we went to Le Town House. On the way I asked my own questions. Nokato answered them frankly. "You appear to have quite a knowledge of African affairs," he said.

"Only what I've gotten from reading newspapers and magazines. It's a fascinating area. I believe it will be the most important one in the world," I said.

"I think so. But of course I'm prejudiced."

What he did not say was that the largest tribe, of which he was Paramount Chief, occupied the territory which had declared its independence. But he realized I knew that.

Several days later, Françoise and I received a formal invitation to dine at his home. We went to an impeccably served haute cuisine meal in the elegant *hôtel particulier* in Neuilly, just outside Paris. There were ten guests. President Nokato apologized for his wife's absence.

"She is in America. There have been problems about schools for our two eldest boys."

"What sort of problems?" I asked.

"They've been in the United Nations School in New York. Now we have to put them into boarding schools. And we want to get them into a good one."

"I know some top educators. We were on the same committee in the Legal Aid Society. I'll write them. I'm certain they'll be able to help."

"I'd be so grateful if you would cable or even telephone them," Nokato said. Later he gave me her address in New York.

Several weeks after this, Archie told me that Nokato's boys were placed in excellent schools in New England. "If they're anything like their father, the school must be delighted to have them," I said.

"The President would like to give you a present," Archie said.

"Please thank him but it's not necessary."

"He asked me to find out what you'd like," Archie insisted.

"I don't want anything, thanks. He's more than repaid me by his hospitality and friendship."

Now a year later we sat at the same oval table in the alcove of Le Town House while the band played, but President Nokato would not be joining us. I knew that a lot of people were blaming me for his abduction, but not as strongly as I was blaming myself. A hand smacked me on the back. My chair was pulled out as I stood up. Archie was facing me. He put his arms about me and hugged me in typical French fashion.

"Man, am I glad to see you." He pounded me on the back until I had no breath left.

Françoise kissed him on both cheeks as he hugged her. He placed his chair between ours and grinned from one of us to the other. He was wearing a beautifully tailored dark gray suit, a shirt with broad blue and white stripes and a dark blue tie.

"Thank you for the beautiful flowers, Archie," Françoise said. "I meant to write you but I was so upset when I arrived that I didn't do it."

"I'll send you some more tomorrow," he laughed. "Right now we need something to celebrate." He got the waiter and told him to bring champagne.

"Ben's been worried," Françoise said abruptly, "that

you might think he was responsible for what happened."

"I am responsible," I said. "I got him together with Maurice Richard."

"Then I'm responsible too," Archie said, "Because I introduced Joe Nokato to you. Life is full of coincidences. Without them none of us would be here at this moment."

Archie went on in this vein until the Dom Perignon arrived: it was the champagne that President Nokato always drank. When some had been put into the tall narrow glasses Archie held up his. "Let's drink to our absent friend and hope that he'll soon be with us again."

After I'd taken a sip I asked: "Where's Madame Nokato, Archie?"

"Right after the hi-jacking she was in Switzerland where the younger children are in school. I heard she'd gone to America."

"I want to talk to her on the telephone," I said. "I should have done it sooner. I've a message for her."

"What is it?" Archie asked and then added: "Sorry."

"It isn't secret. I was the last to see Nokato. I want to tell her how he was."

"Did you see him often while you were in prison?" Archie asked.

"Just twice. The last time was in the shower. It was four days before I was released. Only I didn't know I was going to be released. My regular guard had the day off. The new one got confused about the time of my shower. They were being nicer to me towards the end – I got a shower once a week. I didn't realize how badly I smelled until I saw the new guard's face when he opened the door of my cell. Anyway, the point is that he pushed me into the shower room. Nokato was there having his. We talked while we were both under the shower. It was a good place. We couldn't be overheard."

"How was he? How did he look?" Archie asked.

"Great. He'd been getting heavy. He lost a lot of weight."

"So did you." Françoise slipped her hand into mine under the table.

"It looks better off him. The only other time I saw him, about ten days after we got there, he looked terrible."

"I didn't know you'd seen him twice," Françoise said.

There were a lot of things she didn't know, but there was no point in worrying her about them now that they were over. "The first time the Algerians brought me to Nokato's room. Actually I don't know if it was his room or just where they interrogated him. I was always taken to another room to be questioned. There wasn't even enough space for me in mine." I could see the expression of concern in both their faces. This seemed like a hell of a place to be telling this. But then any place would be, so I went on: "He was unconscious. They'd pumped sodium pentothal or something like that into him. He was talking under the influence of the drug. They'd given it to him because he wouldn't answer their questions, or at least wouldn't answer them satisfactorily."

"What did he say?" Archie asked.

"He fooled them. He talked but he didn't say anything. He was talking in his native tribal language. No one understood a word he was saying. They thought that I'd understand and translate. I told them I understood less than they did."

"Good for Joe," Archie said.

"I've never told anyone about this. Or about the second meeting with Nokato, either." I looked about. No one was paying attention to us. The music was making so much noise that even the latest electronic devices would fail to pick up our conversation.

"So they even gave you drugs!"

"They gave me a lot of other things too," I said grimly. "And it's all my fault it ever happened."

"Ben, everyone who knows you realizes you couldn't do a bad thing or a crooked thing if you tried. You're not responsible for Joe Nokato's being hi-jacked." Archie sounded almost exasperated. "Now, what did he say to you?"

"Just about that."

"Just about what?"

"That I wasn't to blame for the hi-jacking or for Maurice Richard. That it wasn't my fault. That in no event did he hold me in the slightest way responsible." I looked into Archie's black eyes. "I'm not making this up."

"Of course you're not. It sounds like Joe Nokato. He knew you. He realized you'd hold yourself to blame."

"While we were soaping ourselves under the shower so that if the guards came in it would look like we hadn't been talking, Joe said that he didn't think he'd be turned over to General Moki. If they had been going to do it they would have done it earlier. But he didn't know how long the Algerians would hold him. They had stopped interrogating him and had moved him into more comfortable quarters."

"Did he tell you why he'd been kidnaped?" Archie asked.

"He wasn't certain but he thought that Maurice Richard was working for the CIA and the French Deuxième Bureau. They wanted to stop him from overthrowing the government."

"It's certainly better for him to be alive in the Algerian jail than dead," Archie said.

"He is a brave man," Françoise said. "He was extraordinary in the airplane. I'll never forget the expression on his face."

43

"Neither will I," I agreed. "That's why I want to get in touch with his wife right away. Do you have her address, Archie?"

"It's too late. She'll be asleep," Françoise said.

"No she won't. There's six hours time difference between here and New York."

Françoise and I shared the bucket seat of Archie's sports car. He had been in Paris long enough to drive like a Parisian. After turning on some lights I waved Archie and Françoise to the bar and the kitchen while I picked up the telephone. The long distance operator said he'd call me back as soon as he located Madame Nokato.

"Nice place." Archie was standing at the large window looking out over the Seine, the string of lights of the bridges and the buildings across on the right bank.

"I didn't realize you'd never been here," I said. "A bit on the love-nest style." I indicated the delicate petit-point chairs and sofa, elaborate cut glass chandelier, candle holders, the satin wall, the ornate fireplace, the rococo clock and porcelain figurines.

"Can't knock it to me," Archie said cheerfully, gazing about with appreciation. "The view is sensational."

"This is where Paris was born," Françoise said. "The concierge told us that there's a secret passageway in the cellar running to Notre Dame."

I showed Archie the octangular shaped bedroom. Embroidered lace swooped between the poles of the four poster bed, the cover was embroidered to match. The *armoire* was painted the same delicate pink. Under the window was an inlaid Louis Seize desk and chair. The bathroom was almost the same size as the bedroom and about as over decorated.

"One thing bothers me, Ben," Archie suddenly said. "What if your phone is being tapped?"

"That's easy. It is."

44

"Then why make the call here? Let's go to my place and phone," he said.

"I'm not going to say anything secret or private. I'm not going to tell her where and how I saw him."

"That's fine then." Archie looked relieved.

"What makes you think my wire might be tapped?"

Archie made a disarming gesture. "I know enough about police methods here and how Le Service de Documentation Extérieure et de Contre-Espionage, usually called the SDEC, operates."

"That's not a good enough answer," I said sharply.

Françoise looked from one of us to the other like a spectator at a tennis match. She realized that suddenly something was at stake but could not understand what it was or how it had come about.

"No, it isn't," Archie said with a twisted smile. "We can talk about it later."

The telephone rang. I picked it up. The operator told me he had located Madame Nokato at the Waldorf Towers in New York. If I'd please not hang up he would soon have her on. Françoise stopped me from sitting on the bed until she'd pulled back the satin cover. She told Archie she'd show him the rest of the apartment, which consisted of a large kitchen with a breakfast nook.

I heard Madame Nokato's contralto voice. She spoke fluent English with a French accent. I had never met her. At first her tone was cold when I told her who I was. She thawed a bit when I said I had seen her husband not long before I had been released and he had asked me to tell her that he was all right.

"He said that in no event must the schooling of the children be interrupted. You are not to worry about him but just take care of yourself and of the children. Your husband emphasized that he was certain he would be with all of you before too long," I said.

"I am pleased that you are freed, Mr Clancy," Madame Nokato said. "Actually I have heard from my husband. I have had a letter from him."

"I'm very glad," I said.

"I have written to him. And so have the children. But I do not know if he has received our letters."

"Did he give you a specific address?" I asked. "I'd like to write to him, too."

"It is a post office box number in Algiers. If you will wait just a moment I will find it for you."

While I waited I tried to puzzle out why and how he had a post box address. Then I realized it would be better public relations than writing to a jail; the security people picked up the letters in any event before turning them over to the prisoner. She came back on the telephone and gave me the details. I asked how the older boys were doing in school. Her voice took on a brightness: they were doing splendidly and were happy except for what had happened to their father. I gave her my address and telephone number and asked her to please keep in touch about any new developments concerning the President.

After hanging up the telephone I waited and then picked it up again. There was still an echo in it that had nothing to do with the transatlantic cable. "That's all for tonight," I said to whoever or whatever was listening and hung up.

I did not have to repeat the conversation: Archie and Françoise had clearly heard it in the living room where they were waiting. Archie said goodnight. He was discreet enough not to ask if he could drop off Françoise. I told him I'd come by and see him.

"Have breakfast with me tonight. You know where to find me," Archie said, and left.

Chapter Five

With his dignified face, portly carriage and well-tailored suit, Jean Reinach was the ideal customer for Émile's: a man who took seriously the food and drink of a serious restaurant. We spent the first part of our lunch making polite conversation. In the same tone of voice Jean Reinach asked: "What are your plans for the future, Ben?"

When delivered with the delicacy and facial evidence of concern on the part of the questioner no reply is expected. However, I was beyond the point of innuendo and politeness. Having my brains beaten under a metal pail during the past two months had shaken out what little I ever possessed of those qualities.

"I thought I was going to remain working in your office," I replied.

"Of course. That office is there for your use as long as you wish." Jean Reinach raised the stemmed glass, brought it to his nose, smelled the wine with satisfaction and took a sip.

"That isn't what I meant. And it isn't what you meant either, is it?"

"But it is, my dear Ben. That office is yours."

"But I won't be practicing law or working with your firm. Will I?"

"I would not say that, exactly." He cut carefully into the minute lamb chop. He brought the fork to his mouth the way he had the glass. He savoured it with satisfaction.

I pushed myself sideways on the tufted black leather banquette to look at him without straining my neck. With

47

his knife Jean pointed to the untouched steak on my plate and said: "Your food is getting cold."

"That isn't the only thing that's getting cold," I snapped.

His weary gray eyes showed that he understood. "That is not so. My admiration for you and warm concern is undiminished as is everyone's in our office."

"But not warm enough to overcome what's happened." I turned and slashed into the steak.

I was being fired for the second time in less than two years. Paris, the elegant restaurant, the weary sophistication of Reinach were such a contrast to the other time that it made my dismissal in New York stand out sharply; the way a flash of lightning illuminates a night landscape.

I had come straight into Saunders and Croswaithe from law school. Gradually I got the feel of the office and the clients. I was under P. K. Esty's wing: he was a senior partner. He traveled a good deal seeing the clients and I took care of the home office work.

It was satisfactory and sometimes stimulating except that it lacked heart, soul and life-blood. I understood why the partners went off for a few years at a financial sacrifice to work in the government. Corporation law is minus a major ingredient: humanity. Wisely P.K. was the one who made me aware of this by suggesting I fill in for him at a newly formed, free, legal aid organization in Harlem. He did not have the time for it.

One afternoon I was abruptly summoned to a meeting in P.K.'s office. John Gary, the head of Garywood Oil, was in the large corner office, along with P.K. This was the first time I had seen Gary here. Usually we met at his office building uptown or at his Fifth Avenue apartment. Gary grunted at me in reply to my greeting. He was

48

broad, husky, in his sixties, with a heavy mane of white hair. His head hung forward between his shoulders: someone had said he'd gotten that way smelling the earth for oil. His eyes were a dull gray, flat as a fish's.

Sitting behind the desk P.K. was pale and more exhausted than ever as he smiled and replied to my greeting. He was a tall, balding man in his late forties. I had learned that there was no small talk with John Gary. I launched into a summary of the status of the take-over of the other company. John Gary alternated between staring out the window uptown at the Empire State Building and back at me. Every time he glared at me he chomped down harder on his cigar.

"I would say you can make the stock tender immediately," I wound up. "There are no problems with the SEC."

There was only another grunt in reply. I didn't know John Gary well enough to interpret whether it meant yes or no. Placing the file of the proposed takeover of a fertilizer company on the desk, I turned to face Gary. He moved from the window and stood six feet away, swaying like a bull about to charge. I didn't like him and he knew it. He didn't like me either but months ago I had realized that he didn't like anyone. I regarded him as a person with as much soul as one of his refineries. Still no one is all of a piece. I had seen his magnificent Chinese collection on loan at the Metropolitan Museum in the new Oriental wing.

We stood staring at each other until P.K. said: "Why don't you tell Ben what's bothering you, Mr Gary?"

Gary removed the cigar from his thin lips. "I'm not having any God damned communist working for me!"

"I assume you're referring to me, Mr Gary."

"Who the hell do you think I'm talking to, boy?"

Out of the corner of my eye I saw P.K. raise his hand

in warning. "Mr Gary would like to have you explain some things about yourself, Ben."

"I told P.K. I want you fired. If you're not fired my account goes to another firm." Gary pushed the cigar back between his teeth.

"That was Mr Gary's first intention," P.K. cut in.

"It's still my intention," Gary said around the cigar. "But P.K. insisted I hear what you have to say about it."

"About what?"

"About being a God damned Red."

"Mr Gary is referring to your activities in Harlem."

"Oh, that!" I said.

"Mr Gary says that you have appeared in demonstrations at City Hall with various deputations from Harlem. You've been photographed and quoted in newspapers."

"What I do in my spare time is my business," I replied. "When I'm here I work for the office to the best of my ability. And I'm here a lot. I've never neglected your work, Mr Gary."

"That's got nothing to do with it."

"Then what's it got to do with?" I challenged, using his tone of voice.

"I'm not having any punk handling my work who's a nigger lover. This housing crap for them and for the Puerto Ricans! Boy, you've been in my pocket. You've been coming to my house."

"So what?"

"I won't have any friggin' nigger lover around me! Either you're out of this firm or I am. And I ain't stayin' to discuss it."

The door slammed behind him. P.K. winced at the noise. Wearily he returned to his chair.

We regarded each other for a moment. Off in the distance came the mournful hoot of a transatlantic ship followed by the sharp toots of the tugs warping the liner out of its berth into mid-channel. It was leaving and so was I. John Gary and his companies were worth more than a million dollars a year to Saunders and Croswaithe.

P.K. wanted me to take a vacation, to go on leave, and then return to the firm. I thanked him and said it was useless. Gary was mad: in every sense when it came to his prejudices. What I didn't realize was that within twenty-four hours the word was around Wall Street that I'd been fired because I was a Red. I was finished with the big law firms.

I had a message from Mrs Sally Dalton asking me to have lunch in the Lady's Dining Room at the Harvard Club. I had met Sally Dalton a number of times with P.K., usually at dinner parties at his home when she came with her husband, a doctor. She was about forty. She had delicate wrists and ankles. Her eyes were round, quick and knowing, her mouth generous. Even I, who paid little attention to color or style, realized that she dressed marvelously.

Sally Dalton knew what had happened. She told me how hard P.K. had taken it. "You mustn't take too harsh an attitude towards him."

"I don't. My greatest regret is that I won't be with him anymore."

"I felt the same way when I stopped working with him," she said.

Taking another hot popover, I broke it open and buttered it. "I didn't know you'd worked at Saunders and Croswaithe."

"Like you, when I finished law school. I think it was the best two years I ever had."

She talked about P.K., how he had married after completing law school, while in Washington clerking for an Associate Justice of the Supreme Court. Gradually, without anything specifically being said, perhaps by her tone of voice, the expression on her face, I understood that these two people had been in love for years. Now she was engaged in the type of law practice P.K. might have had if he had taken a different course.

"What are your plans for the future, Ben?"

"I haven't any."

"My office has been asked to recommend a lawyer in Paris to follow through on a large estate that is being settled. The litigation has been going on for years."

"I don't know French law," I said.

"It requires knowledge of American law: a good deal of the estate is here. You'd work with Reinach et Frères, the French lawyers."

"In the frame of mind I'm in, it sounds great."

The first month in Paris I followed the dusty labyrinth of French chancery. The Napoleonic Code is different from our law. Jean Reinach, the senior partner, gave me a room in his firm's office. While he helped me, I helped him. He began asking advice and assistance about various matters concerning his American and foreign clients until after a while I was virtually on the staff if not on the letterhead of Reinach et Frères.

Now a year and a half later I was again being asked about my plans for the future. In this instance it was not a question but a statement put politely, that I was fired. Sally Dalton's question had been rhetorical: she'd had the answer for me.

"Jean, I had nothing to do with President Nokato's abduction. I was just the innocent bystander who introduced him to Maurice Richard."

"I know that. But unfortunately there are all manner of ugly rumors that you were handling the President's business affairs and contrived to get rid of him. And that now you have a free hand with his estate."

"That's not true."

Jean Reinach could not have looked sadder if he had been the chief mourner at my professional funeral, which he was. The long aristocratic head and silver hair nodded with sympathy but word was out about me just as it had been in Wall Street. Only this was worse. There are many liberal lawyers in America and elsewhere. But I had been branded as untrustworthy and dishonest. Jean Reinach's firm could be tarred with the same brush if I remained an associate.

"All I have to do then, is to finish up the Benson inheritance case that brought me to Paris," I said bitterly.

"Oh, that's been taken care of while you were away."

"Then there doesn't seem much reason for my sticking around Paris."

"There are many places to visit in Europe and things to see," he said blandly. "You have not made many trips for amusement, have you?"

"No, the traveling I did was not for amusement. But it takes money to travel."

"That should not present any problem." He brushed some invisible crumbs from the starched white table cloth. "This conversation has not gone the way I had hoped, my dear Ben. You Americans rush in. You do not allow one the opportunity to be a bit more –" He gestured with both hands in a circular manner. "Graceful, I think might be the word."

"All right, consider that we've been graceful." I was getting tired of this game.

"You will still be receiving a salary."

"Oh, no! I'm not taking charity."

"Just a minute –"

"You don't have to pay me off."

"No, Ben, I don't. And I am not. You have earned the money. We have not."

"What money?"

"When Maurice Richard expanded his activities months ago, he came to me to explain that he wanted you to handle everything. We would naturally help with the French legal work. This was agreeable to us. We settled on a yearly retainer to be paid by the Swiss bank which handles his affairs. The formal agreement was entered into over two months ago."

Jean Reinach told me how much I was getting. It was more than I'd have made in five years at Saunders and Croswaithe.

"I can assure you that it is all yours," Jean said. "We also have been very well compensated."

"It's for work I won't be doing," I protested.

"Swiss banks are not known to pay unless there is a solid reason. They also mentioned that, due to what had occurred, the projects on which you had been working should be placed in abeyance. Your checks are being sent by them to your New York bank. Perfectly legal and correct, as it is for work accomplished out of France."

I chewed on this and tried to wash it down with coffee and some brandy. It proved to be more difficult to swallow than to chew. The flavour of that much money was fine but I didn't care for the ingredients and how it was cooked. Still I had to admit it had been served with a surprisingly graceful flourish. I doubted if I could digest it.

"How did Maurice Richard come to you as a client?" I asked.

"He came, as most clients do, on the recommendation of someone."

"Who recommended him?"

"He came from Charles Carter Associates, the international firm of accountants. You have had dealings with Attus there. I believe Attus sent him."

"And you had no reason to suspect Maurice Richard?"

"Why should I suspect him? He wanted legal information and help. Everything he asked of us made sense."

"Did you ever ask Attus why and how he had sent Richard to you?"

"No, why should I?"

When I said I'd like to see Attus and learn how all of this had occurred Jean Reinach advised against it. His attitude was that I should consider it all a disagreeable experience with a happy ending: I'd come out of it unharmed and with a large sum of money.

Attus really ran the Paris branch of a world-wide firm of auditors: the chief was an American who fronted for the company. He saw me immediately and welcomed me back. Attus was a neat little man whose gay bow-tie gave him a jaunty air. When I explained why I was here he told me that he had never laid eyes on Maurice Richard until about a year and a half ago. Richard had come to the office for tax advice about setting up companies in various countries. He had given the Swiss bank as reference. After several meetings Attus had told Richard that he should consult an international lawyer. Richard asked him to recommend one.

"And you sent him to Reinach et Frères," I said.

"I did not. It would have been most unethical. We work with many legal firms. Therefore I can't recommend one above another. I provided him with a list, including American and Swiss firms with branches here. Richard chose Reinach. As a courtesy I telephoned Monsieur Jean Reinach and asked him to see Maurice Richard."

So this attempt to back track on Maurice Richard

ended right there. It was a clever and simple way to get the proper introduction to a reputable law firm. Jean Reinach would assume that Charles Carter Associates were Richard's accountants. And it was not chance that made Richard select Reinach: it was carefully calculated like everything else.

Was Sally Dalton a party to this? Had she started me in the pipe-line? The beginning of this chain of events began there. Was it a coincidence that the long drawn out inheritance case abruptly ended when it had served its purpose? I kept coming back to this. It was like having a sensitive tooth with an exposed nerve: I could not keep my tongue off it even though it hurt.

Chapter Six

It was long after shopping hours but the rue Faubourg St Honoré was well lit by the windows of its elegant stores and art galleries. After Place Vendôme the character changed to more mundane shops, cafés, tabacs and inexpensive hotels. As I walked I gradually became calmer and less depressed. I decided that the first thing was to get away from Paris, take everyone's advice and forget the whole thing. Françoise had always wanted to go to Italy and paint. I decided that we would go there first.

My steps quickened when I saw the lights on in the top apartment. Françoise was home: she had the French frugality about wasting electricity. The dirty nylon curtains rose and dropped after Madame Albert, the concierge, saw me. I took two steps at a time; cheating by holding on to the circular wooden bannister and pulling myself up. I got to the fifth floor before the lights went out. I pushed the button on that landing and walked more slowly to the next floor. I rang the doorbell.

Françoise had given me a set of new keys. I opened the upper lock and was inserting the key in the lower when the lights went out. The key did not turn but this was not unusual for a newly made key. I thought I heard a noise on the other side of the door. For a moment I stopped working the key. It was quiet. I forced the key and it turned. The lock slid back once. I turned the key again. With a click the bolt slid back all the way. The knob turned in my hand. The door began to open. With a rattle and jolt the door held. The inside chain was fastened.

"Françoise! Françoise!" I called.

There was no reply. Through the crack of the barely open door I could see that the small foyer was dark; the door leading to the lighted living room was shut. Françoise had to be inside. I banged on the deep purple door, rang the bell, shouted her name. There was no response. For a moment I stood still in the dark trying to decide what to do.

I pressed the button for the stair lights. As they went on I was on my way up the stairs. The fire-door at the top of the steps was in darkness. I felt for the handle. The low clouds in the sky reflected the city lights. Behind me the iron door slammed. It was on a spring. There was no outside handle: only a place to fit a key. The door was designed as a fire escape for the occupants of the top flats: in the event of an emergency they could make their way to the roof and across to the adjoining buildings. But anyone trying to get into the building from the roof would find a handleless locked door.

The edge of the building was bright due to the floodlights placed across the street illuminating the recently cleaned church. Leaning over the low parapet I saw the window ledges of Françoise's apartment and the glow of the inside lamps. The top and sides of the building were faced with large stone blocks set into a pattern with a space half the size of each block between them. I lowered myself over the ledge. The tip of my shoes slid into the recess between the blocks. After the first glance at the street seven floors below I did not look down again.

I was extended at full length against the building. Groping with my right hand I found the crevice between the blocks. I pressed myself into the wall, let go with my left hand to find the matching opening again below and to the side. I moved down and to the right, taking the six inch step between the blocks. I heard the clanging of an ambulance bell, the honking of horns but I shut everything out of my mind, concentrating on the slow movement along the surface of the building. I wanted to come alongside the windows. I did not want to find myself directly over them for I did not trust the strength of my fingers to bear my full weight if I lowered myself down onto the sill. I continued moving diagonally, pushing the toes of my shoes into each crevice. Before moving my other foot I pressed down tentatively to determine if the stone would bear my full weight.

I kept telling myself this was no different than the mountain climbing I had done at holiday resorts. My right foot scraped six inches below seeking the next crevice. There was none. I brought my foot back to its original perch. I felt below with my left foot. There was no crevice. This was as far as the design of large stones went. It ended above the windows of the apartments. I grabbed to my right. I was perched on the last layer of the stone blocks. Out of the corner of my eyes I saw the block of light of the apartment window coming closer. The flood lights placed about the church bounced off the stone to almost blind me.

Finally I was directly over the first living room window. I lowered my hands to grip the insert of stone below. This was going to be the most difficult part. I could not crouch. I had to press forward against the stones or I would lose my balance. The only way I could lower myself was by spreading my legs. My feet were about three feet apart when I glanced to the right at the adjacent window to measure the distance and gauge the height of the window directly below me. I could not spread my legs any farther apart. I dug my fingers into the stone to support my balance. I shifted my weight to the left leg. I slipped the right toe out of the crevice. I could not regain my balance. I felt myself going. I kicked my left foot free. My legs were dangling. The entire weight of my body was on my fingers. It was too much. My fingers were slipping. My grip went. I dropped. The balls of my feet hit the window ledge. My knees bent. I was momentarily in a crouching position facing the window. I threw my weight forward. The window crashed open. There was a scream. I fell onto the cushions of the banquette and went sprawling across the floor.

The screaming continued. For a moment I did not have the strength to lift my face from the carpet. I rolled over. Françoise was huddled in the corner of the curved bench. Her knees drawn up pressed against her face, arms wrapped around, squeezing her into the tightest and smallest position.

I yelled at her. She could not hear me over her shrieks. I dragged myself along the floor. I reached up and grabbed her ankle. She stopped yelling. She became rigid. I pulled myself up on the bench, talking all the while, telling her that it was me. Her muscles were straining so hard as she pressed herself together that I was afraid she might break her spine or a bone in her arms or legs.

There were blood stains on her. Who else was in her apartment? I got to my feet and stared about me.

All the lights in the living room were on. The doors to the other rooms were closed. I staggered to the door of the studio. It was locked. I stumbled across the long living room to the door leading to the minute foyer. This door was also locked. And then I saw the blood on the door and doorknob. I looked at my fingers. The tips were torn. Using my thumb pressed against the side of my forefinger I unlocked the door. The foyer was in darkness. I turned on the light and pushed the front door shut the half inch I had opened it. I managed to slide the safety chain off the rail so that the door could be opened.

I made my way to the kitchen. The yellow plastic dishpan was turned upside down drying. I got it under the tap, put some water in it and went back to the living room. Françoise was still frozen in the same position. I poured the water over her head. She gave a sound like a choke and a sob.

"Françoise, it's me. Ben! You're all right. I'm here."

She sobbed again. I placed the palm of my hand on the back of her neck. She stiffened again. "Don't do that," I said. "You're safe. There's no one else here. Let go of yourself. Darling, you're all right."

I picked her up and carried her into the bedroom, talking all the while as though she were a frightened child who had just had a nightmare. I laid her on the bed, stroked her, talked to her. Gradually the tension left her. Her body uncoiled. Tears were streaming out of her eyes as she stared unseeingly at me. But she would not let me get up. When I moved she clung to me.

"What happened, darling? What happened!" I kept asking.

Her eyes, still unseeing, went to the open door of the closet. As they came into focus she screamed. I put the

60

palm of my hand over her mouth. "Don't do that. There's no one there. There's no one in the entire apartment. What happened? What frightened you?"

I could not get a coherent reply. I decided that she was suffering from delusions by misinterpreting things; putting the most sinister meaning to ordinary occurrences. Mounting a step-ladder I changed the electric bulb over the front door of the apartment, it had burned out. She was certain that someone had rung the doorbell. I agreed that this was possible, but it didn't mean he had disconnected the bulb. It was a coincidence that the staircase lights on the landing and her light were out at the same time, when she tried to look out through the peephole.

She had a sudden dread of the telephone, as though it were a coiled snake. I tried it: something was wrong with it. When I finally got the operator she explained there was trouble with all the telephones in the district; the lines were being repaired.

We left her apartment. Slowly Françoise and I went downstairs, pushing the button for the lights on each landing. At the bottom the curtains of the concierge's window raised, Madame Albert's face appeared. She rapped on the window and quickly came to her door.

"I have your laundry, Mademoiselle," she said. "The laundryman was very annoyed. I told him you were home. He climbed the stairs to deliver it and to pick up your old laundry. He rang and rang the bell. He knocked on the door. He came down and called me a liar."

She glared at Françoise. The concierge knew that Françoise had been in her apartment. I explained that Françoise had been taking a bath. I gave Madame Albert some franc notes: one was for the laundryman, the rest for her. The hairs on the wart on her chin ceased to bristle. She agreed to keep the laundry until Françoise picked it up.

We did not talk in the taxi. Françoise had been imagining that someone was trying to get at her. Still, it did not matter whether it was real or imaginary: it had been real to her. I sensed that she was holding back something.

When we reached my apartment and I had difficulty unlocking the door she saw what had happened to my fingers. She followed me into the bathroom – she could not be alone – and watched me wash my fingers in peroxide and helped put Band-aids over the torn tips.

I'd gotten fragments from her of what had happened but I couldn't put it together. A piece of the puzzle was missing. I started to question her. She began to tremble. I watched her carefully for I didn't want her going into another catatonic state. She could not recall my ringing the doorbell, or my banging on the front door and crashing through the window.

There were blue smudges under her eyes. Her skin was drawn tight over the bones of her face. I had no sedatives in the apartment and told her I was going to get André, my concierge, to get something from a pharmacy to put her to sleep.

"I've got something that the doctor gave me when I came back from Algiers. I was like this then, maybe not quite as bad." She reached for her bag.

"I'll get you a glass of water."

She stopped me from going to the kitchen. "You don't take it that way." My puzzled expression made her continue: "You take it just the opposite way." When I still looked blank she explained that it was a suppository.

While she undressed I sat on the blue satin covered chaiselongue. I talked, but it was just noise designed to calm her, as one speaks to a frightened animal. She left the door open to the bathroom. I got up and folded the satin bedspread, dropped it over the top of the chaiselongue, turned down the sheet and blanket, switched on the lamp on the dressing table, which gave a low warm light, and turned off the bright chandelier.

She slipped into bed. Her auburn hair flowed about the pillow outlining her pale face. Her eyes were wide. The full lips were trembling. I pulled the sheet and blanket and lace cover over her. She would not let me tuck her in. She held out her arms.

"Hold me please, Ben."

I lay beside her and held her. Her lips had the clean taste of toothpaste.

"Close your eyes," I said. "Close your eyes. You're going to sleep. You've got to go to sleep."

Hesitantly her eye-lids drooped and then opened. I continued talking, ordering her to go to sleep until the lids finally covered her eyes. Outside a police car or fire engine went by clanging its bell. Her eyes snapped open and she started shaking again.

"Close your eyes," I ordered. "Don't listen to anything else except me. You can't hear anything but my voice. Just listen to it. To nothing else. You're sleepy. Your eyelids are heavy. You're going to sleep. The medicine is working. It's making you go to sleep. You accept going to sleep. You want to sleep."

The black lashes finally rested on the pale blue tint of her upper cheeks. The trembling was diminishing. I continued talking, repeating what I had been saying. The rigidity was leaving her body. She was breathing deeper and heavier. I slipped my arm out from under her. She moaned but did not open her eyes.

"What happened in your apartment?" Françoise swung her head back and forth. She was asleep but she heard me. "Someone telephoned," I insisted. "He said something that frightened you."

She gave a reluctant nod as her lips formed, "*Oui*."

"You're not completely asleep. You hear me. You can answer. What did the man say?"

"*Il a eu un voix affreux. . . . Il a dit, je dois insister que vous oubliez tout au sujet d'Alger, de Maurice Richard, de President Nokato . . . ces choses ne sont jamais arrivées . . .*" The words died on her lips. She moaned and shuddered. She breathed in heavily, exhaling slowly. She was sinking deeper into sleep.

"The man said something else." I shook her. "He frightened you. What did he say exactly?"

"*. . . quelque chose atroce va arriver a toi . . . a moi . . .*"

I lowered her head to the peach-colored pillow case. There was no point in questioning her more. She could not hear me. I went into the living room. Suddenly I was trembling. I put on an overcoat although the apartment was warm. I huddled in the armchair facing the view across the river but I didn't look at it.

When Françoise had first heard the strange menacing voice she had hung up. The phone rang. She answered it, hoping it was me. The man ordered her not to hang up. He told her that if she could not get me to mind my own business, something worse than hi-jacking would happen to both of us. She slammed down the receiver. The telephone rang repeatedly. I realized that this was about the time I had been calling her. Then came the doorbell. When she went to the door there was no light on the stairs, nor did her newly installed light go on. She was convinced that the unknown man was standing on the other side. And then I arrived and tried to get in.

Chapter Seven

I left word with Jean Reinach's secretary that I was taking his suggestion of going on a trip. However, I didn't mention that I wasn't accepting all of his advice: it was going to be a short trip and to a place I'd previously visited, disastrously. I tried to get Françoise to come with me but the thought of returning there almost threw her into hysterics again. She begged me not to return there. I assured her that nothing would happen to me; besides I wanted to pick up our clothing. The next day I flew to Palma.

Walking into the lobby of the hotel in Majorca brought me back full circle. It was too much of a perfect circle.

I asked for a room but the manager insisted I have the same suite I had had with Françoise, at the price of a single room. The manager looked like the typical gigolo in movies of the thirties that are shown on the late-late-very late television shows. His manner matched his looks. But looks are deceiving; he could not have been more helpful.

"We did not lose any money by your abrupt departure, Mr Clancy. Or by the reservations we were holding for the three additional de luxe suites," he replied to my question.

"Did those three men ever show up?" I asked. "They were due in the day after we abruptly departed."

He corrected me: "They were originally to have arrived the same day you did. I remember Señor Richard explaining that they had unfortunately been delayed for two days. He paid for the suites while they remained unoccupied. We were paid for the whole period even when you did not return from Ibiza."

"Not by Richard. He was in jail with me in Algeria."

"Yes, by Señor Richard." The heavily oiled hair glistened, catching the highlights of the sun coming through the blinds. "We were paid by a bank draft in advance. It was always more than enough to cover everything including meals and drinks."

"Is that usual?"

"It is done," he said, "But it is not usual. Señor Richard's bank did this each time it wrote for reservations. Each time the bank advance was more than substantial. We returned money to them."

"Now what would be the purpose of that?" I speculated. "Richard always had plenty of money on him. Besides you would have accepted his check, wouldn't you?"

"Yes. When the first reservation was made it specified the exact suites. I was not going to give them to him because one was the suite we always held for President Nokato. And then I learned that it was indeed for the President."

I was getting more details and figures but I didn't know where to fit them. The angle of incidence was equal to the angle of something else, but what else? Why would Richard have arranged for his bank to overpay in advance? The obvious answer was that whoever was controlling Maurice Richard did not trust him with that much money. But I quickly erased that: the amount spent on these hotel reservations was nothing compared to what Richard spent when I'd been with him. Then it dawned on me that I had never seen him write and sign a bank check. He always paid with cash. Why had he not written a check on the bank instead of the Swiss bank paying everything in advance?

"It was the International Confederal Bank located in Zurich, wasn't it?" I asked.

He opened the file on his desk marked "Richard, Maurice", and glanced through some papers. I recognized the letterhead upside down. He nodded. "I have never heard of that bank. But then there are a great many banks in Switzerland and they all have money. Such being the nature of banks. Especially Swiss banks."

I thanked him for the information and asked about the next flight to Ibiza. I would be returning this time on the same airplane.

"We miss the President," the manager said. "He is a fine gentleman. Just to look at him makes you feel good. He has such a happy face. *Muy sympatico.*"

"I couldn't agree more."

At the hotel in Ibiza I found the manager. He had a square figure with arms that hung too long. This, added to a wrinkled brow, bald head and flat nose, gave him a simian appearance. I could see the flicker of recognition before I introduced myself. His English was better than my Spanish.

"The day we were here we had lunch in the garden," I said.

"Unfortunately, I was not in the garden that day," he said.

"No, but the waiters were. We had drinks before ordering lunch. Maurice Richard was the only one who was really drinking. He had two scotches. The rest of us had *sangria.*"

Through the window behind the manager I could see the garden. Gravel paths led to the tables, the whole area was bordered with bright colored flowers. The shade was provided by palm and cassia trees, their pods hanging from the branches . . .

At first Maurice Richard had said he did not want to eat.

67

He would wait for us inside; he wasn't hungry. He was dressed in a dark business suit; a contrast to us for we were in sports clothing. Françoise was wearing a bikini under a short wrap around skirt and jacket. President Nokato had put his arm about Maurice Richard's shoulders and insisted that he must have a drink. It would do him good.

So we'd all sat in the garden. Maurice Richard looked uncomfortable and unhappy, like a character who had stumbled into the wrong play. People at other tables, even the pilots hidden out of sight behind some bushes, were wearing sports shirts. The two, ever present, bodyguards whom the Spanish government had assigned to President Nokato were discreetly sitting on the other side of the flower bed facing the four of us: Nokato, Richard, Françoise and myself. President Nokato firmly informed Richard that this was his party.

The drinks came. Richard knocked his back and quickly had another. He was pale. Françoise and I were concerned about him. He assured us that he was fine but he would eat nothing. He remained sitting with us until a bellboy appeared on the steps. Before the boy had reached the table Richard excused himself and hurried into the hotel, the boy at his heels. We were eating and drinking. I did not think anything of it at the time. However I had thought a lot of it since then.

"Richard received a telephone call," I said to the manager. "I want to find out from whom."

The hotel manager's brow wrinkled and he looked even more like a monkey. Abruptly I thought of something: "Now I realize Richard didn't receive a phone call. He must have placed one. He was waiting for it to go through. That's why he didn't want to sit with us. That's why he disappeared for a few minutes when we first arrived here, at the hotel." My English was going too fast. I slowed down. "The telephone operator! She would have a record of all calls made from here, would she not?"

"Si, if it was not a local call to someone on this island," he agreed.

"Let's just hope and pray that it wasn't. Could you please ask her to check her records for that day. It was about three o'clock, I'd say, when he made the call."

While he went in to talk to the operator I paced up and down the shaded veranda, in and around the green and yellow covered wicker furniture. When he reappeared he had a slip of paper in his hand. He would not talk until we returned to his cubicle of an office and he closed the door. He handed me the piece of paper on which were written some numbers.

"It is a telephone number in Palma," the manager said. "The operator remembered it well because the guest gave her a very large tip. He insisted the call was urgent. He was angry with her because the lines to Majorca were engaged and she could not immediately obtain the number. He kept telling her it was vital. It was most important. And then, when she did get the number, he spoke for only a few seconds. She was afraid he had been disconnected. He told her it was all right. He had completed the call. But she remembered he was even more nervous than before."

"Is there anything else she remembers?" I asked. "Anything. Everything she has told you is important. Any little thing else."

"I shall ask her if you wish." He got up. I gave him a large peseta note to give to her.

When he returned he shook his head. "The only other thing she can think of, is that Señor Richard was irritated when she told him she would put the telephone charge on the lunch bill. He paid for it right then."

For a moment I could not understand this. Then I remembered that Nokato had insisted that he was picking up the tab. Richard did not want him to know about the telephone call. I thanked the manager and shook hands. He replied that he was pleased to be of service and handed me back the bills I tried to press into his hand.

I was breathing more quickly as I got into the taxi to return to the Ibiza airport. Everything appeared brighter and sharper, the way things do when you're about to start a race. I had picked up the trail. I was off in search of Maurice Richard's masters.

The manager of the Palma hotel was not in the hotel when I got back. I told the receptionist not to disturb him at his home: it was not urgent. I would see him when he returned to the hotel at dinner time, about an hour before midnight. I went up to my suite to lay down and rest. I stretched out on one of the twin beds.

Turning my back to the empty bed I stared at the telephone alongside the reading light on the white and gold night table. The slip of paper was in my pocket. I had memorized the number. I had a plan. I went over it again in my mind. I could not afford an error.

Shifting on my back I stared at the ceiling. On the floor just above was an identical suite to this one. I had had the suite above on my first trip to Palma five months ago. President Nokato had been in the adjoining suite both times. The next time we returned to Palma, Françoise had been with me and we had been given this suite. Richard had taken the one above with the connection door to Nokato's. Why?

On our first trip to Madrid we had eaten at Horcher's the

first two nights. Richard liked eating there. The second night he had given a large dinner party for some government officials and bankers. I was talking to a steel haired man with rimless pince-nez glasses, who reminded me of photographs of Woodrow Wilson, when a hand as broad as my back hit me across the shoulders. Everyone was getting to his feet, nodding and smiling to the man behind me. I turned to see President Joseph Nokato and lost my hand in his enormous one.

"How long have you been here, Ben?"

"Since yesterday."

I introduced him to Maurice Richard and to the others at the table. President Nokato knew a few of the guests. Everyone knew who he was.

"You should have let me know you were coming." He sounded hurt.

"I didn't know it myself," I explained. "I'm working with Mr Richard and we suddenly had to come here on business."

"Madrid is my stamping ground. I'll show you the town, and your friend, Mr Richard, of course."

I tried to explain that we were only here for a short trip and had a lot of work but President Nokato would have none of that. He gave me his telephone number and got the name of our hotel. He insisted that we get together for lunch tomorrow.

Nokato went back to his table on the other side of the restaurant where he was dining with a magnificent looking girl. She had jet black hair gathered low on the arch of her long neck, superb skin, huge black eyes, wide mouth. Only the top of her dark red dress showed above the white table cloth but that was more than enough.

When our party broke up President Nokato called me over. After introducing me to Señorita Lola Tone, he insisted that I join them. Richard smilingly waved goodnight and called that he would see me in the morning. We had an appointment at the Ministry of Tourism.

Madrid was as much President Nokato's stamping ground as it was the flamenco dancers'. We went to a place that was more cave than nightclub. At first the clacking of the castanets, the crashing of the dancers' heels and the high wailing hit me like the sound of an off-key boiler factory. After a blanket of several brandies it became so harmonious that I found myself clapping in rhythm with the rest of the audience. It did not permit much conversation. It didn't matter. I could see that the girl was enamoured of Nokato and he wasn't finding it difficult to reciprocate. He was happy. The thing that seemed to have made him even happier was my showing up unexpectedly. The ubiquitous bodyguards were at a table in the back of the nightclub and when we rode in Nokato's black Lincoln Continental. I soon got as used to them as if they were additional shadows.

The next morning I told Maurice Richard that he was expected to lunch at President Nokato's. Richard declined, explaining that a lunch appointment had been arranged with an official from the Ministry of Finance.

"Then I'd better be there too," I said.

"I'll let you know what's discussed."

"But this is one of the principal reasons we came to Madrid," I protested. "I'll put off Nokato."

"You can't do that. I'll get the official, and the Minister probably, to see us again later today or to-morrow."

Chapter Eight

President Nokato had a large apartment in an old building near the centre of Madrid. From the street it did not look like much but inside it was spacious and elegant. Nokato enjoyed the Spanish way of life: the hours and climate suited him although he missed certain aspects of Paris. At lunch on my first visit to his Madrid residence there was a half dozen people, including Lola Tone. The President's ADC was a small, wizened man of undetermined age with a shrewdity in eyes so dark and large they appeared to have no surrounding white. They stared at me appraising, calculating.

After the large meal, he, Lola and the others disappeared, leaving me alone with the President in a small library off the sitting room which was large enough for an investiture.

"The war in Europe and in the Far East did a great deal for me and for my country. I was a boy growing up in our village far in the interior of Africa. When I was a child my closest association with Western culture was the five gallon tins in which petrol came to us to be used for our kerosene lamps. At the age of puberty – it comes earlier in Africa – I was initiated into the tribe: circumcized, and other things which were even more painful, but equally as important for the step to manhood. But instead of moving into tribal life my grandmother insisted I be sent to the missionary school. In those days it was a long way off, trails and canoe passage through the territory of another, and, hopefully friendly, tribe."

He described his growing up. His father was Paramount

Chief of one of the strongest tribes in a large secluded territory. But it was his grandmother who had been the leading figure in his early life. At the missionary school there were either gifted teachers or he was an outstanding student: it was probably both. He finished the entire curriculum in record time. The head of the school was eager for him to continue his education in Britain and so was he. His grandmother endorsed this idea and plans were made. Before they could be implemented war broke out in Europe and it was decided he would study in America. While waiting for this to be arranged, the United States arrived on the lush plains and jungles of his home. The New World came in the form of an emergency landing airfield, an airways communications system and a weather station. The Americans were preparing alternate air routes to North Africa, Europe and across Africa to the Middle East and Asia.

The tall, adolescent African boy fresh from missionary school with his command of spoken and written English, was one of the first to be employed by the detachment of the US Army Air Force Engineers. He helped recruit labor from the tribe and bossed them. With the building of the airfield the tribe leapt from the ritual native life of thousands of years into the twentieth century.

In the past, explorers and missionaries had been through this territory. They were followed by adventurers and Arab slave traders. But none stayed and none brought anything of value with them. But the young Americans managing the emergency airfield demonstrated what Western civilization had to offer.

"I remember the first night they showed a movie." Nokato roared with laughter. "I knew about films. I'd heard about them, read about them, but I'd never seen one. I told my father and the members of our tribe what to expect. They couldn't grasp it. We were all invited to

74

come and see the show. There was a sign over the screen, 'Loew's Broadway.' When the picture appeared on the white screen and started talking, kids fell out of the trees. Everyone ran for home. Eventually they got used to it, although they always regarded it as witchcraft. I learned how to thread and run the projector. I helped the mechanics on the line when planes limped in and had to be repaired. I hung out with the weathermen and in the radio office. I was going to school, a real school, right there on that landing strip."

His deep voice and mobile face revealed the nostalgia he had for the excitement and humor of those days in the hot, humid jungle of his homeland. With the arrival of every airplane and with every new American, his knowledge increased.

"Abe Lincoln might have had a log cabin and a fireplace," the President said. "Young Joe Nokato had a bunk in the shack behind the mess hall and kitchen on the base. Not because it was comfortable or more pleasant than being in my thatched hut in my village but because it had electricity. I could read at night, all night, if I could keep my eyes open. I knew everything about that installation."

Along with the dispensary, its drugs and two corpsmen – the base was not large enough to have a doctor assigned – came crates marked Special Service. In these crates were the motion picture projector, films, baseball equipment and even one with skis. For Joe Nokato the most interesting ones were those with the books and magazines.

Thirty new books arrived every month, oblong in shape, different covers on their paper backs, printed in double columns. Half of the volumes were novels and current non-fiction, the other half were a mixture of classics, history and popular educational books. The fiction held no interest for Joe Nokato for he had no frame of reference for the problems and characters. The others he read every night to the rhythm of the generator and the shrill calls of the animals in the bush. Some nights he watched with fascination a game the visitors played called poker. He learned to play it.

During the day he was busy supervising the native labor and making himself as useful as possible. All the while he was watching, observing and learning from the efficient strangers who were more than willing to share their knowledge with the native youth with his infectious smile and quick intelligence.

"I learned something new every minute, certainly every hour and every day. The planes were being ferried across Africa to India, Burma and China. I still remember the first Air Transport Command C-46 that made it in on one engine. It had to stay until a new engine could be flown in and installed. The pilot was a small elderly man. At least he seemed so to me at the time; he must have been at least forty. He did something I'd never seen. He set up a little stand on three legs on which he put a large sheet of paper. He dipped little brushes into various pads of color that were in a tin box. He was busy all day painting. I brought him to our village. I still have the picture he painted of my father in full ceremonial robes and mask."

As the President spoke, painting his own pictures of young Joe Nokato, it became clear that his early education had not been aesthetic. He had learned partially by lecture, partially by personal instruction, a good deal by reading, but mainly by empiricism. The basic rules of capitalism were demonstrated to him. Later he realized that he had been brought up in a society that was more communist than any in the so-called civilized world.

He became an expert scrounger: the American military term for legitimate pilfering. It started in a small way by his appropriating usable items which the visitors neglected or threw away. It grew larger as the airfield enlarged and over-flowed, when the base began running down with the end of the war. None of the Americans cared what happened to the majority of the stores and equipment. By the time the last airplane left, Joe Nokato was the wealthiest man in the territory. He had a jeep, a supply dump of petrol, oil and spare parts, refrigerators which ran on kerosene, boxes of Army emergency rations, medical supplies, several radios, phonographs, records, a complete library and stores of every description. He had become accustomed to wearing chino trousers and tee-shirts although it took longer to become accustomed to shoes.

The commercial airlines falteringly took over the Army Transport Command. This airfield was left for the jungle to close in on and the territory to subside to its former state. But Joe Nokato knew it never would. "Our tribal world wasn't Sanforized," he grinned over his coffee. "The world had shrunk. Before the airfield closed I used to ride the American Air Force planes back and forth to the capital of my country. It was a colony in those days. I met a lot of my fellow countrymen. And a lot of Europeans who were governing us. I talked the colonial government into enlarging the airport in the capital. That was how we became one of the hubs of commercial aviation."

He was at an age when there is no such thing as death or dying, when there is an intolerance of illness and disease, when the whole world is in front of one. The obvious qualities of initiative and leadership marked Joe Nokato. When the first post-war scholarships became available he was chosen. He was disappointed at not being able to go to the United States to study. He went to England where he spent three years at Cambridge. He worked hard there. He got his cricket Blue. His ability oddly enough was derived from learning baseball from the Americans; the British experts deplored his peculiar but highly effective style. When he finished university he was torn between returning home and remaining for an extra year of post-graduate work at the London School of Economics. His father had died, he was the logical choice to succeed him. He received a letter from his grandmother dictated and translated into English by his younger sister; there was no written language for his native dialect. The old lady urged him to remain in Britain to complete his education; it was more important for the future than becoming Paramount Chief.

"She was right, as she always was. My only regret was that she died before I returned," he said.

On his return he was a marked man. His country was in a political turmoil with the restlessness of the approaching end of colonialism. When he tried to hurry things along he was put into jail. It was really this which launched him on his political career. Until then, he had been sneered at by his countrymen as a European and a turncoat. But having the colonial power arrest him for political activities proved that he was a patriot. Like Kenyatta of Kenya and Nkrumah of Ghana his followers rallied to him while he was in jail. The time in prison provided him with an important hiatus in which to think, plan and refine his studies but unlike Nehru, Mussolini, Hitler, and other political prisoners, he did not publish anything after his release. When the country ceased being a colony and became a new nation, he was freed to head the first government.

"Why did you send your boys to school in America?" I asked. "You received a fine education in Britain."

"Yes, I did. But you see I always liked the Americans

and the way they operate and run things. I know how and what they're thinking. The color prejudice is greater in the States. I didn't encounter much of it when I was in Britain. It's just really beginning to take hold there. I decided it was better for my boys to learn about it and get it full blast, first hand in America. It'll make them realize and appreciate that their future is in Africa." Leaning forward he emphasized this point by repeating: "Africa. We are the future."

"Not Asia?" I asked.

"No, not Asia. Japan can expand only so far. It's limited because of lack of material resources. Although there is much to be learned from them. China is just the immediate threat to the world, but big as it is it is too weary, too old, too civilized. We're young. We haven't been exploited to the point of exhaustion, although there are many who will say we have been in our mines and in expropriating our land. Most important we haven't been self-exploited like the Chinese with their emperors and war lords. If we go about it correctly we never will be. All of what is happening now in Africa is only the beginning, the first phase of our true existence."

Still those days on that emergency airfield were the happiest period of his life. He talked about a book he had read at that time. It was an autobiography by an American journalist. In it he had found an insight, a key, into men and their behavior. "There are no good men and bad men; there are only strong men and weak men," Nokato quoted with such emphasis that I understood that this was his credo. Somehow this did not ring true to me but I did not argue about it. I wanted to have my reasoning sound and arguments marshalled, when I discussed it with him.

On taking over, General Moki's administration found certain discrepancies as well as things of which it did not approve. General Moki and his followers exploited this as corruption. Nokato had made long term deals with big American and European companies for oil and mineral rights and for establishing industries. Now it appeared as though these agreements would be swept away.

Following the coup d'état the economy of his country became stagnant and began to slip. Stern police measures were taken against protesters. Starting in Nokato's own province, among his tribe, the largest in the country, a groundswell of support began for his return. Although he deplored it, Nokato realized that the only way he could return to his country was by a revolt. It would have to be a revolution launched from the outside. It would gain momentum with the support of his followers. The revolt was imminent when we had been hi-jacked.

I was fascinated by what President Nokato told me. I liked him enormously and he knew that. Still I wondered why he spoke so openly to me. This bothered me. Something about it was in the back of my mind. It was like a bee trapped behind an opaque glass trying to reach the sunlight. At the time I put it to rest by telling myself that he found me sympathetic and felt like talking. Probably he had bored his entourage with all of this. I was a fresh audience.

Chapter Nine

The buzzing was insistent. It took me a moment to realize I was alone in the hotel in Majorca and another moment to realize it was the telephone. I reached over and picked it up. It was the manager. I thanked him for returning my call and asked what time it was. When he told me that it was a half hour before midnight it was my turn to apologize. I said I'd see him in the morning.

"You have telephone operators who speak English," I said to him the next morning. "I gather they are local girls."

"Two of them are. Neither of them is especially pretty. But we have a waitress who comes from Barcelona who is young and is most attractive."

"I'm not running a beauty contest," I said. "The point is that someone born and raised in Majorca would have a different Spanish accent than someone say from Madrid or Barcelona, wouldn't she?"

He nodded. Now he was interested and not cynically amused. I told him I didn't want to see the telephone operator in my suite. He picked up the telephone. In a few minutes a middle-aged woman came into his office. She had dark thick hair, a thin waist and sharp, coal black eyes. She had the natural dignity of the Spanish. Her name was Carmen. The manager begged to be excused and left us alone.

When I told her what I wanted, Carmen moved to the telephone on the desk. I asked: "Can you dial direct?"

"No, but Maria will get the number for me," she said looking at the slip of paper which I'd obtained in Ibiza.

"No, that won't do. I want it to come as though from a private house. The idea is that you've dialed the wrong number. When they answer you ask who is at the other end. Then you ask what number it is. When they tell it to you, say you're sorry, you've got the wrong number and hang up."

"That is very simple, Mr Clancy," she said. "Would you not also like me to ask the address?"

"No." I did not want to explain that this might alert whoever answered at that number. "It has to seem as though a wrong number has been obtained by you. If you ask quickly, the person will automatically give his or her name."

Apparently she was accustomed to strange requests from the guests of the hotel. She explained that there was a public pay telephone in the employees' section. I followed her into the area of the hotel where the corridors ceased being decorated and quiet. The telephone was in a narrow cement-floored corridor filled with the smell of the kitchen and the distant clatter of utensils and dishes.

I held the notebook for her and gave her a pencil. Through the receiver I could hear the telephone ring. A man's voice answered, saying something quickly, not the usual hello. Carmen was writing even as she was giving her line in Spanish. I could make out the man's reply. She begged his pardon and hung up. I could have kissed her. She was wonderful. She printed the name on the pad under her handwriting.

We returned through the white-washed corridor, through several sets of doors and emerged into the cubicle where she worked. The other operator was busy running both switchboards. Quickly Carmen found a telephone directory and looked up the name, José Santana. On my pad she printed the address and after it, "Plumber and Bathroom Supplies".

"We were most fortunate, Mr Clancy, that it is a business. There is more than one Santana in the telephone book."

"I'm fortunate that you did it all so well." I thanked her again and she thanked me for the tip. "Just where is this address?"

"It is in the main part of Palma. I think I know the shop although I have never been in it. It is not too far from the cathedral and the main square."

"I'll find it. Thanks again, Carmen."

"Mr Clancy, would you not like me to go there with

you? What if the gentleman who answered the telephone does not speak English?"

"You're right. It would be most helpful. When will you be free?"

"I was told to be at your service by the manager. I am free now," she smiled.

The narrow, cobblestone street was barely wide enough for the taxi. The wares of the butcher, grocery and vegetable shops over-flowed onto the narrow sidewalk forcing the pedestrians to walk in front of the taxi. We jolted to a halt before a plate glass window displaying a purple bathtub, toilet, washstand and bidet. I helped Carmen out and paid the driver. I followed her into the store, a bell tinkled in the back as she opened the door. The shop was jammed with plumbing fixtures. On the walls were mirrored cabinets, assorted taps, hooks, railing, racks, toilet paper holders, poster displays of matching bathroom fixtures in yellow and green, but none in white.

A portly man with bushy black and gray hair, wearing heavy framed glasses perched on the end of his short nose, waddled forward. He was wearing white coveralls and a white jacket, he looked like an elderly hospital intern. He nodded to us and greeted us. We replied. In Spanish, Carmen said that I was planning to build a house and wanted to obtain some idea of the prices. The man listened, nodding all the while, rocking back and forth from heel to toe and then spluttered back some Spanish, which I understood to mean that he would be pleased to help and would provide an estimate not only of the fixtures but also of the cost of installing them.

"Is this gentleman the proprietor?" I asked Carmen.

Before she could translate the man nodded again and replied in slow English: "Si, I am the patron."

"Ah, you speak English." I was trying to determine how good his English was.

"I speak a little. I have many English who have plumbing from me."

"Do you know Maurice Richard?" I asked.

He stopped nodding. His head shook. There was no flicker of recognition on his face. "I do not know Señor Richard. But I am most grateful that he has recommended me."

"He telephoned you from Ibiza."

I wondered how the portly plumber got under pipes and into small spaces when working, until I remembered the apprentice system on the Continent; as the patron, Señor Santana would not do any of the actual labor. Now the patron was nodding and again rocking back and forth, like a doll with a heavily weighted bottom which cannot be knocked over. "I have many customers on Ibiza and the islands. I am very large agent. Is there anything here that is of fancy for you? I will also show you catalogues."

"Maurice Richard telephoned you from Ibiza about two and a half months ago. Don't you remember?"

"I do not remember. What did Señor Richard wish?"

"That's what I want to find out from you."

With the back of his forefinger Señor Santana pushed the heavy glasses towards the bridge of his nose. He regarded me carefully. "You are not here to buy?"

Carmen talked very rapidly in Spanish. Apparently she said the right things for he became mollified. He replied to her. She turned to me and said: "Señor Santana would be happy to assist you in any manner he can. He does have many customers and has a large business. This establishment here is but his display place. He has a large building also with a big staff."

Señor Santana rocked back and forth in agreement. He stared at me over the top of his glasses.

"About two and a half months ago you received a telephone call from Ibiza from Señor Maurice Richard," I persisted. "He did not speak long. Only a few words. It is my guess that he asked you to telephone to Algeria. Did you call Algeria?"

"Never in my life have I telephoned to Algeria," replied Señor Santana.

Carmen led me to the highly glazed purple toilet in the shop window. "Do you not think this would be what Madame would prefer?" she asked. I caught myself nodding. I almost started rocking: it was infectious. "We should also look at the catalogues as the patron suggests," she went on: "You can in that way compare the prices with what it would cost you to import these things to Spain."

"I have imported," the patron was following all of this. "I have imported from England. From France. From Germany. It is most expensive. We make all very good here. If you will please to compare. It will not cost so much."

We went through the charade of comparing prices. Enthusiastically Carmen discussed the bathrooms of the non-existent house. I did not believe that I had been given a wrong steer in Ibiza. Still there was no doubt that José Santana was who and what he said he was. That he was an accomplice of Richard's did not appear likely. That he had been used unknowingly, as I had been, seemed logical. Reaching into my pocket I brought out the loose-leaf page of information and photograph circulated by Interpol, which Inspector Albert Giraud had given to me.

"This is Maurice Richard," I said. "Do you remember seeing this man?"

The back of the forefinger pushed back the glasses. Santana stared down at the photograph. He was motionless. And then he began to rock. "Yes, now I remember. But his name was not Maurice Richard."

"That's not important. He did telephone you. You did something for him after that telephone call. What was it? You called Algiers."

"Please to be calm, Señor. I will tell you all that I know. It is a few things." Santana pointed to a brilliant yellow bathtub that was barely large enough for a child. "That is one of our popular baths. Very excellent color. Very comfortable."

Before he could insist that I slip it on for size, I agreed that it was all of these things. He began assembling catalogues and mimeographed sheets along with a large illustrated calendar. My impatience must have been too evident for Carmen shook her head warningly. I heeded her; she knew what manner of man he was. We must play this out. Either she was a natural actress or pricing plumbing items was something she always wanted to do. When he handed her the brochures and printed material she asked the right questions, borrowed a pen and jotted down details.

Señor Santana slipped everything into a used Manila envelope and handed it to her. "Here is also my card." He gave one to each of us. I shoved mine into my pocket.

Carmen assured him he would be hearing from us. Casually she mentioned that I would appreciate his letting me know about Señor Maurice Richard, whose photograph he had recognized, when he had time to recall the occasion.

"I do remember it now." Santana was rocking again. "That man did come to see me. He gave me money. A large amount. He said it was only half. He would give me the other half when I did the telephone call. He never returned."

86

"I'll pay it. How much does he owe you?" I said quickly.

"Thank you, no. It was already more than sufficient for what I did."

"What did you do?"

"This gentleman of the picture. He was French or Italian but he spoke beautiful Castilian." Abruptly the rocking ceased. "I remember now. His name was not Maurice Richard."

"What was it?" I asked.

"Very strange name. Ben Clancy."

Even Carmen, good actress though she was, registered her surprise. I asked: "What did Ben Clancy want you to do?"

"It was as you said. He did telephone to me. I did not know it was from Ibiza. And he did only speak a few words."

"What did he say?"

"He said, 'This is Ben Clancy. Telephone Madrid.' "

"That's all?"

"That was all. I then telephoned Madrid and gave the message."

"What was the message?"

" 'The goods are en route.' *Basta*. Finish."

"What was the telephone number in Madrid. Can you remember?"

"No, I can not." The rocking had stopped. "Please, Señor."

I had grabbed him by the arm and was shaking him. "I'm sorry," I managed to say. "I've got to have that telephone number. Can't you remember it? Please?"

Santana brushed the sleeve of his white jacket. I had wrinkled it. "I have written it down. If you would please to wait."

I followed him behind the mock-up of a stall shower

with a glass door, to where several shelves had been cleared of plumbing joints, chrome pipes, taps, nuts and bolts, to serve as a desk. Picking up a large register he opened it. He wet his index finger as he turned the pages. He mumbled to himself as he read down the notes until his finger pointed: "*Ecco!* 'Ben Clancy. Telephone Madrid.' " He picked up another of his business cards, copied out the telephone number in Madrid and handed it to me.

As we left I tried to pay him the remaining half of the amount of money that Richard had promised him but Santana would not have it. He said that he looked forward to hearing from me and my sympathetic assistant in the near future. He would be pleased to serve us.

When we reached the hotel Carmen handed me the large envelope with the bathroom catalogues. I thanked her again and gave her what I figured was the second half of the payment Richard had not made to Santana. She assured me that it was not necessary. I insisted that she had earned it. I told her I wished I could take her with me to Madrid. I had to figure out how to get the name and address of the party Santana had telephoned for Richard.

"Why not let us do the same as we did here?" Carmen suggested. "I can say that I have the wrong number again. I will try to get the information from whoever answers."

"But we'll be calling long distance from Majorca," I reminded her.

"All the more reason for me to be annoyed at getting a wrong number. I will be very upset and insist that I must know who is talking, so I can complain to the long distance operator that I got this number."

It seemed like a sensible solution; it would not alert Richard's contact in Madrid; it would give me a head-start in Madrid, to know where I was going. I followed

Carmen into the oversized cupboard. She took her position beside the other operator, put on the headset, threw a switch and told the operator she wanted Madrid. Then she gave the number on the card.

"I'm sorry we can not offer you a chair, Mr Clancy," Carmen said while we waited. There was barely enough room for me to stand. I assured her I didn't mind. Suddenly she brought her hand up in warning. "It's ringing," she said.

It rang for a long time. Carmen shook her head. "There is no reply." She disconnected the line. "I'm sorry."

"Try again," I suggested. "It is possible the Madrid operator gave us the wrong number."

She brightened and got to work. "That is always possible." She again gave the number to the long distance operator.

"It's ringing." We waited. She had her hand moving towards the switch when she froze. "Hello!" Carmen asked what number she was talking to. Her eyes were wide with excitement as she nodded to me apologizing for having been given the wrong number. She listened for a moment and then thanked the party at the other end, before releasing the line.

"It was a man," she reported. "He was annoyed. He said that they are closed. He hung up before I could ask any more."

She was disappointed. I assured Carmen it was not her fault. There was no point in trying the number again, I did not want to alarm whoever it was at the other end of the telephone. At least it established that there was someone there. If they were closed then there was a time when they were open.

Carmen followed me out of the windowed cupboard which held the switchboards. I said goodbye to her and again told her how helpful she had been. She said that she had enjoyed it. It was a change from just hearing voices over a telephone.

"One favor I would like to ask of you Mr Clancy. If you do not mind."

"Anything."

"Might I please have the lovely magazines and calendar and the information about the bathrooms, if you don't need them?"

Chapter Ten

I flew first class to Madrid from Majorca because tourist class was full. I recouped some of the extra cost by drinking champagne while I tried to figure out why Maurice Richard had selected José Santana to be his drop in Palma. I understood why Richard had to have an intermediary in Palma: it would take too long to get the call through from Ibiza to Madrid and he risked discovery; it was simpler to pass the key words from Palma to Madrid and from there to Algiers; the lines of communication were better. But why the plumber as part of the relay?

I took out the card on which José Santana had written the telephone number of the contact in Madrid. I turned over the card, read Santana's full name, his occupation, the address and telephone number of his shop and work plant. Something struck me. I called the stewardess.

"Could you please translate the printing on the bottom of this card." She took it from me. "Just under the telephone numbers."

"Twenty-four hour service." She flashed me a wondering smile which gave no indication whether or not she gave the same service. I was certain she didn't.

I studied the card, with grim satisfaction, rocking back and forth in my seat like Santana. Maurice Richard had picked the plumber because he would always answer the call, he even had two telephone numbers. Undoubtedly whoever it was in Madrid would give the same night and day service.

In Madrid there was no reason to go to the same de luxe hotel which Maurice Richard and I had previously used. A few more free spenders like Richard and all the countries in Europe would be on their feet and running. Now, looking at it from a different perspective, I realized that this had been deliberate, it was the right way for him to operate. It camouflaged Richard: no one asked questions of a man who spent money without hesitation.

I had someone in mind as interpreter. I went to Nokato's apartment. Lola was having none of it. She came at me like a wildcat; screaming, scratching, kicking; her lips curled. I backed away while trying to explain. The onyx ashtray crashed into the picture on the wall behind me. Grabbing her arms I got one behind her back. I forced it up until the pain was too great for her to kick and bite. She was sobbing with rage.

"Listen to me." I was standing behind her. I wondered if the polite thing to do would be to replace her left breast inside the dress, but since she showed no signs of being lady-like I decided I didn't have to be a gentleman. "Would I be here if I were responsible for hi-jacking your boy friend? I was hi-jacked too. I want to know who the hell did it."

Either what I said sank in or her arm was hurting; when I released her she stopped struggling and fell into a large chair. She was still sobbing, her long black hair hanging in front of her face. "I want to get him out of

Algeria as much as you do," I said after I'd pulled my clothing into position. I was wishing she'd do the same. Her legs were as perfect as her breasts.

Slowly Lola sat up, absent-mindedly pulled the bodice of the dress over her breast and pushed the hair back from her face. I never did learn whether Lola Tone was a name concocted at the time she'd won a beauty contest several years ago in her Central American country or if it was her own name. She had met President Nokato during an international beauty contest when he was on a trip to London to appear on the BBC. She didn't win the contest but she won him. Her English was good but she felt more at home speaking Spanish. After meeting Lola, Nokato had begun to move his base of operations from Paris to Madrid.

"Why did you come here?" she asked.

"To get to the bottom of this. To get help so I can get the President out of Algeria," I replied. "The President always had a staff around him. Where are they?"

"They come around once in a while. Most of them are spies," she said with scorn.

I nodded. "President Nokato knew that." I didn't add that he had told me he knew which ones were in the pay of General Moki and which were leaking information to the Russians, to the CIA, to the Deuxième Bureau, to the Belgians and to other interested nations. It was a pity he had not given her some indication of the ones, if any, he trusted. But then Lola was not involved in either his political or financial life. "I need assistance."

"Have you found out something?"

"I've got a lead. There's some information here in Madrid. I can't get at it by myself."

"You can not trust anyone else. I'll help you."

This was what I had anticipated. "Maurice Richard sent word to Algiers by someone in Madrid that he was about to hi-jack the plane. The message was either cabled or telephoned to Algiers from here. I've got the phone number in Madrid. But only the phone number."

"You don't know who it is?"

"No."

"What is the number?"

"What's the telephone number here?" I asked in reply. "There has to be more than one. The President would have a private line."

She gave me the other telephone number as well as the phone number of the office which Nokato had in Madrid. None were the same as the one Santana had given me. That eliminated the idea I'd had that Maurice Richard might have been working with one of Nokato's Madrid entourage.

"I thought of getting hold of one of the President's aides to help me get the address of the telephone number from the Spanish post office."

"I don't trust any of them," she said fiercely. She stood up. She walked to the telephone on the table. The broad brow above the narrow arches of her eyebrows had a minute wrinkle.

"Yes, he'd be the one," she said abruptly. "Dr Gonzales had excellent connections with the highest government officials," she explained. "Joe always said that not only was he completely honest but was also sympatico and helpful. What is the matter?"

"I'm just wondering what reason you'll give Gonzales for wanting the name and address. For only having the telephone number?"

"Don't worry." She saw that I did. She thought for a moment and then said: "I'll tell him I found I'd written down this number and can't remember where I got it or what it means. I'll tell him I don't want to be embarrassed by calling someone I shouldn't, if you know what I mean."

I knew what she meant. I gave her the telephone number. She wrote it on a pad which had the Presidential crest printed on it. She dialed a number. I could follow most of it when she asked for Dr Gonzales, gave her name, and in a moment was put through. Even if I'd had no knowledge of Spanish I'd have been able to follow the lengthy conversation by the expressions on her face and the tone of her voice. She was sorry to bother him but she had nowhere else to turn. . . .

She hung up the telephone and said that Dr Gonzales would call her back in a few minutes. She glanced at me in a thoughtful manner, excused herself and left the living room. I walked about restlessly. I picked up the onyx ashtray, weighed it in my hand and was glad she hadn't played baseball as a girl. I didn't think she had played much with dolls either.

The telephone rang. I moved towards it. It stopped after the second ring. She had picked it up in another room. Eventually I heard the click of the bell as the other telephone hung up. It had been a long conversation considering the precise bit of information Lola had requested. She did not return for another ten minutes.

She was wearing a white dress of loosely knit lace that set off her magnificent skin and revealed her figure. Her hair was braided and arranged against the nape of her neck. Her earrings were a delicate design of gold which contrasted with her heavy gold bracelet. She had on lipstick but no other makeup. At another time, another place and another situation she would have been breathtaking.

"Was that your friend who called?" I asked.

"Yes, I've got the name and the address." She did not explain the long conversation. She didn't have to. "Who is it?" I asked.

"El Club Bunnie."

"What?"

" 'The Bunny Club'. Now you understand why I could not get Señor Gonzales off the phone. He wanted to meet me there. And he was more than curious how I had such a telephone number. I'll have to think up some sort of story to tell him when I see him."

"I'm sure he can hardly wait."

"Well, I can," she snapped. "Let's go."

"Where?"

"To El Club Bunnie."

"Do you think it's open?"

"No, it's too early for that sort of place. But this is the cocktail hour. After we've had dinner we can go there."

When I gave the address the taxi driver was startled. Very carefully he asked if we had the correct place and address. Lola assured him we had. The taxi driver spluttered a lot of Spanish which was returned rapidly by Lola. The driver shrugged as he turned around, put the car into gear and started off.

"What about the Club Bunnie?" I asked.

"The driver said it is no place for a lady," Lola replied. "I told him that I was not a lady."

The driver was right and she was wrong. Garishly hand-tinted photographs were displayed along the cement walls of the sloping entrance. Originally this must have led to the cellar of the large, recently built, apartment house above. When we reached the level portion of the passageway the photographs became more artistic, if that was the word, changing from girls dancing flamenco to art poses of nubile gauze-covered ladies. I held open the door for Lola.

We were in a large, square white-washed room broken up by pillars helping to support the building. At regular intervals between the walls and the square dance floor were small round tables and chairs. There was a six inch high platform along one side of the dance floor for the musicians. The room was empty except for a bartender. A white jacketed waiter disappeared through a door as we came in.

The bartender made the traditional circular movements with a cloth on the bar and had the traditional weariness and wariness of his trade in his eyes. He did not try to hide his surprise at seeing us. He greeted us and wanted to know what we'd like to drink. Lola said sherry. A bottle was opened and placed on the bar. We declined his invitation to sit at one of the tables. The place was as inviting and as cosy as the mess hall of a prison.

With the taffeta rustling of skirts, the clatter of high heels and the aroma of musky perfume, five girls came in. They were like tropical birds emerging from pens into a cold, rainy aviary. They did not look pleased at seeing Lola. They surrounded us. Their voices were melodious as peacocks, their movements as deliberate. They tried to tear Lola off my arm. They insisted that I buy them drinks. I nodded to the bartender. Five bottles of sherry popped up on the bar. From Lola's reaction and my limited Spanish I realized that the conversation was as gamey as the denizens. We were pulled to a table. Another table was dragged up.

In passable English the bartender loomed over us to say that the dancing would not begin for another hour. However, if I wished one of the girls would dance for me in private.

Lola projected a quality into her voice that brought respect, or at least attention. No, her friend was not interested in seeing anyone dance alone for him in a back room. He liked her dancing well enough.

"Why did you come here?" one of the girls spat at her.

"To see the dancing, of course," Lola replied smilingly. "We heard you dance flamenco expertly."

It was the right answer. Dancing is like driving; everyone who does it thinks he does it well. Lola made a few pleasant remarks with a nice smile on her face. It had a soothing effect. The ladies ceased resenting her.

One of the black-plumed girls said something to a waiter. In a few minutes three men appeared. An elderly, fat, bald man and a boy young enough to be his grandson were carrying guitars. The third man carried himself as though he was wearing a brace which held his head back so that he looked down at the world in disdain. All three wore the long, tight hipped black trousers, sash, and white flowing shirts of the flamenco. The musicians sat on straight-backed chairs, bent over their guitars, watching their fingers. The male dancer stood with one foot on the seat of a chair. The few inches of platform made him appear taller and thinner as he stared motionless at us.

Lola's attitude was undoubtedly the correct one, if you can't beat them join them; she began to clap her hands to the rhythm of the music. Two of the girls stepped onto the dance floor, their castanets clucking away, as they swayed to the chords of the guitars. It all had the unreal, overly bright, jerking quality of a piece of film going through a hand-cranked toy projector. Occasionally the action would speed up, then slow down. It stopped abruptly when I asked one of the girls for the telephone.

"No telephone here," the girl said with irritation when she was certain this was what I wanted.

"You must have one," I insisted. "It's very important."

Lola was occupied, trying to keep the hands of the male dancer off her. He had condescended to join the group. I was beginning to wonder if there had not been a mixup about the telephone number and the address. This joint and Maurice Richard did not add up. Besides I did not like the way the atmosphere was building. Several more waiters had appeared and were watching us from beside the bar. No other customers had arrived.

Thinking that the girl I was arguing with needed assistance, the largest and toughest of the waiters appeared behind me. She said something quickly to him which I could not follow. The din of castanets, stamping of heels, the wail of flamenco singing and guitars made quite a racket for two guests. The table was covered with sherry bottles. They seemed to come automatically every ten minutes. Out of the corner of my eye I saw that the disdainful male dancer had Lola against a concrete pillar. She had a strained smile on her face. None of this was going to lead to a sociable evening or even an informative one. I decided we had better get out of here while I had enough money on me to pay and before the party got rough.

"You are asking to use the telephone?" a man's voice came from behind me.

Turning, I stared up into a face which had a huge purple blotch. The features were irregular: deeply hollowed cheeks with the bones of chin and eye sockets protruding. I nodded. The man with the purple face jerked his chin in the direction of the service door. I excused myself to my hostesses and got up. I stopped at the pillar and told Lola that I was going to make a telephone call. She ducked under the dancer's arm and moved in front of me.

The man led the way. He walked like the dancer, his torso arched back, elbows pressed close against his sides. He did not bother to see if we were following: he could hear our footsteps.

At first the passageway was wide. The light came from dim bulbs covered by red lampshades. A double line of large photographs, like the ones in the entrance, moved along with us on both walls. We passed rooms, the doors were open. By the dim, colored light within, blue, purple, red, I could see that each featured a bed. We pushed through another door where the sound of refrigerating machinery echoed along the bare passageway. The few bulbs in the ceiling gave a faint light. We went up a dark clammy staircase, along a small corridor which led into a wider cubicle with another staircase. We passed this to go down a short flight of steps and into a wide alcove with still another stairway. I was no longer certain which floor we were on. This area was better lit, looking less like a rabbit warren. I figured that we were in the large apartment building over the El Club Bunnie. Our guide threw open a large door and we entered the carpeted and wallpapered foyer of an apartment.

He hurried us through another door and closed it behind us. The room was obviously an office. The walls were covered with framed, signed photographs of bull-fighters and flamenco dancers. A steel safe the size of a walk-in refrigerator occupied the remainder of the wall where the door led to the apartment. A large desk took up another side of the room. Three straight-back cane chairs faced the desk.

"I should have left a trail of bread crumbs behind me," I said.

Neither Lola nor our guide seemed to know the Grimm Brothers' fairy tales: they both stared at me. "I will get you back," said the man.

"You speak very good English," I said. I was in no hurry now. I was certain I had found my man.

"We have customers here from many different countries. It is necessary I should speak with them."

"You're the manager of El Club Bunnie?" I asked.

"I am the owner." His face was sharp enough to cut and so was his manner. "You desired the telephone, no?"

"Yes. I have an important call I must make. I should

99

have made it earlier. But your place was so distracting I could not get to a phone."

His reaction revealed that flattery would get me nowhere. Gracefully he moved about the desk, bent over, his back held stiffly. I was certain he could touch the floor easily with the palms of his hands. He unlocked the bottom desk drawer, lifted out a telephone and placed it on the desk. He had either seen too many gangster films or feared the help would run up his telephone bills.

Taking the few steps to the telephone I stared at it, seemingly trying to think of the number I wanted to call. I was searching for its number. There was none. It was like looking at a clock with no hands. I tried to stall, fumbling in my pockets for the number, all the while trying to think of an approach to this new problem.

I lifted the phone and heard the tone. I began dialing. Our host watched as though it was a roulette wheel. To take the strain off I said: "I'm calling my hotel."

I heard the operator answer and give the name of the hotel. I said: "This is Mr Jack Jones. I occupy room seven eighteen. Are there any messages for me?"

Holding the receiver close against my ear, I seemingly listened carefully. Then I said: "He did? But he didn't leave a number for me to call him? . . . Are you sure?" Our host could not hear the hotel operator say that there was no one named Jack Jones occupying that room. I continued talking over her objections: "When he calls tell him I'm at this number." Abruptly I glanced up. "What's the number here?"

He responded automatically. Then a frown came to his face. It was apparent that he wished he had not given it to me. I repeated the number to the operator, or rather to the dead telephone for she had hung up. I went right on talking: "I'll be here for another ten or fifteen minutes.

After that I'll be back at the hotel. Tell him, if I miss him to leave his number and I'll call back."

It did not seem strange to anyone that I was expecting telephone calls at two o'clock in the morning. This was Madrid where the matinée hour was eight p.m. and right now was the height of the evening. Hanging up the telephone I extended my hand. "Thank you. My name is Jack Jones as you heard."

"Louis d'Alamo," he said briefly shaking my hand.

"And this lady is – "

"I know who is this lady. Señorita." Lola held out her hand and he bowed over it. "It is an honor."

"*Gracia*," Lola acknowledged. She shot me a quick glance when he bent over her hand. I nodded. This was the telephone we had been seeking.

Either Louis d'Alamo's field of vision was extraordinarily wide or he was naturally suspicious. His gray eyes flicked from me to Lola and back again with the rapid movement of a reptile about to strike. "I will let you know when your telephone call comes," he said. "If I may escort you back now. Or perhaps you have had enough of our entertainment?"

"I wouldn't say that," I hedged.

"And how has it come about that you have honored us here?" he asked.

"I was told about your establishment by a friend of yours," I said.

He did not understand the innuendo of referring to it as an establishment. "And who is my friend?"

"Maurice Richard."

His eyes widened. For an instant I could see beyond the hard surface. It revealed that the name had registered; so had a number of other things including who I was and why I was here.

"Maurice Richard is being held in Algiers," he said

quietly. There was force behind the words as though he was warning me. "And your name is not that which you told me. You are the American who was with Richard and President Nokato on that airplane."

"That's right. You know everything. Including the fact that on the day of the hi-jacking you received a telephone call here from Palma. In turn you either telephoned or cabled Algiers to expect the hi-jacked plane. With whom did you get in touch? And when did Maurice Richard arrange this with you?"

Picking up the telephone he replaced it in the bottom drawer and took a key container from the inside pocket of his jacket and locked the drawer. The extension of the telephone was probably in the apartment: he too had a twenty-four hour service. It seemed to me that he had more than the key container in his hand when he returned it to his pocket.

"Mr Clancy, you have made a mistake. I suggest you forget it."

"I'm not mistaken. I want to talk to you about this."

"If you insist."

"I insist."

D'Alamo's left hand reached under the desk and fumbled for something. I realized it must be a button and that he had pushed it as a signal. I didn't know what he was signalling or to whom. By now I didn't care.

"Suppose we have a drink and discuss how much I owe you." Meaningfully I accented the last words.

He stared at me blankly before nodding. He moved to the door and held it open, ushering us back into the bare corridor. This time he did not lead but pointedly remained behind us, giving instructions as to where to turn and when to go up the steps and when down them.

It seemed to me that we retraced our steps quickly. We were back in the red-lit corridor with the rooms for private instruction on either side. Moving ahead of Lola I threw open the door.

While we went to the table I quickly examined the room. The door, through which we had originally entered, was closed. During our absence customers had arrived. Several tables were occupied, girls were seated with the guests, all men. One of the girls was on the floor, dancing. As we sat down the large bartender came to our table. I gave Lola a nod to indicate that everything was all right. Out of the corner of my eye I saw the bartender making the same sort of gesture to d'Alamo. Lola and I accepted when he asked if champagne would be all right. My apprehension returned. I looked about again. No one was paying much attention to us. I turned back to our host.

"I found the man who telephoned you from Palma. He told me the message he passed on to you. The message Maurice Richard gave him." My words had as much impact on him as the two guitars being played next to us. "You don't deny this, do you?"

"I don't deny anything. Nor do I agree with what you have said."

"Then I'd better talk to you tomorrow when you've had a chance to think it over. We're just wasting your time right now." I pushed back the chair. It did not move. Turning my head I looked up into the face of a waiter. He had his hands on the back of the chair.

"I have much time," d'Alamo was saying. "I would like to know how you came to find this man you said telephoned me."

"I saw him in Palma. He told me that Richard had paid him to pass the message to you. Only he didn't know it was you. He only knew the telephone number."

"And you were clever enough to trace the number?"

"That's right."

"You never thought that he gave you the wrong number?"

"No, I never did. And neither do you."

The bartender set the ice bucket with the champagne on the table. He worked on the cork. It blew up to hit the ceiling but the sound was lost in the noise of the place. Two more girls and the male dancer joined the first girl. Eight castanets, plus the stamping of heels, added up to a lot of decibels. The bartender poured a small amount of champagne into d'Alamo's glass. He drank it and nodded. The bartender filled our glasses and then our host's. At least the wine was not drugged. We raised our glasses, Lola watched warily. I noticed that she brought the wine to her lips but did not drink. I was thirsty and did. I congratulated d'Alamo on the champagne.

It was as though I had pressed a switch that called for gracious manners. He began asking Lola about herself, how long had she been in Spain and how did she like it. All the polite questions a native asks a stranger. Lola was a good enough actress to enter into the spirit of the game. I joined in while trying to figure out this abrupt change. I had the answer five minutes later when four men entered by the back door.

The wailing that passed for singing, started again. One of the guests got a girl onto the dance floor. The four newcomers were at the bar. They were all the same type of gangsters. They stared across the room at us with a tightness in their movements that made me realize they had been summoned by the button pushed in d'Alamo's office.

D'Alamo's eyes flicked like the tongue of a snake to the men at the bar and back to Lola. The response was almost as rapid. The youngest thug pushed off from the bar, skirted the swirling skirts of the dancers and moved towards Lola. He had long black hair. Sideburns reached his chin making his face seem as narrow and sharp as a hatchet. He said something I couldn't hear. He took her by the wrist, pulled her to her feet and started towards the dancing. Lola tried in vain to jerk her arm free. I was on my feet. The bartender and two waiters came between me and the dancers. My chair was shoved against the back of my legs and I sat down.

Between the waiters I caught a glimpse of the dance floor. Lola's partner did not go in for flamenco. He had his arms about her. She threw me a distressed look. I spun back to the table. There was an empty chair where d'Alamo had been seated. His glass was gone.

"Where's your boss? Your patron?" I called to the bartender. He regarded me blankly. I pointed to the empty chair and shouted again.

The bartender shook his head. "There is no one there, señor."

"I can see that," I shouted. "Where did he go?"

"There has been no one there, señor. You have been drinking too much. Or taking too many drugs." He leaned over to make certain I understood. I understood all right. By now Louis d'Alamo was leaving the building. He would go to a well lit café where everyone could see him and later testify that he was not at his own place when the unfortunate incident happened to the American visitor.

The chair was jerked out from under me. Stumbling backwards I tried to maintain my balance by clutching at a diaphanous mass of black. It gave. I caught the edge of the next table. A girl was pointing at a tear in the side of her bodice, and screaming at me. The bartender grinned. Grabbing her black dress he tore it to reveal a crimson brassiere holding too much flesh. The slash of lips in the girl's powdered face showed her dismay. The bartender pushed me into her and gestured to the girl.

He and two waiters hustled us onto the dance floor. I was engulfed in the stink of cheap perfume, powder and sweat as she put her arms around me and we were among the dancers.

The other three thugs were no longer at the bar, nor were the customers at their tables. They surrounded the dance floor along with the waiters and the bartender. The flamenco dancers swirled about me and my partner and about Lola and the ape who was clutching her. The castanets vibrated, the heels of the dancers struck the floor, the guitars played as though they were amplified, the singing reached the pitch of caterwauling.

I stopped struggling and let my body sag. My partner's grip relaxed as she leaned back to see what was wrong. I pushed. She fell against one of the girls. Lola's partner had his back to me. I tore her from him. I grabbed Lola's arm and we moved in the direction open, the corner of the room. The castanets ran down until only one clucked on like an absent-minded hen. The singing stopped.

The men pushed past the girls. Slowly, like a semi-circular wave they followed us. Lola and I backed up. As we passed a table I grabbed a bottle in each hand. A growl came from the men. The guitar playing became softer and then died away. I heard the sound of heavy breathing and realized it was me. With the bottle in my left hand I motioned Lola. She got behind me.

There was a hollow resonance in my right hand. The bottle had struck the wall. The semi-circle was closing in. I flicked my wrist. The bottle hit the stone wall with a crash. I did the same with the bottle in my left hand. I held the jagged end of the bottle outwards and began swinging them. The men stopped. I heard a click and then another. There was a gleam of light on the switch-blade knives. For an instant we were frozen. Then one gleam changed. Lola's dancing partner was shifting the position of his knife. The handle rested in the open palm of his left hand. The point of the blade was between the forefinger and thumb of his right hand. I waited for him to bring the knife up to throw it. I dropped the wrist of my right hand, getting ready to flick underhanded the jagged glass into his face.

There was a shout. Everyone turned. I could not see over their heads. There was another call. A door slammed. The guitars started as though a needle had dropped into the middle of a phonograph record. The dancers were on the floor, the castanets were snapping. The men and girls were sitting at the tables, being attended by waiters. The four thugs slipped out through the other door. The bartender and another waiter were pushing us into seats. I dropped the broken bottles under the table.

Abruptly the main door opened. The bowing and grinning doorman appeared. Three uniformed policemen and another man who looked vaguely familiar, brushed past him. The policemen scanned the room. The civilian waved when he saw us. He called something to the police and hurried over to us. My knees felt rubbery as I got to my feet. The man was beside the table speaking rapidly. Lola nodded. Two of the policemen came up and began jabbering.

"Do you want to make a complaint?" Lola asked me.

"I just want to get the hell out of here."

Lola said something to the police. The man not in uniform helped her to her feet. She took his arm and mine and we walked to the door. I saw one of the police talking to the bartender and he wasn't praising him. The bartender, with the wide smile of an innocent shark, was making expansive gestures to indicate that everything was lovely here.

The three of us did not speak going up the incline to the

street. At the curb, washed in the blue neon light that spelled "El Club Bunnie" was an empty taxi, behind it the police car. Our new companion darted ahead to open the door of the taxi. Then I recognized him: our taxi-driver. I shook his hand and thanked him. He asked where we'd like to go. Lola said we wanted to go home and gave the address. The comforting silhouette of the driver slid into the front seat. The taxi swung away from the curb.

"Did you understand what he was saying earlier?" Lola asked.

"No."

"When he dropped us our taxi-driver decided we wouldn't be staying long. He knew what sort of a place it is. So he waited for us. When we didn't come out he got worried. He went down to see if we were all right. The doorman wouldn't let him in. The doorman said the place was closed."

Lola slid against me as the taxi took a sharp turn. We were on one of the main boulevards. The sidewalks were filled with people. She didn't move. I put my arm about her.

"So he went to the police and told them that something was wrong?" I concluded. Lola nodded.

The taxi pulled up in front of the apartment building. It isn't often one gets to meet one's good fairy; it's even less often one can repay him. I handed mine a wad of bills. He protested. I assured him it wasn't enough. Besides, the evening's entertainment, if it could be termed that, had cost nothing: somehow the bill had been overlooked in the rush.

Before Lola could put the key into the lock a sleepy-eyed young maid opened the door. The lights were on in the apartment. Lola thanked the maid and sent her off to bed. She curtsied and scurried away. The drapes were drawn in the living room.

Lola indicated the bar. I made a couple of stiff drinks. I brought them to the couch. She had kicked off her shoes and was curled up in a corner.

"There's no doubt that Louis d'Alamo was the one who relayed the message to Algiers," I said. "And there's no doubt he was going to make this the end of the trail for me. By the time the ambulance and police got there it would have been explained to them that we were on drugs and had gotten into a fight with the girls and other patrons."

"Should we not have had the police arrest them?" Lola asked.

"It would have been their word against ours. They'd have produced evidence like the girl with the torn dress, and the broken bottles. We were lucky to get out whole."

We both drank to that. I leaned back against the couch and let out a soft sigh. I knew how a fox must feel who's been chased by hounds and escapes.

"One thing we have proved is that this isn't a cold trail." I sat upright. "D'Alamo could have stalled or made up some story. Why was he so determined to stop me?"

"Because you were determined too. And you wouldn't have believed his story."

"But I wouldn't have been able to prove anything except that Santana telephoned him from Palma on Richard's instructions. No, d'Alamo was ready to finish me off. If nothing else it shows that the people working for Richard are loyal. Or else they're still on the payroll." My voice ran down as a new thought struck me.

"And what, Ben?" Lola asked.

"And the whole thing is still operating. It's still going on but in a manner I don't understand."

"Why? What for?"

"I don't know. I thought that hi-jacking Nokato was the end of it. Now I'm starting to wonder."

"What are you going to do now?"

I explained that tracing the telephone number wasn't the only reason I'd come to Madrid. I told her what I was planning to do and how I was going to go about it. Lola regarded me thoughtfully. I apologized again for having gotten her into this.

"I wanted to help," she said.

"You did. A great deal. I'm certain that it was your being along that got me in to see d'Alamo. I don't think he would have seen me if I'd been alone or with someone else. He knew you're Joe Nokato's girl."

"I am his girl." That thoughtful expression did not leave her face. "Joe is a fine man. I only wish he were here."

"So do I."

"But he isn't. And you are. And I have been alone for a long time and for too many nights. It is something I am not used to. It is also something I do not wish to get used to."

Chapter Eleven

Lola was not the only reason I remained in Madrid longer than I had planned. I was retracing my visits to the various officials, bankers and financiers I had met with Maurice Richard. If it had all been a hoax then the men I'd met were either in cahoots with Richard or also had been duped.

I telephoned the offices of various government officials.

The secretaries did not know who I was and referred me to other offices. When Lola telephoned I was boiling. She listened sympathetically and asked me to meet her for cocktails at the bar of the Castellana Hilton at eight-thirty.

The place was jumping with Americans, British, Italians, Germans, every nationality except Spanish. All appeared to belong to a club composed of three film companies making westerns; the bar was the assembly point after each day's work. The light was dim but not that dim: everyone turned to stare when Lola glided up to me. She slid onto the bench beside me.

After she had ordered a drink she asked if I'd had any luck. I told her I had gotten in to see a couple of men I had thought were bankers and financiers. They had turned out to be lawyers who weren't very busy. They were surprised at my reappearance. I had learned that they were frontmen, the legal Spanish names: certain property sales and investments could only be made by Spanish citizens. To get around that, a foreigner put the investment in the name of a Spaniard who could be trusted.

Before I could warm up to the subject Lola said: "We are meeting someone. Dr Gonzalcs."

"Isn't he the gentleman you phoned yesterday who got the name and address of the telephone number?"

"Yes. As you heard, he was interested in having cock-tails or dinner with me." The manner with which she said this with an innocent widening of her eyes made me grin understandingly. "After you told me about your diffi-culties I called him. I know he would prefer meeting me here. He will not run into many of his friends."

"I'm not so sure he's going to be happy seeing me," I said.

"Don't worry. As I told you he is a great friend of Joe's."

I noticed a short roly-poly man peering near-sightedly at the tables as he moved cautiously in the dimness of the bar. Lola called to him. His face creased into a smile and he waddled across to us. After he'd kissed her hand she introduced me to him. He apologized for being late as he took a chair facing us.

"It is difficult to become accustomed to the American custom that when you say a certain time that that is the time and not forty-five minutes later," he said in perfect English.

I could almost hear the click of the shutter behind the iris of his eyes as he made a mental note of what he saw and heard. Yet there was something about Dr Gonzales that I liked. There was an inner warmth coupled with tolerance gained from experience: he would never be surprised by anyone's actions, motives or character. There was a black band of mourning on his upper left arm. I expressed condolences. He thanked me and explained that when one reached his age someone in his family was always dying; it was customary to wear mourning for a year.

"Is there any news of Joe?" he asked after he had been served his drink.

"Mr Clancy was the last to see him," Lola replied.

His unblinking eyes did not register surprise. "Was he in good health from what you could see, Mr Clancy?"

"I saw all of him. The prison guards made a mistake and we met in the shower and talked. He was physically and mentally fine."

"Ah yes, you are the Mr Ben Clancy who was on the airplane with the President." I realized that he'd known who I was from the moment Lola introduced us, but he was not going to say anything about it until I did.

Either Lola had remarkable powers of intuition or was indiscreet to such a degree that it paid off, for she blurted out: "Mr Clancy was an innocent victim. Maurice Richard used him to get Joe on the airplane. Mr Clancy wants to find out who is behind Richard and why he did the hi-jacking."

"You had big plans for Spain, Mr Clancy. Not only was it a grave shock to have this happen to the President but it was also an end to those ambitious plans."

"They weren't my plans and projects," I said. "I was working for Richard and whoever was behind him."

"That is not the way we understood it," Dr Gonzales replied. "Richard made some visits here before you arrived. He explained to various ministers and departments that you were one of the heads of an international syndicate. He was merely an employee. You were the key figure."

He was polite enough to let me think this over for he could see the shock on my face. He turned to Lola and asked a number of questions which revealed that he understood that President Nokato's entourage had virtually deserted her. He agreed with her that it was no great loss. I pulled myself together and at a lull in their conversation mentioned that various officials who had been co-operative before now refused to see me.

"With all due apologies, Mr Clancy, you must see it from their point of view. They do not know yours. Possibly they feel that they wasted – perhaps that is too strong a word – spent, much time already with you and feel it would be a further waste spending more."

I felt myself flushing and was glad that the bar was not well lighted. "How can they be so sure of that?" I demanded.

"You mean you are prepared to continue?"

"There is great merit and potential in those projects,"

I hedged. "I think money can be raised and the projects gotten under way."

He knew I was ad-libbing. He also knew that what I said was true. "When you are prepared to talk I can assure you that all doors will be open to you just as they were before."

"If I may speak frankly, sir, I don't understand how they were so open to Richard. Surely your government knew who and what Richard was."

"He appeared to have excellent qualifications and recommendations," Dr Gonzales said.

"Who was behind him? Who was so powerful and important that his recommendation was enough to overcome all that your police and immigration authorities must have known about Maurice Richard? They had the Interpol file on him."

"I can't tell you that offhand. I don't know."

I leaned forward to give greater weight to my words. "A man who's served a jail sentence for kidnaping is permitted, in fact welcomed, into top government offices to talk to your most important people. How is that?"

"There is one very important thing upon which you place too much emphasis."

"What's that?"

"That Maurice Richard was a criminal." Dr Gonzales's eyes looked wearier and yet tolerant. "He served his jail sentence and therefore he has paid for his crime. Why should we not permit him here? It was not as if he was an embezzler or a confidence man and therefore might do the same thing here."

"He was a kidnaper and he did do the same thing," I said.

"So we found out too late. And so did you. We were all taken in by him. The people in our government are not stupid. And neither are you."

"Mr Clancy meant no insult towards the government," Lola interjected.

"I understand how Mr Clancy feels. He must realize that the officials with whom he dealt feel towards him the way he does towards Richard."

The waiter was standing in front of the table. Lola had barely touched her champagne. Dr Gonzales thanked me and declined another drink. I wasn't thirsty for anything but knowledge about Richard. The waiter drifted to the next table.

"We have a proud and fine history of political asylum," Dr Gonzales said firmly. "This was shockingly violated when President Nokato was abducted from our country. Naturally at first it was thought that you were involved, but careful checking indicated that you were not. You want to find out how this happened and why."

"Do you blame me?" I asked.

"I do not blame you. We, on our part, are not so much interested in that as we are in securing the release of President Nokato and in making some amends to Señorita Tone."

Turning back to Lola he indicated that this was the end of the discussion I was so keen to pursue. I could sense that Lola was having as difficult a time reading Dr Gonzales's intentions as I was. How much was friendship for Joe, how much was old world gallantry, and how much was he a man on the make, only she would be able to find out. He did not appear to be disappointed that the cocktail appointment with Lola had not been a tête-à-tête when he rose to say goodbye. I wondered if he had not known that he was going to find me with her. He appeared to know everything except when the President would be released.

Shortly after Dr Gonzales left, Lola and I decided we were hungry. She took me to an undistinguished looking restaurant which made up for its lack of decor by having superb grilled seafood.

"What is worrying you, Ben?" Lola asked after we had been sitting quietly for some time.

"A lot of things."

"Of course. Was it something that Dr Gonzales said?"

I nodded. "There's one thing he didn't cover and which I forgot to ask about. Why, if Spain is such a sanctuary and political haven, did the Spanish government assign two policemen to guard Joe?"

"I never thought of that," she agreed. "Didn't he have bodyguards in France?"

"Not to my knowledge. What were the Spanish expecting? Do the other exiled heads of state go around protected?"

"I don't know," she said. "I don't think so."

"Then why did they do it for Joe?"

Chapter Twelve

Two days later I returned to Paris. I dropped my bags with André, my concierge, and went on to the Embassy. Ralph must have had a meeting with some visiting congressmen that day: he was wearing his most sincere three-button, oxford gray suit. "You're a credit to the taxpayers," I said.

"Thanks," he grinned. "How did it go?"

I told him how it went, and ended by asking: "Who is Señor Gonzales?"

"I think I know who he is although I've never met him. Let me check." Two quick telephone calls and Ralph said: "That's the guy. He's an *eminence grise*. He operates between the Spanish government and foreign private enterprise. Actually he runs one of the biggest private banks in Spain. He knows whereof he speaks."

"Whereof?"

Ralph looked sheepish. "That's what happens when you write too many reports and brief too many people."

"I seem to be briefing you."

"That's good." He tilted back the swivel chair and put his heels on top of the desk. I was walking rapidly about the room as though action would help my mind to function more quickly.

"Dr Gonzales gave me a slight insight. Enough to let me understand that if you can't lick them, you join them." I leaned against the desk. Ralph slid down in the chair so that his head was against the back. "I worked damned hard on those abortive projects. I came up with new financial and tax angles. There's a hell of a lot of money in this."

"You plan to go ahead?"

"Why should all that work go down the drain? Property development in Spain, if handled right, can't fail."

Ralph sat upright. "Although you never said anything to me about it, I gathered you were on another track when you and Nokato were hi-jacked. And it didn't have to do with property in Spain. I got you a lot of economic information about the developing countries in Africa."

"That was the old Ben Clancy. It was a wild idea."

"I hadn't seen you so excited about anything since you got the scholarship to law school."

I shook my head. "What I'm talking about now is something that's feasible. I'm going back to see those bankers in Zurich. That is, if they really exist. And if they're who and what they claimed to be."

"What do you mean?"

"The men I met supposedly represented the International Confederal Bank."

"Is there such a bank?"

"They've got nice stationery with their letterhead. They exist as far as mail, telegrams and telephone calls are concerned. They picked up the tab for everything including the chartered airplane. But I've never been to the office. I don't know if Laurel and Hardy were really bankers or funnymen Maurice Richard rigged up for me to talk to in Zurich."

"Laurel and Hardy?"

Sitting in the chair at the side of the desk I picked up a pencil and made marks on a long, yellow, lined pad that meant nothing to anyone but to me. "That's what I call them. Their names are Oliver and Hardt. They supposedly checked my reports. Studied and made comments before forwarding them to the head of the syndicate, Mr Johnson, in New York."

"If they're stooges of Richard's do you think you'll find them?"

"They'll have gone to cover but I've got some idea of how to smoke them out."

Before leaving Ralph's office I called Françoise using the signal we had agreed: the phone would ring twice, I would hang up and then dial the number again. She answered the moment it rang the second series. I assured her I was fine; that the trip had been all right. I told her I couldn't come right over: I had another appointment this afternoon. I'd pick her up in about two hours and would bring her suitcase with her things from the hotel in Majorca. We were having dinner tonight with Ralph and Mildred.

The expressionless receptionist at Interpol headquarters had me wait in a different but identical cubicle. Inspector Albert Giraud appeared. After the usual handshake I apologized for disturbing him. He waved it aside and took me to his office.

"We are very much interested in your hi-jacking," he said. "We are working with IATA in trying to evolve methods to prevent hi-jacking of aircraft."

"This one was worked out carefully. There was an accomplice on the ground. His name is Louis d'Alamo and he runs El Club Bunnie in Madrid," I said.

It took several of the loose-leaf books, the cross-checking of names and crimes and the verification in the Spanish criminal police file before Inspector Giraud was able to pull yet another binder out of the shelf. He opened it on the desk. "Is this the man?" he asked.

I stared down at the flat shadowless identification photographs. The profile made me nod. Giraud read off the description. The name over the pictures was not Louis d'Alamo but he had occasionally used it. At the moment he was not wanted. However the color of the tab labelled him as a potentially dangerous criminal.

"Yes, that's your man." Giraud looked up from reading details on the other side of the page. "He served three years in the same prison in France with Maurice Richard. They undoubtedly met there."

"Was he in for kidnaping too?"

"A form of it, you might say." Giraud pulled the centre metal rings apart of the loose leaf book. He plucked out the page devoted to the man I knew as Louis d'Alamo. "It is politely known as white slavery although it does not necessarily have to be white."

"He's still doing business at the same stand." Giraud's high forehead wrinkled. I went on: "To put it politely he's still running a house of prostitution although the girls also have to be able to dance flamenco."

Being with Inspector Albert Giraud made me feel better. He was like a touchstone: he gave forth the truth.

He was what he was: an international policeman who had no involvement with me or with what had happened to me, except as it fell into the terms of reference of Interpol. We had had no previous personal relationship. Of all the people I knew he was the only person I trusted completely. After he had meticulously returned the books of the files to their correct places in the bookshelves he said, "I have an appointment near the Madeleine in forty-five minutes. If you have nothing better to do, why not walk over with me. We can have a drink before my appointment."

We sat at the sidewalk café watching the cars and pedestrians. I told him I was going to Zurich to try to pick up the trail of Maurice Richard. I did not believe Richard had acted alone.

"He is capable of committing an involved crime alone," Giraud said. "Eleven years in prison gives a man a lot of time to think. To go over the mistakes which got him into jail. I would say that some of the most daring and carefully executed crimes such as the big bank robberies are worked out by men in confinement."

"But the hi-jacking of President Nokato doesn't make sense viewed that way. Where's the payoff? Maurice Richard didn't kidnap Nokato for patriotic reasons. I can see him doing it for someone who paid him enough. He certainly never planned to hold Nokato for ransom."

Giraud looked sceptical. "Did you ever meet Richard in Switzerland?"

"Yes." I hesitated. "Let me think. I went to Switzerland for the first time about two months after I started working for Richard. I had problems concerning Swiss tax and banking laws. Richard suggested that we go to Zurich. The chartered plane would pick us up at Le Bourget. But early that morning I got a phone call from Richard; he'd been called to New York. But I was to use the plane as planned. 'I was only going to introduce you to the Swiss bankers,' he said. 'I don't understand high finance. I'm really only the office boy for all this.' "

The waiter brought another glass of milk for Giraud and a minute cup of coffee for me. He slipped the bill under the ashtray.

"You're right," I said. "Richard never did go on any trips with me to Switzerland."

"He wouldn't go to Switzerland with or without you."

"How do you know that?"

"The Swiss are very particular about the people they let into their country. They don't appear to pay attention when you enter but they check on everyone. No, Richard would never have dared go there. They would have turned him back or even held him. And you would have found out who he was."

During the next weeks I saw quite a bit of Albert Giraud. I phoned him whenever I returned to Paris. Usually I needed information about someone who had been associated with Maurice Richard. But often it was just to see him, I liked his company. We'd meet at a small restaurant near the Bourse or, if he had a mysterious rendezvous, it would be in a bistro in one of the working class arrondissements. Invariably the talk would touch upon restaurants and hotels in the United States until I got an inkling of what this was all about. Albert Giraud wanted to quit his job and become a maître d'hôtel in a good New York restaurant. I told him that I was certain New York was filled with head-waiters who would adore being inspectors of Interpol.

He had begun working in cafés when he was a boy. Before joining the police he had worked in London, where he had met his wife. He had been called upon to use this early experience during state banquets when he would double as a waiter. He had been seconded from the

Sûreté to Interpol. He did not find anything glamorous about being an international detective: the hours were long, the work routine, the pay low. He and his wife lived in Versailles where it was less expensive than Paris and where the air was healthier.

One of the most amusing contradictory aspects of Albert – we soon were calling each other by our first names – was his extreme suspicion of everyone. Invariably, before checking our coats at a restaurant he would make certain I'd left nothing in the pockets, not even a pair of gloves. After what had happened to me, and was still happening, I joined his club. I was beginning to have doubts about the trustworthiness of everyone including Ralph and Mildred and Françoise.

Chapter Thirteen

We reached Zurich late in the afternoon. Françoise had never been there. Not knowing how long we'd stay I opted for the nearest hotel across the small bridge from the bahnhof. We were given a large corner room with twin beds pregnant with puffed eiderdowns. While Françoise unpacked, washed and put on fresh make up, I took the telephone directory to the fading light beside the window. International Confederal Bank was listed with a telephone number and a street address I did not have. I had written to a post office box: this was the custom not only with Swiss banks but banks in virtually every country. It was too late in the day to telephone.

Then I looked up the name, Oliver. The one I wanted was under his initials with the added information that he was a banker. I found Hardt in the city of Zurich directory too. So far so good: I would find out tomorrow whether the faces I knew went with those names.

Next morning I left Françoise in the hotel room buried under the eiderdown having chocolate and brioche. I told her I had some shopping I wanted to do and that I'd be back before lunch. She had the newspapers and some magazines to keep her company. It was cold. The wind was coming off the Alps where it had snowed again during the night. Zurich and the lake were roughly like a shallow soup plate with the misty hills as the sides. I had studied a map of the city and had calculated the walk. The numerous clocks on banks, churches and in the shop windows made certain I'd be on time for my self-made appointment. At a large department store on Bahnhofstrasse I turned and walked towards a new office building that did little to advance Swiss architecture. It appeared to have been planned by a child; it was square in shape, oblong windows regularly placed with an oblong glass entrance in the middle.

I got out of the automatic elevator at the sixth floor to face a set of heavy wooden doors marked "International Confederal Bank". When I pushed one open I realized they were metal doors painted to simulate wood. I wondered if this was a warning of what was to come.

The anteroom reminded me of my dentist's except that here the magazines were in German and French. A frosted glass window slid back and a bovine girl with a muddy complexion and rimless glasses stolidly bid me good morning. How she knew that I was to be addressed in English was one of those instincts the Swiss have.

"I'd like to see Mr Oliver and Mr Hardt. Or either one if the other is busy," I said.

"Do you have an appointment?"

"No, but I'm certain they'll see me. Please tell them that Mr Ben Clancy is here."

My name meant nothing to her. Yet I had telephoned this office often until two and a half months ago. Perhaps this was a new receptionist, more likely I had telephoned to a private number.

"Would you please take a chair," she said. I glimpsed the small, desk switchboard beside her but could not see anything else. She closed the glass partition. I stood there, I could hear nothing. I sat down and studied the brogues I was wearing; they'd been highly polished during their night's wait outside the hotel room.

It had not been like this the first time I visited Zurich.

That morning the car and driver had been waiting outside my apartment building as Maurice Richard had told me it would be. At Le Bourget a long-legged English girl in the dark cap, tight fitting short skirt and short jacket of an airline stewardess introduced herself as a member of the crew of my private aircraft. Quickly she shepherded me through immigration. A small bus drove us to the bay where a twin-jet plane was parked. Aside from the British flag and the international registration number painted on the fuselage, there was no other identification. The pilot and co-pilot also in uniforms were waiting at the aircraft steps. They saluted and asked if I was ready to leave. I was shown into the cabin: later to become written indelibly on my memory. It was similar to the cabin of a yacht; easy chairs near the forward section, couches on either side farther back which made into berths, a door at the rear leading to the toilet. I assured the stewardess I was fine as she fastened my safety belt and the engines started. I didn't want anything to drink but I wouldn't mind coffee and a roll after we were in the air.

When we reached Zurich there was the same efficient

procedure. Before leaving the plane I told the pilot I didn't know when we'd return to Paris. He said he'd telephone me at three that afternoon. The suite at the Hotel Bar au Lac was elegantly ostentatious. I gave the operator the number Richard had instructed me to telephone. A woman's voice answered and announced in German that this was the International Confederal Bank. I asked for Mr Hardt or Mr Oliver. When I gave my name I was put through to a deep bass voice with a guttural accent: "Hardt speaking. Good day, Mr Clancy. I hope you had a pleasant trip."

"Couldn't be better," I replied. "Your city looks charming with the view from here of the lake."

"Zurich can be beautiful if the weather is good."

"I'm sorry that Mr Richard could not come with me. He had to go to America at the last minute."

"It is only important that my colleague, Mr Oliver, and I meet with you. We have studied the preliminary reports you sent us. We would like to discuss our suggestions before you write the final report."

"I am at your disposal. I can come right to your office."

"We would not think of inconveniencing you, Mr Clancy. We will come to you," he announced firmly.

I told him to please call me on the house phone when they arrived and I'd meet them in the lobby. But we didn't meet downstairs; we never met anywhere but in the hotel suite. It seemed to make sense for it was large, comfortable and private and the room service was perfection. In all the times I went to Zurich to work with the two bankers we never met anywhere else but in the living room of my suite in the hotel. I wondered if the two Swiss bankers really did exist: perhaps they were ghosts who only materialized in my hotel. Did they dissolve into the lake mist when they walked out of the door? They had impressed me with their thorough knowledge. They were two-legged computers who had not been wired for small talk or emotion, although they had been programmed for a few gestures of politeness. There was not the slightest grain of humor or warmth in either of them. The fact that Oliver was long, lean and had wide eyes while his colleague, Hardt, was large, rotund and had a stubby moustache, made me think of them as Laurel and Hardy.

At that first meeting they demonstrated their professional ability. They threw back facts and figures as well as laws. They explained that Mr Johnson and his group in America were waiting for our combined efforts on the matters under consideration. Would it be possible for me to go through everything and have another discussion? We agreed to meet here the next morning. It was almost five o'clock when they left.

We finished the next afternoon after a satisfactory session that ran through and included lunch. Oliver and Hardt agreed with my way of handling the complicated alignment of companies; it would afford the widest latitude and operation on a global scale. Hardt said they did not feel our time had been wasted. This was high praise coming from them. We agreed to be in touch by telephone and mail. They would have my new report typed up immediately and forwarded to Mr Johnson.

No mention was ever made of Maurice Richard receiving copies of reports or of being included in subsequent conferences. When I mentioned this to Maurice Richard at our next meeting he said that he was delighted not to be included. He was basically a front man, or as he depreciatingly put it, an office boy, for Mr Johnson. That explained why he was moving about so swiftly at the commands of his superior, handling matters which could not be accomplished by telephone or cable.

I had checked my diary of the past year. I had been to

126

Zurich seven times. The routine with Oliver and Hardt had always been the same. Ten days after the first trip Jean Reinach had called me into his shabby office, the decor for old family law firms was the same in France as in Britain. Reinach had shown me a letter of appreciation from the International Confederal Bank expressing its client's approval of my work and enclosing a large check as a retainer. Jean Reinach wanted to turn the entire sum over to me but I'd refused. I explained that I never would have had this account if I had not been accidently working on something else out of his office. I left the money matter to him. He was more than generous. Everything seemed bright and gay, Paris was the way I'd heard of it in songs and stories. I was on my way.

The frosted glass of the receptionist's window slid open. The girl's voice brought me back to the present. A buzzer sounded at the door. I pushed it open to look down a long corridor. A dumpy woman was walking towards me. She was wearing what appeared to be a man's double-breasted suit altered for her into a coat and skirt. She expressed regret for having kept me waiting: I wasn't expected. You can say that again, I thought.

We entered a door that had a number but no name on it, but then the Swiss keep everything financial anonymous. I followed her into a secretary's office. She knocked on the other door, turned the knob, opened it and asked me to enter. Hardt was sitting in a deep office chair, his back three-quarters to me, studying a sheaf of papers. I heard the click of the latch behind me as I started towards the desk. He put down the papers. The large round head raised, then slowly turned towards me. I stopped. There was a resemblance in size, girth and coloring, even in the moustache. But this man was not Hardt.

He saw the shock on my face and merely blinked the lids over his protruding cow-like eyes. Getting to his feet he held out his hand. "Herr Fischer," he introduced himself. "How do you do, Mr Clancy. Will you not have a seat please."

"How do you do," I replied automatically after shaking hands and let myself down into the chair. "I'm sorry to bother you. I asked to see Mr Hardt or Mr Oliver."

"Unfortunately they are both away."

"When will they return?"

"In several days I believe, but I am not certain. Is there not something that I may do to assist you, Mr Clancy?"

"I've only dealt with Mr Hardt and Mr Oliver."

The shoulders inside the padded suit shrugged. "I am certain that if they had known you were coming, they would have arranged their schedules."

I was tempted to say that I doubted that. I also wondered why they always traveled in pairs, but I realized that that question would get me nowhere in this anonymous world. I was here. It was up to me to get as much out of everything as I could. If there was no blood in the turnip, still there was something that served in a similar capacity. I was determined to stick to my new resolution: in a sewer a sewer rat is the best fitted to survive.

"I don't know how much you are familiar with my dealings with Mr Oliver and Mr Hardt," I began.

"We keep records of everything, Mr Clancy."

"I investigated a number of investment and growth opportunities for a client of your bank, Mr Johnson."

"Ah yes, Mr Johnson," the big head wagged.

"I don't know what the current status is of these enterprises. I've been out of touch with things for the past two and a half months."

"So I was given to understand," Fischer blandly agreed.

"I'd like to know where these projects now stand. Perhaps Mr Johnson and his group are no longer interested. I want to make certain. It would be unethical to discuss these things with other parties."

Herr Fischer's small mouth was open slightly and he was breathing in and out like a goldfish. It all made sense with the straight-laced, hard-shelled attitude he affected. I was a lawyer who had done certain work for a client. Nothing had happened with the projects. I wanted to make certain the original client had dropped them before suggesting them to another client.

Before I left there was a thaw in Herr Fischer. I stressed that I felt that Hardt and Oliver should be consulted. I would feel better if I could discuss it with them for they too had contributed to the various projects. Herr Fischer said he would have them telephone me in Paris when they returned in a few days.

"I'm taking a vacation," I explained. "I'm going up to the mountains. I don't know exactly where. Suppose I telephone or send you a telegram and let you know where I am. Then you can notify me when Mr Oliver and Mr Hardt are back. I'll see them on my way through Zurich."

We shook hands on this. The programming for politeness was switched on, Herr Fischer wished me a pleasant holiday, and I began it by leaving that corridor of numbered doors.

I waited for the traffic signal to change to walk across the wide road at the foot of Bahnhofstrasse. I entered the big stone building with its gables and ever-present clock which gave it a sort of Christmas card quaintness. Inside there was the intermittent echo of loudspeaker announcements and the special smell of railroad stations. At an information desk the man told me without consulting charts that there was plenty of snow on the higher mountains. He pulled out some brochures. I could make up my own mind. He suggested I make a hotel reservation and pointed out the public telephone.

Before calling I again looked in the directory, wrote down two numbers and dialed the first one. There was no answer at Hardt's house. At Oliver's a woman told me in fluent English that he was away for several days. She didn't seem surprised when I avoided telling her who I was. She suggested I call his office and leave a message there. She gave me the office number: it was the same as that listed in the directory.

Chapter Fourteen

I never understood the fascination of trains because I was raised in the decline and decay of passenger rail service. Still, traveling on a Swiss train gave me an insight into their appeal. There was a warmth, comfort and stimulation watching the passing scenery. By comparison flying was like being stuffed into a metal container and shot through a pneumatic tube. At the toy-like station a porter with the name of our hotel on his cap picked up our bags. I stopped at the post office and sent Herr Fischer a telegram telling him where I was.

Skiing is a unisex sport. Wearing helmet or cap, sunglasses or goggles, as well as the rest of the outfit, skiers are as unidentifiable as vizored knights in armor. Skiing is one of the few sports where women look as good as men. We swung down the middle run in wide arcs, not hurrying, enjoying every moment, knowing that eventually we would arrive together at the bottom with a feeling of happiness: a paraphrase of our yesterday's sport when the sky had darkened and the snow came down outside the balcony of our room.

"Why did you not tell me you skied so well?" Françoise called above the clank and rattle of the ski lift.

"You never asked me," I laughed at her swinging in the chair ahead of me. "Why didn't you tell me you were so good?"

"I wanted to surprise you."

The sound of her voice echoed over the abrupt indentation below us. There was a sharp crack. We watched a cascade of last night's snow, which had not merged into the icy under layer, shake loose, gather into a miniature avalanche and crash to the bottom of the ravine. The sun made the snow a dazzling blue white. We wore dark goggles. When we got off the chair lift we were on the highest point overlooking the valley. There was no one else in sight. The few ski tracks that took off at this point revealed that not many people had been here today. It was like being on top of a fresh world. Far below the miniature village connected to us by the thin metal lines of the lifts and the marks of the ski runs. The horizon showed a succession of mountains like frozen waves. We pushed along the top of the ridge.

I stopped to wait for Françoise to catch up. I'd always been better at cross-country runs than at downhill racing. The slope was steep. Above, the rise was abrupt, leading to a direct fall of rock. When Françoise reached me I pointed to the run we could take across the virgin snow. At this angle it would be very sharply down hill.

"It'll save having to go back to the trail at the chairlift," I said.

Françoise studied the slope before answering: "It is fine

131

for me. I like downhill racing. Would it not be too much of a drop for you?"

"I don't think so. I feel like going fast. Forgetting everything."

As I swung my skis around something caught my eye. A man – although it might have been a woman – was standing not far from the ski lift. He wore a white ski outfit with a peaked Alpine cap. He had on dark glasses but was too far away to distinguish his, or her, features. He was watching us. I motioned to Françoise to start. She pushed off. I dug my sticks into the snow. As I did I heard a sharp crack. I looked to my left. The person in white had taken off his gloves. He brought the palms of his hands together; it sounded like a pistol shot.

I was moving slowly, not having pointed very sharply down the slope. Françoise was below, to the left of me, picking up speed. Then I sensed before I heard, another noise: it was a rumble. I yelled: "Françoise! Look out!"

She glanced at me over her shoulder. I pointed behind me. "Go! Go!"

I was pushing hard on my sticks, lifting myself up and forward. I had almost caught up with her. We started to pick up speed. Out of the corner of my eyes I saw the distant figure in white standing on his skis, putting back his gloves. He was watching the race he had just started. His entry had given us a head start. The rumble became deeper, more persistent, along with it another sound: a cracking noise. I glanced over my shoulder. On the steep crevice above us the top snow was sliding, gathering up the other snow in front of it, gaining momentum.

We had two advantages over our opponent: we had a head start and we did not have to go straight down. As we sped diagonally across the slope we were moving faster than I had ever skied. I could feel the rush of wind on my back as the air was pushed ahead by the following avalanche. The rumble of snow was growing to a roar. Snow was shooting up between our skis. We were both crouched in egg shape offering as little wind resistance as possible, our sticks held parallel to our skis.

It wasn't fast enough. The first wave of snow caught the back of my skis and shot ahead of me. I struggled to keep my balance. The river of snow reached Françoise. There was a wave of wind on my right. Then a roar. I couldn't keep upright. I felt myself going and leaned forward to get as far away as possible from the centre of the avalanche. Then I was down in the snow, sliding face forward. I formed my arms in a wide circle over my head so that there'd be a hollow space to breathe when the snow covered me. My momentum was slacking. I could feel more than hear the shriek of wind and the noise. Everything was white. I could see nothing. Then the sound was gone. I could move my arms. The snow offered no resistance. Bringing my gloved hands to my goggles I cleared away the snow. I could see the sky and the mountains. I raised my head. Françoise was lying ten yards ahead of me on top of the snow. Fortunately the ski-bindings had held, I got my skis in position and rose. Just a few yards from where we had fallen was the path of the avalanche. The echo came to us of the crash as the tons of snow fell into the deep ravine below. And then it was still.

I bent down beside Françoise. Putting my arm about her I held her. I looked towards the line of masts that supported the wires of the lift. A row of empty chairs were swinging as they clanked up and down. The man in white was gone.

When I reported what had happened to the hotel proprietor he was horrified. He insisted that I must go immediately to the senior guide of the area and tell him about it. The senior guide was the proprietor of the shop where we had rented our ski outfits. His weather-creased face did not move while he listened to me, his pale blue eyes unblinkingly fixed on mine.

"That was a most dangerous place to ski," he said.

"I found that out," I snapped in irritation. "Why did that man deliberately clap his hands to start an avalanche?"

"One of the duties of the guides is to get rid of extra snow that might cause larger more dangerous avalanches. Especially after a snow storm near a ski run. Any sharp noises can start the snow," he explained pedantically.

"But why do it with us right under it?" I demanded.

"Perhaps he did not see you," the senior guide said.

There was no point arguing this: he had seen us. "Who the hell was it, is all I want to know?"

"I do not know, Mr Clancy. I have already checked all our guides. It is true that they do wear white ski suits and such caps. But none of the guides was up there at the time you mentioned."

We didn't ski anymore that day. We walked to the big café facing the skating rink to sit quietly having a drink. It was all calm, charming, normal and delightful until I thought about what had happened. A wave of fury rose inside me that brought bile to my mouth. Only one person, only one organization, knew we were here. This was their way of showing they had received my telegram.

Chapter Fifteen

We spent the next days skiing but stayed on the usual slopes and at the discotheques. I had not realized there were so many people here: they were not on the ski runs or the ice-skating rinks; they saved their strength for the dance floor. In après-ski outfits the girls looked great and the men handsome, bronzed and athletic. There is something about high altitudes which makes me feel as though I'm running a slight, yet agreeable fever; it gives me twice the energy I normally have. We folded before midnight: the dance floor and ski slopes weren't the only enjoyable activities.

It was the best time we had ever had together. I told Françoise the version of our near accident I'd gotten from the senior guide. She did not connect this with what had happened at Ibiza. It dawned on me that then, as now, I had been waiting for the Swiss bankers, Oliver and Hardt. And again with almost dire results. I said nothing of this to Françoise. She got in a happy, carefree frame of mind. She began talking about herself, something she had never done.

She told me of her childhood, her loneliness after the death of her mother when she was six. Her unsuccessful attempts to gain affection from her meticulous, stern aunt and father who was engrossed in his medical practice. She spent her vacations in the mountains where her mother's closest friend lived with her husband and children. She learned to love the mountains, to ski and to climb. When she returned to her father's house – even as a child she never thought of it as home – she conjured up those happy times by drawing and painting them. Her talent was revealed in school. Her paintings were sent to Munich to the International Children's Library which sponsored a yearly exhibit. One of her paintings of the mountain village in winter was chosen by UNICEF for a Christmas card.

"So you see, at ten, I was a world-renowned artist," she said with mock despair. "After that, everything was an anticlimax."

"Everything?"

"Well, not quite," she answered. "I was too young then to know about things like this or even to imagine them. I was a very innocent child. But I did know then that I was going to be a painter. While other little girls were imitating their mothers, playing with dolls and thinking about what it was like to be a mother, I was putting down colors and designs on paper."

"There's nothing to stop you from being both is there?"

"I never wanted to," she said quietly.

"Even now?" I propped myself on an elbow. I looked at the pale face, high cheek bones, vivid blue eyes framed in auburn hair and wished that I could paint her as I saw her now. She could read my thoughts.

"I don't know, chéri," she answered.

"Why not? Is there anything better than this? Than in just living and in just being together?"

"I don't believe there is. But it won't last."

"Why won't it?" I asked irritated.

"Because you won't let it. Because too much is going on inside you to permit you to live in peace with yourself. And with me."

Her arms went about my neck. She pulled me down to her warmth and to the taste of the salt of her tears.

The fourth morning a telegram arrived from Fischer in Zurich saying that his colleagues would be in the office the following Monday and would be pleased to see me that afternoon. I made train reservations and tried to forget about it for the next four days. I didn't succeed. I'm not too good at compartmentalizing my thoughts and emotions and unfortunately the two overlap. A picture kept recurring of me walking into that office next Monday afternoon to be confronted by two men bearing the names of Oliver and Hardt whom I had never met.

We caught the small clog-train that crawled down the mountain sides to meet the Zurich express at the cross station. We walked across the wide street from the station to the hotel. I told the receptionist I did not know how long we would be. We might leave late this afternoon, tonight or tomorrow.

This is where I came in, I thought to myself, when, for the second time, I entered the International Confederal Bank and the frosted glass slid back and the bovine girl peered at me. The circle was still there: walking down the same corridor, following the same secretary in that dandy altered man's suit, into her office, the knock on the door, her opening it and telling me to enter. Turned away from me the same figure was sitting in the office chair studying papers. The door clicked shut.

"Herr Fischer," I said as I walked towards him.

The papers dropped from the hands to rustle down onto the desk. The chair swung towards me. It was not Herr Fischer.

"How nice to see you, Mr Clancy."

Hardt was standing holding out his hand. At the same time another door which I had not noticed, opened and a long thin figure walked in, also holding out his hand. It was Oliver.

I caught my breath. They were smiling, telling me how glad they were to see me. They hoped that I was well and apologized for not having been in Zurich when I'd paid my earlier visit.

"We are sorry you took the trouble to come here." Hardt resettled himself, filling the chair behind the desk.

As I sat down opposite him I thought that if they had had their way I wouldn't have troubled either them or myself. I would have passed through Zurich in a pine box.

"We telephoned the Bar au Lac but were informed there was no reservation for you." Oliver had seated himself facing the narrower side of the desk. "We would have come to see you at the hotel."

This was closing the circle too neatly. Still it gave an indication that we could pick it all up from where we had left off. It was similar to a rocket-ship re-entering the earth's orbit. I estimated the correct angle of re-entry. I decided on an oblique approach. I did not want to try a head-on attack and be immediately destroyed or a too shallow one and be bounced off. I set my course.

I assured them that I was well, that what had happened was most regrettable. We agreed that we were all surprised about Maurice Richard. I pointed out that the hi-jacking would not have taken place if they had arrived in Majorca when they were supposed to have.

"We were delayed by Mr Johnson," Hardt replied.

"We received a cable telling us to wait for him to join us here. We would all fly to meet you in Majorca," Oliver added.

"Did Mr Johnson show up?"

"No, there was no point in his coming when all of you disappeared," Hardt said.

"Have you ever met Mr Johnson?"

The two Swiss bankers glanced towards each other. There was a flash between them. When they looked back at me there was no expression in their eyes.

"Mr Clancy, we do not talk about our clients," Oliver said.

"I'm asking a very simple question. You're not a

138

doctor or a priest. I'm not asking you to betray your code of ethics or to reveal something professional."

"But you are."

I wondered if this meant the code of ethics or revealing something professional. I decided it was both. "Look, I put in a lot of hard work on the various studies and reports I was asked to do. I think I'm entitled to an explanation after what happened."

"What happened was not the fault of ours." Hardt sat as straight as the back of the black chair and there was about as much expression on his thin features.

"It was the fault of your client, Mr Johnson," I snapped. "Richard was working for him."

"Mr Johnson and his associates regret that very much. You can imagine what a shock it was to them to discover the sort of man Richard was."

"It was more of a shock to me and to my friend, President Nokato," I replied. "I find it difficult to believe that Mr Johnson and his associates, who were so careful and thorough about everything, did not know who and what Richard was when he was hired."

"I can not answer that, Mr Clancy. I don't know what our client knew. We are employees, so to speak, of our client. We do his wishes to the best of our abilities."

"Is it possible then, for Mr Johnson to be some other person?"

"What do you mean, Mr Clancy?"

"That Mr Johnson is a false name, not the client's real name. That it might be more convenient to refer to him by that name rather than as a number?"

"It is possible," Hardt replied after a significant pause.

"Then that name could be the same as a numbered account in the bank?" I went on.

"That is correct."

We sat staring at each other. I had worked out my next move. I didn't have to do any acting. "Look, I've been used as a tool and a dupe. I've gotten a friend involved in a harebrained scheme that got him hi-jacked and confined. My reputation has been smeared. And you expect me to sit still and not want to know who's behind all of this?"

"Maurice Richard was behind it. Our client regrets having employed Maurice Richard," Oliver said.

They were either too clever or too polite to mention that I was being paid off through the retainer with Reinach and Frères, or maybe they figured that Reinach was keeping all the money and they didn't want to reveal this to me. They probably couldn't have cared less. It was not their money.

"Well, I may not be able to do anything about how and why this all came about." I adopted an air of defeated petulance. "But I'm damned if I'm willing to let all my hard work go down the drain. Ethically and professionally I was working for Mr Johnson and his associates. If they're not going to move on these projects I want to."

"Our colleague, Mr Fischer, told us that you had made this proposal." The expression of the two Swiss bankers was less formidable. My previous outburst had had as much effect on them as throwing pebbles at a tank.

"What about the Pan-African scheme? Mr Johnson and his group were certainly steamed up about that. It was top priority. Is that going ahead?"

"We have no reason to suppose it is not," Oliver said.

"Nor have we any reason to suppose it is," Hardt amended. "President Nokato was important to it. His abrupt removal has caused complications."

"I should hope it would." I was honestly indignant now. "It would be a terrible thing if someone else replaced him."

"We actually know nothing about this," Hardt cut in. "Were you thinking of carrying that through, Mr Clancy?"

"I should say not. It would take millions of dollars just for openers."

"We were led to believe you wanted to know about the Spanish projects."

"That's right. The Spanish government is still willing and eager to go ahead. The conditions I negotiated still stand. It's a viable proposition. The interlocking companies will work. The tax incentive is attractive. I should think that Mr Johnson and his group would be interested in moving on it."

"We thought that it had merit, too." Hardt's big head nodded. "But you must realize that we initiate nothing for our clients."

"However," Oliver picked up, "we did get in touch with Mr Johnson and appraised him of your interest after your conversation with Herr Fischer. We were informed that Mr Johnson thanks you for calling it to his attention. He and his associates are no longer interested. You are free to take over the entire thing and to act on your own behalf."

I had failed to make the entry into that impregnable circle. I felt that I had the right angle. I made a new approach: "Would your bank be interested in entering into this venture?"

"We are not that sort of bank, Mr Clancy. We are not like the British and American merchant banks. We handle our clients' accounts. We invest for them only at their explicit instructions."

"Surely you're asked by your clients to make recommendations?"

"On those occasions we give our clients a number of choices. We will certainly bear in mind your proposal when next we are requested to suggest a sizeable amount for investment."

"Your project would tie up a considerable sum of money for a long period," Oliver amended.

"Exactly what kind of a bank is this?" There was no change in their expressions. "I should have asked this question long ago. You don't have to answer."

"We prefer to answer." Oliver spoke stiffly.

"You are free to examine the charter of incorporation at the government offices of the canton," Hardt said. "We are subjected to strict regulations."

"We will save you the time and trouble of having to look it up by giving you this information," Oliver added.

"We would be pleased to have you as one of our accounts."

They were turning the whole thing around on me. There was nothing I could do but play it their way. The circle was still there. No matter how or where I ran my hands along its circumference I could detect no flaw or crack whereby I could break into it. They also informed me that they would be pleased to furnish me with copies of my own reports, even letters which I had sent them, in the unlikely event I might not have them in my own files in Paris. They had an underling bring a large envelope with a brochure, prospectus and material about the International Confederal Bank. When I finally left they shook hands with me and told me the bank and they were at my service at any time.

Françoise and I caught the evening flight back to Paris. I read the information about the bank. It was all as clear and as anonymous as Oliver, Hardt and Fischer. That brought me right back to zero, a nice round shape. Still, we were alive, with no thanks to them. Now I knew what death looked like: he was an unidentifiable figure in a white ski suit clapping his hands.

Chapter Sixteen

I realized that Mr Johnson could be anyone except me. He could even be Maurice Richard except that Richard was in jail in Algiers along with President Nokato, and could not answer questions and give orders to Oliver and Hardt in Switzerland. Whether or not Françoise had accidentally been at Café Procope or had deliberately picked me up the night we met, I tentatively put to one side. She no longer was afraid to stay at her apartment. She discarded the canvases on which she had been working except for the strange portrait executed with blobs of paint. She put that on the top shelf in her studio where it glowered. She had made sketches of our trip, now she was transcribing them onto canvas, but they weren't all of Switzerland; some were of the French Alps as she remembered them as a child. She was excited, stimulated and felt she was making a great step forward with her work. She was again the amusing, independent girl I'd met that first night, although I had ceased being the wide-eyed American boy.

One evening I had dinner with Inspector Albert Giraud in a huge brasserie that had the tiled impersonal decor of a subway. That impression vanished when the food was served. I kept answering Albert's questions about American restaurants: it was a harmless fata morgana.

"Albert, is there any way of getting information about a small bank in Switzerland?" I asked.

"The Swiss are co-operative in police and criminal work," he replied. "But information about their banks is something else."

"I'd like to know about the International Confederal Bank located in Zurich."

"International Confederal Bank," he repeated. "I'll ask but do not expect anything."

"You've been very helpful about everything." He waved this aside. "I think it only fair to tell you that I'm not in the CIA."

"I know that. I checked after your first visit and was told you weren't."

He did not volunteer what else he'd been told or who it was who had told him. "And in spite of that you've still helped me?"

"Why not? You're sympathetic. I understand what is troubling you. It has been a shocking thing to have happened."

I said goodnight to Albert at the Metro. I too had a late rendezvous but it wasn't on a dark, windy corner as Albert's probably was. I returned to my apartment. I emptied some ice into the Thermos bucket and put it on a tray with glasses and whisky and carried it into the living room. I sat at the big chair in the corner window looking out at the dark ribbon of river hoping it would open to give me a glimpse of what I wanted to see. Finally I went downstairs to open the outside door. I was five minutes early. Archie arrived exactly on the appointed minute. He assured me he did not mind meeting here, the nightclub could get noisy and was not private.

"Have you heard from Madame Nokato in New York?" I asked after I'd closed the door.

"Yes, she was pleased to have that chat with you on the phone and news about Joe." I took Archie's top coat and hat and put them in the cupboard. "She's had a letter from him telling her not to worry."

"You hear from him, too, don't you?" When he nodded and we'd gone into the living room and he'd helped himself to a drink I asked: "How are you involved in all of this, Archie?"

He looked surprised. "I thought you'd figured that out."

"Well, that gives me the answer," I said.

"He backed me. I didn't have the scratch to open a joint like Le Town House and to keep it going. It's out of the red now but it lost dough for a while."

"It was a good investment on his part."

"It's also the unofficial headquarters for the pro-Nokato and other insurgent African movements."

"Did you know what I'd been discussing with President Nokato?"

"Yes. He told me when I saw him in Spain. I'm his right-hand man."

"Was, you mean."

"No, not was! Am!"

It was unusually quiet, even the distant and constant noise of the city's traffic was momentarily gone. I stared across the overlapping yellow pools of light coming from the lamps.

"Who told you to introduce me to President Nokato?" I asked.

"No one. I think you were at Le Town House one night when he dropped in."

"No one in New York or here told you that I should meet him?"

"No."

"And you just happened to look me up because your aunt wrote you about me?"

"That's right. I heard from her and others in Harlem what a good guy you were. After he met you, Joe Nokato wanted to know about you. I got more information. I heard some sort of story about your being fired because of the work you'd been doing in Harlem."

"That's neither here nor there."

"But it is. It meant something to me and it meant something special to Joe. That's why he asked you to help him with his boys. He trusted you."

"I wish the hell he hadn't. Somewhere I was put into that pipeline so that Joe would end up in Algiers."

He took a sip from his glass before replying: "You think I did it."

"You're the direct link."

He walked across the room and draped the coat over the back of a small chair. "To me, Joe is President Joseph Nokato, the father of his country. He's as important as General Charles de Gaulle was to the French during the war. He not only symbolizes, but he is, the future of my country."

"Your country! You're an American," I said in amazement.

"Am I? I didn't feel like an American when I was there. I feel even less like one living here."

"But you were born and raised there."

"If that's what makes an American I've got even better qualifications." I had never before heard bitterness in his voice. "I've represented the United States. I didn't win every time but I didn't do too badly, either."

"What sport?"

"Well, it wasn't swimming. Did you ever stop to think that we're among the best in all sports except swimming? I mean aside from equestrian events and sailing and such. Those take dough. You can't do them on empty lots or in the streets. And we don't compete in rifle and pistol shooting. Still we're getting pretty good at that now that we've gotten tired of being the targets."

"I never thought of it that way."

"I come from Maine. I was taught in school to believe in the Bill of Rights and in the Constitution: freedom,

146

equality and justice regardless of creed, religion and color. Oddly enough, I do believe in them. I played the game the way it was taught to me. I even made Phi Beta Kappa. Now that's a fraternity with no discrimination or prejudices. Only the gold key they gave me didn't unlock any doors. I wanted to be a Rhodes Scholar. I had the qualifications but I didn't make it. I've lived with my aunt and uncle and cousins in Harlem. I saw what was happening and what was being planned. The only way to equality was Black Power, violence, kill Whitey. How else can you change Harlem, Chicago, the South? So a few thousand or a few hundred thousand, or a million of us are killed. In the end there'll be progress and a fair deal. It makes as much sense, even more, than most wars. But Maine and the New England traditions are poor breeding grounds for anarchy and violence – at least in me.

"One thing I knew: I wasn't going to do the reverse and be an Uncle Tom. I'd taken courses in psychology and talked and worked with psychiatrists. A Negro with a mental breakdown is the same as a white man with schizophrenia or depression except that his basic problem springs from our physical one. Plus the basic conception engendered by the whites that we're inadequate. For us it is abnormal to be normal, to achieve something, to be competent. You have to overcome not only the way society regards you, but your own inadequacies. I took the easy way out."

"You came here," I said.

Archie shook his head. He unbuttoned his collar. "Later, much later. No, I enlisted in the army. They wanted me. I was sent to Officers Candidate School. Being in the military service frees you from ambition because advancement, if it does come, doesn't matter too much and besides it's out of your control. Everyone knows how much you earn and you know how much everyone else does. You don't have to worry about what suit or tie to wear to work in the morning. It takes all the strain off you except for one thing: it can't change the color of your skin.

"I was the ideal live recruiting poster for my people. Except that the poor bastards didn't have a chance to be recruited: they were drafted. I couldn't sit back while they were sent out to Vietnam so I volunteered."

"I didn't know that."

"Why should you? I'm not proud of it. Out there I learned that I hate killing. I don't want to shoot anyone. I hate that more than I hate all the other things put together. And brother, that's too much hate for one man to have. Like a double negative it neutralizes itself. I didn't want to stay in America when I finished my tour of duty. I got discharged because I knew I'd hate all white men and before too long I'd be shooting them before they could shoot me."

I didn't bother to throw in words or sentences to encourage Archie to talk. There was no holding him back: the dam inside him had burst from all the pressure of the accumulated years.

"There is going to be violence in American cities. There has to be because people can't continue to live like that, like pigs and cattle because we're not pigs and cattle – we are people! Now there's a wave of unemployment coming for those who do menial jobs and we can't move into the higher jobs. The mechanization of everything from the cotton fields to assembly lines and even household work means that the need for cheap labor is finished.

"The police are preparing for it. That's not the way to settle the terrible problem in the United States even if it is time for a revolution. Because it won't be a revolution: it'll be another civil war with unequal sides and right will not prevail." Archie laughed scornfully. "I hear myself saying these things and I realize I've been saying them to myself for years. But I didn't prepare myself to say them aloud. If I had I'd have marshalled my facts, presented them logically, point by point and not let it spill out of my guts like vomit."

"I'm flattered that you say these things to me."

For a moment he stiffened. He stared at me. There was no softness now in his eyes. "I'm not going to say that you're different. Every person is different. But I know you. I know what you've done. I know what's happened to you. You're like me. You're an idealist and you've been hurt. But you're not going to take it lying down. Well neither of us are. You're going to fight. That's why I'm telling you all this."

"Go ahead. I'm with you."

Archie suddenly stood still and stopped his weaving in and out of the maze of furniture. He smiled at me. The smile was in his eyes and deep down inside him. He sat in the chair again, facing me.

"Maybe violence is the only way for America. We'll soon know because it's about to happen. But as I said, I want no part of it, not if I can help it. And in this case I can help it. I didn't come to Paris just to escape. I came to prepare for what is going to come and perhaps to make it all come easier and with less death and destruction.

"I was going to be a sociologist. I thought that the best field for me because that's the one my problem comes under. It didn't help but it did teach me to think along certain lines, to ask questions and to do research. Where and how did all this start I asked myself? I knew only too well where it was going. In order to arrive at a solution, if there is one, I had to go back to the beginning."

"Where was that?" I was fascinated. What had happened to me was nothing compared to this.

"I asked my mother where she'd come from. And my father where he came from. I was able to trace my family on both sides as slaves to two different plantations, in the slave days. I went down South. I found relatives living near those farms. I lived with them. I had to beg my way into the country courtrooms and city halls where the old records are kept. I had to get rid of my uppity northern accent and do an imitation of the way the men in the courtyard thought a nigra should talk." He finished the last with an imitation of what he meant.

"I couldn't trace my father's family back beyond a few years before the start of the Civil War in 1861. It seems I had a white great, great, great grandparent which wasn't unusual. Did you know that by law in those days no slave husband could protect his wife against sexual and physical attack by a white man? And a mother couldn't protect her child from physical and sexual abuse. It was a deliberate attempt to break down and abolish the unity of the family. Still the slaves were supposed to go to church and be Christians."

There was irony in his voice: "I'm just presenting this to you as a sociologist but I should add that the white ancestor was a woman. That's on my father's side. The infant was turned over to a foster mother on a distant plantation. I never discovered who was the real mother. I had better luck with my mother's family.

"I went to Washington. There may be a lot of bad things about the American government but there's nothing wrong with the Library of Congress and the Archive Building. I had a letter from my old university professor saying I was doing research. I sure was. The files were opened to me. I learned a lot reading basic documents as you've just heard, about slavery in those United States. All those prejudices spring from slavery. Did you know it was forbidden to teach slaves to read and write? That practice has continued in the South until only a generation or two ago.

"Finally I found the log book of the ship that had brought that ancestor of my mother's to America. It wasn't in much detail: ship's logs never are but it gave me the Captain-Owner's name. It's a famous one in the history of the American revolution that was fought for liberty and justice. I went to Connecticut, to the port of that ship, even saw the house the captain had built. The place is a backwater now. The end of the great three-corner trade of slaves, molasses and rum finished it. I uncovered the detailed diary the Captain had kept. I found entries for the very trip that brought that boatload of slaves to America, even a line about my ancestor and what he sold for when he was landed in Baltimore. Most important of all I found out where the Arab slave traders had captured him and others of his tribe. He came from the same place and the same tribe as Joseph Nokato."

Archie let this sink in while he put some ice into his glass and added mineral water. He took a big gulp. I could only shake my head in wonder. "Is that why you looked up Nokato in Paris?" I asked.

"This was all before President Nokato had left his country. I went there. I went into the jungle, up the river to the villages of that tribe. I saw people who looked like my mother and sister and one of my brothers. Then I returned to the capital. Through the American ambassador I met President Joseph Nokato. I explained what had brought me to his country. I wanted to renounce my American citizenship immediately and become a citizen of the country from which my ancestor had come. President Nokato persuaded me not to do this, at least not for a while. He explained that I would be more useful and helpful to his country as an American. He sent me to

Paris. And when his second term of office as president finished about a year later, he followed. He had a plan,' Archie concluded significantly.

He knew I understood but still I asked the rhetorical question: "President Nokato's plan and yours was to set his country up as a homeland for the American Negroes just as the Jews did in Israel?"

"That was my original thought but Joe explained that it wouldn't work. The premise was wrong. Liberia had originally been formed supposedly for that very purpose, to bring the Negroes back to Africa from America. Our problem is different from the Jews. In the first place we don't have the unity of tradition and religion that the Jews have although God knows we've had the persecution.

"Still we're ahead of the Jews in one respect: we don't have to fight for our Promised Land. It is waiting for us, peopled by us. It is Africa. It is the home of all black men. It is a big enough bastion to hold all of us. From there we can emerge to be as strong as the Asians and the Caucasians in the Occident. We are not going to be wiped out like the Indians were in North and South America. We'll come together because we have a common cause."

"Where did you come to this idea of Pan-Africa?" I asked.

"You should know, Ben. You're the one who sold it to Joe Nokato only four months ago. Until then I believed that if we could get just one country established with that policy we would have made a giant step. We'd have achieved enough in my lifetime. Then you came along with your grandiose conception and got Nokato committed to it."

"The hi-jacking of that airplane put an end to all of it."

"I refuse to believe that," Archie snapped. "It's the

only hope for the black man, not only in America but throughout the world."

"That's not what the Black Panthers and the other militant groups think."

"I know what they think and why. I've been with them. I've talked to and read Baldwin, Malcolm X, Eldridge Cleaver, Stokeley Carmichael and the others. They've taken that stand because they believe it's the only way to gain our rights in this generation. The minute they see what we're doing the whole emphasis will change."

"What if we don't get a chance to do it?"

"I refuse to believe that the most beautiful sight is black men wearing black berets, powder-blue shirts, black leather jackets, black trousers, shiny black shoes – and each with a gun."

Chapter Seventeen

Nothing gives you a quicker perspective of your problems than finding someone who has greater ones. Archie had been living with his all his life; mine were more recent. We both reacted the same way in assuming combat postures, determined to resolve them. However, I did not realize I had given Archie hope that there was a solution to his. Getting up from the chair I walked across the living room through the yellow circles of light. From the large window in the corner I saw two flashing lights which were moving too fast to be satellites. It was as easy to reach out and touch the lights of that airplane as it was to transfer into reality the plan that had given Archie such hope. In the reflection of the window I could see Archie standing in the middle of the room facing me.

"I didn't know that President Nokato had told you about the Pan-African Movement," I said.

"He told me everything. I was in charge here. I was waiting word from Majorca whether or not to dispatch the airplanes with arms and mercenaries or whether to call it off. I never heard. He was gone."

"Who else besides you did Joe talk to about this?" I asked.

"No one that I know of. Did others know?"

"Well, Maurice Richard knew. The Swiss bankers who were coming to join us in Palma knew. That's what the meeting there was all about. And Mr Johnson, whoever he is, especially knew. Because he originated the idea. That was the bait that got Joe to step onto the plane that was to be hi-jacked."

"Was he abducted to prevent him starting the revolution or from being the head of the Pan-African Movement?" Archie asked.

"From starting the revolt," I said firmly. "The Pan-African Movement didn't mean a thing really."

"You don't believe in it anymore?"

I hesitated. I recalled that I had not received an answer from the Swiss bankers that this plan was dead. In fact I had been outraged that it might go ahead without Nokato as the leader of it. Dimly I heard Archie saying: "You mean the whole idea was a fake? It was a fraud, to suck him in? I don't believe it."

When I had received the cable from Maurice Richard in Tokyo asking me to read the articles about a new religious movement in Japan I didn't know what he had in mind. I was concentrating on the Spanish project. I had dismissed the two magazine articles from my mind when, four days later, Maurice Richard arrived in Paris and

154

asked me to meet him in his suite at the Hotel George V. He wanted to know what I thought about the Soka Gakkai in Japan based on what I had read in those two magazine articles.

"From what I can gather, there are a number of religious and semi-religious movements in Japan," I said. "Soka Gakkai sounds like a Japanese version of Moral Rearmament grafted onto Buddhism or Shintoism but I'm no expert on either Japan or religions."

"Mr Johnson would like you to fly out to Japan and take a good look at the Soka Gakkai movement." I had learned enough about dealing with clients to say nothing until they had given a complete explanation of what they wanted. "It would also be a good notion for you to read up about some of the new contemporary movements like Scientology and others," Richard went on.

"Like what?" I was not certain I had heard correctly.

"You haven't heard of Ron Hubbard, the founder of the Church of Scientology?"

"No."

"I've got a file on it. It's especially interesting to know how he figured out how to found it and its doctrines. But that approach isn't quite the emphasis Mr Johnson suggests. You'll also find material about Moral Rearmament and others."

"That, I have heard of," I was able to say.

"Soka Gakkai is the most interesting. It's the only one for you to examine first hand. The suggestion is that you will do a paper for Mr Johnson and his associates."

"On what?"

"On how to form an all-embracing movement which every black African will want to join. Which will imbue in him a fervor and zeal for that organization."

Maurice Richard's attitude was not that of a man giving the directive for forming a world-embracing movement. It was that of a man who has decided on a trip and wants recommendations about the route and hotels. He appeared to find nothing unusual about the request he had put to me.

"I've been knocking my brains out about the Spanish deal," I said.

"Mr Johnson wanted me to inform you that he and his associates are very impressed by the way you handled the proposed Spanish project."

"Then why don't we do that instead of starting a wild goose chase to Africa by way of Japan?"

After lighting a fresh cigarette from the end of the old one he stubbed the butt in an ashtray. "Mr Clancy, I do not ask questions of Mr Johnson. I do what I am asked to do."

"But what happens with the property development plans for Spain? Do we just flush them down the drain? I'll have to account to a number of people in Madrid if it's suddenly abandoned."

"We are not abandoning it. It will be realized in time. You can explain that there are certain unforeseen developments which are delaying matters. If you wish I can drop a few words in the right places."

"What's behind all this? Don't tell me that Mr Johnson and his friends want to start a new church in Africa?"

"If it accomplished their purpose I am certain they would."

The telephone rang. A telephone was always near Richard. It was his umbilical cord. He told the operator to put through the call. From the conversation I knew it was the British pilot of the private airplane. Richard told him they would probably fly to Rome this evening but to telephone him again at six o'clock in case there was a change of plans.

"I expect to hear from Mr Johnson," Richard said to

me after he had hung up the telephone. "I never know where he will want me to go."

"Just who is Mr Johnson?" I asked.

"I told you when we first started working together that he is one of the wealthiest men in America. He has a number of associates equally wealthy. They are interested in investing enormous sums in enterprises that will pay off with large profits and still have the least possible amount of risk." Richard walked over to the bar set up on the buffet. He ignored the whisky and gin. He opened a bottle of mineral water. "Will you have something?"

"No, thanks." I waited for him to continue.

"Mr Johnson and his group test every element as well as every contingency before they commit their money." Richard leaned against the buffet. "It's in the new countries, the developing nations, in the centre of Africa where the potential lies. They are moving from the dark ages into the twentieth century in one step. Many companies and big interests have been burned by investing too soon before the governments are stable. There is too much unrest. If a calm came to those dozen or more new countries there'd be enormous prosperity."

I said: "Just how do you attain it?"

"What is needed is a creed, a movement, possibly a form of religion that isn't dogmatic. If we could get the people in Central Africa to rally to a basic principle, an essential cause, to understand that they all have the same problems, that united they can find the solution then there'll be stability."

"In other words this isn't being thought of as a political movement?"

"So far nothing has been thought of in specific terms. It would seem difficult to have a political movement due to the many individual nations, not to mention the interests of the various political parties. The solution is to have a movement, an organization, that ignores boundaries. One that unifies all people no matter what their country."

"Peace, it's wonderful!"

Richard did not get the irony in my voice. He nodded. "Peace! That is what every person wants no matter how well or poorly educated he is. And no matter where he lives."

"Unless of course he manufactures arms or is a professional soldier."

Richard regarded me with new respect. "Yes I think you have hit the correct note. Peace. How do we start an international peace movement in Africa?"

"You tell me."

"No, you're going to tell us," Richard replied.

"You've come to the wrong guy. Tell Mr Johnson what he needs is a combination of Bertrand Russell, Lumumba, Martin Luther King and Gandhi."

"This is not philanthropy. Mr Johnson is only interested in the financial benefits."

"It'll be all right, won't it, if in the process, the natives get some benefits?" I asked.

"Naturally. How else will they be able to unless they prosper and have wealth? Developing nations generate economic prosperity. Look at Japan and Germany after the war."

"They seem to have bred a few other things with it." Still, despite myself, I was getting caught up in the potential of all of this. Good can come out of evil. Why shouldn't something along these lines be feasible? All Mr Johnson and his associates wanted was to get richer.

A package of smoked cigarettes later I agreed to explore this new concept. Richard explained that research material on various peace, religious and other groups had been accumulated for me to study. There were also reports and studies on various foundations in the United States.

"Can we set up a foundation?" I asked.

"You can propose anything that will accomplish the mission I outlined but foundations are generally non-profit organizations," he said meaningfully.

"This could cost fifty to a hundred million dollars, maybe more. Have Mr Johnson and his associates that kind of money?"

Richard side-stepped this neatly: "If the plan is formulated correctly there is no reason why non-profit foundations and governments shouldn't contribute. Right now, much of the money they're putting up for aid to needy countries is being mismanaged and dissipated so that it is not achieving stable government nor helping the people. I should think they would welcome an organization or movement they could trust to accomplish their aims." I listened carefully when Richard spoke: it was like a tape-recorder playing back his master's voice. "The United States is pouring out money. And so is the United Nations through UNICEF, UNESCO, Food and Agriculture and other branches."

"You can't tell me that smarter and more experienced people than I haven't explored these problems and made suggestions," I said.

"Let us say that their spectrum was too broad, too theoretic. Yours is narrower, specific and practical."

"Can I call on people to advise me?" There was something highly chimerical about the whole thing and yet this very stolid man sitting across the table from me was in dead seriousness and so was his boss, and my boss, who was paying for all of this.

"It's not a good idea at this point. This is a preliminary

survey. It is a similar approach to Spain: you studied the project, proposed an attack, drew up a program. Do the same thing with this."

I thought of the people in Spain who should be notified and gave the names to Richard. He knew them for he had introduced me to them.

"When will you leave for Japan?" he asked.

"Isn't it possible to get all the information I need without my going to Japan?" I asked.

"No, it is something you have to see to understand. Soka Gakkai has swept across India, which proves that it doesn't necessarily have to be grafted onto Buddhism, for India is not predominantly Buddhist. And it is catching on in Western countries as well."

Richard gave me the name, address and telephone number of a Hungarian in Tokyo. He would familiarize me with Soka Gakkai and would fill me in on other movements that were similar. This man was expecting me. I was to keep in touch with Maurice Richard via cable or telephone. We agreed that it would be best if no one, including Jean Reinach, knew that I was on a trip to Japan. I would tell everyone that I was going to America because of certain complications with the probate of the Benson will that had brought me to Paris.

"If you want anything, or more information, please telephone the Bank in Zurich. If you want to get in touch with me leave word with Oliver or Hardt," Richard said in farewell.

"Can't I see Mr Johnson while I'm passing through New York?" I asked.

"I don't see why not, if he's there. Let me know when you'll be in New York and I'll arrange it."

While studying the material given to me by Richard I realized that there was more to the directive I'd been given than economics, finances and governments. It all boiled down to the individual African at whom all of this was directed. How would he react? What was his potential? If you asked John Gary and others you'd get a prejudiced reply. I knew how wrong they were but I needed as much scientific proof as possible.

I tracked down a number of studies about race and intelligence. Ultimately I settled on a UNESCO study, first done in 1951 and revised in 1966. It was a document on race by an international panel of scientists, geneticists, anthropologists, psychologists and sociologists. I put down the key findings as an essential part of my first paper to Mr Johnson and his associates: they might have the same prejudices as John Gary and Adolf Hitler: "The range of mental capacities in all races is much the same. Given similar degrees of cultural opportunity the average achievement of members of each ethnic group is about the same. All human beings possess educability and adaptability, their traits more than anything else have permitted the development of men's mental capacities. Racial discrimination has no scientific foundation in biological fact.

"Differences in the achievements of different peoples must be attributed solely to their cultural history. Neither in the field of hereditary potentialities concerning the overall intelligence and the capacity for cultural development, nor in that of physical traits, is there any justification for the concept of inferior and superior races."

I nailed that on the masthead of my new venture. I was now prepared to tackle Mr Johnson. I received word back from Richard, via a cable from Istanbul, that Mr Johnson would not be in New York.

I went through New York in a hurry. Three hours after landing at Kennedy Airport I took off for Japan.

Chapter Eighteen

I was sent to Tokyo to take an intensive course in religion from a Hungarian whose family name was written in his country's history. Berci, as he insisted I call him, was delighted to meet me and especially delighted to talk about our subject. He was like an overflowing pitcher; he wanted to pour out some of the contents so he could replace it with more.

I had read enough about Soka Gakkai to know it had been started by a Japanese school teacher about the time of the outbreak of war in Europe in 1939. The founder had been thrown into prison in 1944 for preaching anti-militarism. He had died in jail before the end of the war. The defeat of Japan in 1945 brought about a multitude of creeds and dogmas. Soka Gakkai was just one of them until ten years after the war when it shot far ahead, attaining a following in Japan of more than fifteen million people. It had a strong representation in the National Diet and in smaller local governing bodies. It had become a political entity as well as a religious one. It was spreading throughout Asia and had reached America.

Berci had me see the Soka Gakkai organization in action. I traveled to the shrine and world headquarters at the foot of Mount Fuji where every day thousands arrived for a two-day period of worship. It was staggering in its organization and wealth. And even more staggering in the fervor of its believers. I visited temples in Tokyo with Berci. All the while I was attempting to resolve how Soka Gakkai – it was an all-embracing movement as much as a religion – could be developed in Africa. I quickly came to the conclusion that it could not be directly transplanted: certain aspects were too fundamentally Buddhist. Still there was a similarity in the problems of the individual in Japan and Africa. And certain basic aspects of Soka Gakkai could be applied to Africa under a different label.

In the 1940's the destruction by bombing, including the first atomic bombs, of Japan, followed by the swift economic recovery caused dislocation of much of the population, the loosening of the traditional family ties and religious belief. Similarly in Africa there was now the erosion of the tribal system; the new economic and political structures were destroying the basic traditions of the people. In the cities as well as in native territories the African population was rootless due to the impact of mechanization, new methods of agriculture and husbandry.

No amount of reading and study in Paris could take the place of what I observed in Japan. I watched the worship in the temples, the small group meetings under the tutelage of a leader – similar to group therapy – talked to priests and believers and continually asked questions of Berci and received sage replies. I began to understand how the gregarious type of worship of Soka Gakkai could appeal to Africans. There was a sense of belonging, with enormous appeal for the lonely: it provided an essential feeling that others cared for and would help you; and you would do the same for them under the guidance of the leaders. Wherever a believer went he could join a group, part of the mass movement, to which he could swear his allegiance and in turn get succor and sympathy from fellow believers. There was considerable self-cure and guidance by temple priests and group leaders. This would fit into the African tradition of chief and witch-doctor. Every member of Soka Gakkai proselytized, stressing the economic and social as well as the spiritual advantages to

163

be obtained by joining. And all turned out fervently to get votes to elect their political leaders in order to influence the government of the country.

Without being obvious, Berci asked me questions about myself. I did not mind answering. I had been asking myself a lot of questions, too. I told him almost everything of importance. I knew that gradually he was able to build a picture of me. I didn't know if it was flattering or not.

On my last night in Tokyo, Berci invited me to his home for dinner. The door was slid open by a Japanese woman wearing a deep blue kimono. She greeted me and removed my shoes. I replaced my jacket with a richly embroidered kimono. She led the way into an inner room facing a courtyard with an exquisite miniature garden. From there we entered another room facing the garden. Here Berci greeted me. He was dressed in Japanese attire. We sat opposite each other on straw mats.

We were served by a girl who made me wonder if there were drugs in the food and saki. She was the Oriental equivalent of "The Blessed Damozel". I began to understand what the great poets meant by beauty. She felt my eyes on her when she served us but her expression never changed nor did she react to anything we said. Berci pretended not to notice my reaction. Several times he spoke to the girl in Japanese. She brought various treasures which Berci explained to me. There were carvings and small Chinese statues of warriors on horseback, silk paintings, vases of delicate colored glaze. Much as I appreciated their beauty my gaze returned to the girl. Nothing was her equal.

"Hungarian women are among the most beautiful in the world. Do you not agree my dear Ben?" Berci asked.

"No," I replied taking my eyes from the sliding door. "The girl who has been serving us is."

"Yes, I agree." The smile could be seen between the moustache and beard.

"She's Hungarian!"

"Half Hungarian."

"You're Hungarian. You mean she is related to you?"

"She is my daughter. Her name is Evy. She speaks perfect English. Not like me, with an accent. That was my wife who showed you in."

"I am honored," I said.

"We are honored." He bent forward from his waist. "It has been very gratifying having you here, my dear Ben. I am always pleased to talk. I talk too much. Most people are not interested in what I say, so I have written books. Not many people are very interested in them either but they have achieved some respect from orientologists and those interested in Oriental art. Now that I am older I find it more difficult to write. It is less tiring to talk. It has been especially gratifying to have been able to talk to someone who is not only interested, but who has understood what I have been saying and has a love for what I love."

I felt guilty: I had been betraying him for I had not come to him for this. My ends seemed practical to the point of vileness. He read my mind for he went on: "You came here for specific reasons, with preconceived opinions. But you are not leaving with them, Ben. All that you have seen, all which we have talked about has left a mark on you. You have placed yourself in the role of a man of action. But basically you are a scholar, Ben. I do not know what reason brought you here. It does not matter."

"It does to me. I am different and a better man for having known you and for having been with you."

His hooded eyes regarded me in the soft candlelight. He nodded slightly as though he were a Buddha come to life; perhaps he was my Buddha, for I had become his pupil.

"We shall never see each other again," Berci finally spoke. "It is written so. I know. But I am content. I have made a friend. It is difficult to make a friend when you are old. I have. And it has made me happy."

I had a lump in my throat which would not dissolve: for the friend I had found, for the father I never had had, whom I had just found and would leave, but would never lose.

From the darkness of the wall the girl materialized as the door slid open. Berci motioned to her. She melted down onto the mat between us.

"Evy," Berci pronounced it as though it was "Avy", as Europeans do, "Evy, this is Ben."

Her movements changed, becoming less fluid and slightly more angular, more Occidental. Holding out her hand she smiled at me. It was like holding a trusting bird: it was quivering, about to flee and yet it stayed.

"I'm pleased to meet you, Evy," I said.

"I am happy to know you too, Ben." Her voice was the way I thought it would be: musical, with a mezzo quality that gave it the same intensity as her violet eyes.

The woman who had welcomed me to the house joined us. She was introduced to me as Berci's wife and Evy's mother. She sat on my other side. The candles burned down, others were lighted, burned down and still we sat and talked and looked at each other and I understood what Berci's philosophy meant. At last I felt at peace with myself and in harmony with those who were with me.

Berci had met his wife when she was hardly more than a child. Her father had been an important Japanese industrialist. He had come to the United States with one of the first post-war trade missions. I had not realized that

Berci had been an engineer with a number of remarkable patents to his credit.

I had not understood that I could remain in this celestial atmosphere until Evy's mother said something in Japanese. Berci's head lifted in a start, he had dozed off. I apologized for overstaying my visit; I must get to the hotel, I had not packed.

"You've been here too short a while for the things you wanted to learn," Evy said.

"A lifetime would not be enough." No one contradicted me. "But I can't unfortunately."

"I would like you to have a small token, a remembrance of your visit," Berci said.

"It isn't necessary," I protested. "I already have more than one. I shall never forget being here."

"You would make me happy if you would take some token from me," Berci insisted. Both his hands opened, spreading themselves to indicate all the treasures which had been brought out. I followed his glance, his eyes momentarily rested on the exquisite girl sitting between us. "Please, my dear Ben, I would be happy if you would select whatever you wish."

I looked at the ivories, the small statues, the silk paintings, the jewelry, vases, porcelain. Always my head turned back to the girl beside me. Her eyes never left me. I looked into them, the circumference was blue turning to purple at the iris. Her mother was watching me, a faint gentle smile on her lips. I could see the resemblance. Evy had her mother's carriage, perfect facial bone structure and the translucent texture of skin, straight black hair; her mother wore it in the traditional Japanese coiffure, Evy's fell down her back, a small crimson ribbon holding it in place.

"If I may be personal," I spoke hesitantly. "There is one thing. One object I would like."

"I would be pleased if it were more than one," Berci replied after his usual pause.

Raising my index finger I held it upright like the statues of Buddha before pointing it at Evy. I heard Berci breathe in deeply. A responding soft sigh came from his wife. Evy was motionless.

"I would like the ribbon you are wearing in your hair."

Without taking her eyes off mine, they had suddenly enlarged as though her face had contracted, Evy's long thin fingers went to the back of her head. She brought the ribbon away from the black hair and placed it on the low platform in front of me which had served as the table. Her hands returned to the back of her neck. I heard a minute click. Her hair cascaded in front of her face as she bent forward. Beside the ribbon on the platform she placed a small gold hair-clip.

"Thank you. I only asked for the ribbon."

I picked it up. Evy placed the gold pin in my hand alongside the red ribbon. I looked at her. I could not see her features: her hair covered her face.

Her mother said something in Japanese. Berci and Evy nodded. I waited for him to translate. Berci said: "You must accept both. The barrette was a birthday present from her grandmother. It is very precious to Evy. She is pleased that you chose it."

"It will be precious to me too," I said.

Both women uncoiled to stand up, their kimonos flowing about them. They bowed to me. I rose as did Berci. His wife spoke again in Japanese. By the tone I realized she was saying good-bye to me. Evy never spoke, nor did I see her face and eyes. She slipped away. A few minutes later Berci slowly led me through the rooms around the inner courtyard to the front door. He embraced me in European fashion, putting his arms about me. A taxi was waiting at the door. I got in. The door to the house closed.

When I reached my hotel I found a cable from Maurice Richard saying that he would be waiting in Paris when I arrived tomorrow. Automatically I had turned on the lights upon entering the room but the sky was bright so I turned them off and walked towards the window looking out unseeingly at Tokyo. I was not sleepy. I looked again at the deep red hair ribbon on the bureau top and the gold clip beside it. There was the faintest aroma of Evy in the ribbon. Her name engraved on the gold clip was almost worn away. I slid the ribbon into an envelope with the hotel name printed on it and placed it in the special compartment of my briefcase where I carried my passport. The barrette I slid into my wallet.

When I returned to Paris my apartment appeared cluttered, vulgar and ostentatious. It was several days before I stopped comparing it to that house in Tokyo. Had it not been for the hair-clip and the ribbon I might have thought it had been a dream. In the next weeks Berci and Evy began to recede in my mind. Maurice Richard had never remained this long in Paris. He had been on a trip to the Central African countries and he filled me in about them. He also had some specific directives from Mr Johnson.

As I listened to Richard talk about his African trip I understood why the timing of this project was right. There had been almost continual upheavals in more than fifteen African countries since 1960 when independence had been granted them. Many of the early leaders who had fostered the independence movements like Nokato, Nkrumah, Kasavubu and others, had been swept aside by young, little known army officers. Following the pattern of Nasser in Egypt they set themselves up to govern their countries without any ideological political reference. If

169

they were anti-anything it was the regime they had over-thrown. Despite the best will in the world their countries were in virtual bankruptcy.

Until something was done to stop this endless cycle of revolts, poverty and economic chaos, the situation would become worse. The leaders of even the poorest countries with no exports, kept themselves in power by utilizing the tricks of dictators: distract the people by giving them an enemy, real or unreal. Thus along with anti-colonialism came the fight against apartheid even though discrimination was more than a thousand miles from the country; even though a way to end apartheid was to prove that they could govern themselves.

We needed a movement that ignored these artificial political and economic boundaries. It must appeal to all the people. It must have aims so general and catholic that no political leader would dream of banning it from his country. On the contrary, he would embrace and sponsor it, for it promised to help him without endangering him. It should have a mystic, religious significance that would be broad enough to pass for ethics and morality. Also it should have a practical application so that every member would feel he was gaining personally. The movement must appear to be benevolent. But like communist organizations it was controlled from the top although it appeared to be vice versa.

I worked the paper over and over, boiling it down to arrive at a doctrine that could be understood by the most illiterate. It was called the Pan-African Movement. Its central planks were peace, economic improvement for the individual through assistance and self-aid. But it lacked one thing which Soka Gakkai had: there was no spiritual unity. I did not have a religion on which to graft it as the Japanese movement had in Buddhism.

There was only one way to overcome this: to select a

leader with such a strong charismatic personality and with such a world reputation that he would evolve as the spiritual head; as India had made of Gandhi; as the Communists had made of Lenin. I was convinced that if we got the right leader the plan would work.

Funds from Mr Johnson and his group would get the pumps primed and it would all be part of the organizational structure. Having heard Ralph Roberts and other members of the Embassy staff discuss US foreign aid, I knew that a donor is regarded with distrust, dislike and disrespect. Something for nothing is not appreciated whether dealing with individuals or with nations. The movement must appear to be self-supporting. When people and governments inquired about the financing they would know that there were strings attached. They had to work for what they were getting: just as with the World Bank and other such international organizations the money when borrowed had to be returned with interest, and with concessions.

Chapter Nineteen

During the weeks after Françoise and I returned from Switzerland I felt that I was in an automobile racing an express train. I was barely level with it. If I could get across the track before the safety gate came down I'd have the answer to the abduction of Joseph Nokato.

Inspector Albert Giraud told me that the International Confederal Bank had quietly changed hands about two years ago. That was all he could find out. My investigations in England got me nowhere. The air charter company was collecting insurance for its impounded aircraft held in Algeria. The pilots who had flown the hijacked plane had been paid a nice sum from the British Sunday newspaper for their story. Their attitude was that it had been unfortunate and unpleasant but it could have been worse. It wasn't for me: I had a stigma.

It was twilight with that dull slate sky special to Paris. The lights were coming on in the shops, the street lamps were not lit. Puffs of dust rose under my shoes. I walked with shoulders hunched, gathering my muscles and thoughts tightly together. The Tuilleries were strangely deserted, the trees dark splotches, the benches empty. I paused for a moment opposite the small Arc de Triomphe to look through it. Off in the distance at the top of the rise of the Champs-Elysées was the perfect match for this arch, bisected by the nearer Egyptian obelisk at the Place de la Concorde. Somehow it failed to brighten me as it invariably had. I drifted past the entrance to the Louvre. A group of chattering school children all dressed in blue spilled out and into a waiting bus like a flock of sparrows about to roost. My footsteps echoed on the cobblestones under the low archway leading to the police station. On the Rue de Rivoli the shop windows peered out from under the eyebrows of the arcade.

I waved a greeting at Madame Albert behind the window of the concierge's apartment and added my footprints to the oval depressions of wear on the circular wooden stairs. I pressed the light button twice en route. For a moment I stood on the sixth floor landing, facing the deep purple-colored door with the tiny peephole. I found the keys and entered. As I did, I caught the aroma of a cigar. I heard a man's voice without distinguishing what was said, and then Françoise's laughter. I quietly stepped back onto the stair landing and drew the door closed before ringing the bell.

The door opened. Her eyebrows arched in surprise as

172

she pointed to the lock and turned an imaginary key. I jerked my head towards the front of the apartment, at the same time said loudly: "Hi, Françoise. Hope I'm not interrupting anything."

She kissed me, pulled me into the flat and closed the door. "Of course not, mon cher. I want you to meet Monsieur Roger Farrar."

She was wearing a light blue pants suit, the wide bottoms of the trousers contrasted with the tightness about her waist and hips. The color of the material set off the redness of her hair: she looked like a fashion photo in *Elle*. Her face was filled with excitement and it wasn't at seeing me.

A man leaned against the fireplace mantel, a long cigar in his hand. He was tall, thin, wore a short cut Italian style jacket with slanting pockets, a horizontal pink and white striped shirt with a white collar and dark blue tie. The thick sideburns were as long as a Mississippi river-boat gambler's: his countenance with its long, arched nose, thin pointed chin, flashing teeth gave that dashing impression. We shook hands when introduced. He was almost a foot taller than I but that wasn't the reason I didn't like him.

"Roger is giving me a *vernissage* at his gallery," Françoise said.

"You're both to be congratulated," I said.

"He wanted to see my things so he would have some idea of the space required. We were talking about how to hang them," Françoise went on.

"Well, home is where you hang."

"I am sorry. I did not understand," Roger Farrar said.

"It's just a joke. A pun on an American saying," I replied.

"Could you please explain it. I go to America often. I would like to know." He spoke as though he had learned his English from Sir Laurence Olivier, not in the United States.

Nothing is more deadly than explaining a quip which wasn't very funny to begin with, but I was trapped. "There's a sort of saying that home is where you hang your hat."

They both looked at me blankly. On a table was a tea tray with the white Rosenthal china, slices of brioche and jam.

"Wouldn't you like some tea, Ben?" Françoise asked. "The kettle is still hot."

Before I could reply she had snatched up the pot and disappeared. "Mademoiselle's work is *formidable. Excellent.* I had not realized her range until now," Roger Farrar said.

I wondered if he was talking about her painting. Pushing himself off the mantel he entered the open door of the brightly lit studio. I followed the trail of Havana cigar smoke. Canvases were all over the room: on chairs, along the floor, on the day bed, tilted against the wall, on the easels and the work table. I was surprised at the number. The majority were complete and were of various mountain scenes. But they were not of the mountains we had seen in Switzerland. There were only a few snow scenes, most were summer and spring landscapes. There was a gay color in the kinetic style. There were several portraits Françoise had painted including an excellent one of Mildred Roberts holding her infant. The lustrous skin tone had the translucent quality of a Renoir.

"This is what I mean." The visitor pointed the cigar at Mildred's portrait. The light caught the star sapphire ring on his small finger.

"I always liked that too," I agreed. "Where are the Paris scenes? She did some nice water colors showing the view out of the window." I pointed to the window. I had the feeling I was standing on the dock watching Françoise and her guest moving away on a ship.

"I must get her to show me those," he said.

"Then she hasn't shown you everything?"

"Not yet," he said. "She is shy. But she will. Of that I am confident."

So was I.

A professional expression came across his face, his eyes had an appraising look as he turned again to the paintings. He made comments to Françoise in French.

Françoise moved to the big work-lamp on wheels and turned the shade so the light poured onto the upper book-shelves. They were examining those ugly globs of heavily-troweled paint that I'd noticed when I'd just returned from Algiers. Studying it from this angle I realized it was a cubist portrait of a man. It had some of Van Gogh's type of madness in the eyes which the sickly greens and yellows heightened; this was a depressing, ugly, unhappy man.

"Why have you not finished it?" Roger Farrar asked. "It is interesting and startling."

"I've been meaning to ask you," I said. "Who is that?"

Farrar stared at me with astonishment. Françoise winced and then looked away unhappily.

"Don't you know?" Farrar asked.

"If I knew I wouldn't be asking."

He stepped back, out of the direct beam of the strong light. Although I could not clearly see his face I knew his expression had changed. Turning I stared at the portrait. Then I looked at Françoise. Her eyes avoided mine. I knew the answer.

"It's me," I said.

"It is a painting of you," the Frenchman's voice came from behind the broad band of light.

"It's the same thing," I snapped.

"No, it is not, if I may correct you, Mr Clancy. You are you. This is paint put on canvas to represent how the artist views someone."

"That's right. Me! It's how she views me."

I don't quite remember how or when Roger Farrar left the apartment but when he did I said, "He must be a successful dealer."

"He is. One of the best young ones," she said quietly.

"Then you're made."

She knew what I meant for I faced her as I said it. A flush rose in her face. She kept her eyes on mine.

"It is one thing to have an exhibit. It is another to get good notices so that people will buy," she reminded me.

"You'll have it all. Farrar wouldn't handle you if he wasn't sure you would. He's not the type who wastes time. He's a man in a hurry."

Deliberately I turned and stared at the now identified portrait. I felt Françoise standing beside me.

"And what are you, Ben?" she asked.

"I don't know, Françoise, I guess I was a guy in a hurry once. Maybe I still appear to be one. But it's interesting to suddenly see yourself through someone else's eyes and not recognize who you are."

She held out her arms. "Please Ben, let me explain."

"Sure."

I held her in my arms. Hers went around me. I felt her hair against my cheek. I released her.

"That painting, Ben," she began. "It did not start out to be of you."

"I'm not so sure it's finishing that way."

"I was haunted by faces when I came back from Algiers. I kept seeing them in my dreams. I had to paint what was bothering me. I found myself doing it. I didn't know who it was at first. As you know I do not paint in that style."

176

"Well, I never had my portrait done that way either. So we both started out together."

"Please Ben, I am serious." Her hand found mine and held it as though she was watching a horror film. "I kept painting it until I realized that it was going to look like you. That is why I never finished it."

"Well, you must now. You heard what the man said: it's good."

"You also heard what he said. It is not you. It is a painting. It is something that came to me at night. A face. And I have painted what I imagined. Not you."

"As long as I don't have to pose for it I can't complain." I didn't add that she had painted other scenes from her imagination too: happy and bright and gay, not the reverse as this one was. "But you have done something for me in that painting." I went on before she could ask what it was: " 'To see ourselves as others see us!' "

Her eyes filled with tears but then she always cried easily. "Please, my dear. It is not you. It is what haunted me. And now it is gone. It does not bother me anymore."

"No, it just bothers me." I stood up. "But I'll get over it. Let me know when you and your friend hang me."

Chapter Twenty

From the corner table Mildred glanced about the restaurant. On the walls were an assortment of weapons dating from Charlemagne to the Franco-Prussian War. Individually, none of it made sense, but somehow it all came together with the large stove and copper pots in the corner of the restaurant where the cooking was done, and towards which the tables and chairs were oriented like a piano on a concert stage. There were six tables. The patron, wearing the traditional chef's *toque blanche*, was a short, round man whose large belly was an advertisement for his art. There was no menu. He discussed the dishes he would make. Mounting the raised platform he gave a virtuoso demonstration of cooking.

"Albert Giraud!" Ralph repeated when I told him who had recommended the restaurant. "He's at Interpol, isn't he?"

"You sent me to him," I said.

"I've never met him," Ralph said. "If nothing else, he knows his eating places."

"He also knows his job."

Mildred was not one for subtleties. "Where's Françoise?" she asked.

"Busy," I replied.

"You've had a fight."

"How did you deduce that?" I asked.

"By the absence of the lady."

"Nothing serious, I hope," Ralph put in.

"I just discovered that Françoise and I see things differently. Especially each other. Those two months apart seem to have given us a different perspective of each other."

"That's odd," Mildred said. "I had a feeling it had brought you closer together. Shared experiences do."

"I'm not so sure we've been sharing the same experiences. I don't know what actually happened to her in Algiers. She never really talked about it."

"We all change after certain experiences," Ralph said quietly. He had always assumed the role of my conscience. I remembered doing the same for him when he couldn't decide between Mildred and Dorothy. He had never regretted his choice. "You were different, Ben, after that trip."

"Which trip?"

"It was about a month or two before the hi-jacking. You disappeared to New York for a couple of weeks on business. When you came back you went around in a daze. Something happened to you."

"Oh, that trip." I tried to push it out of my memory but it had been returned more and more. I had never communicated with Berci.

The patron brought the first course to the table, a fish soufflé that had risen to twice the height of the round dish. Deftly he divided it between us. I was washing down the last bit of soufflé with the wine when Ralph casually asked if any of my trips had taken me to Central Africa. I told him they had not.

"The new countries there are very interesting economically," he said. "The potential is enormous."

"I didn't think that was your area," I said.

"It isn't really. But a study came in from the Department asking for my personal comments. It isn't a department paper. It must have come from Rand or some other think-tank where the bright boys sit around and project the future in various places from Mars to Manhattan."

"And this paper is about the emerging, undeveloped Central African nations, I take it." I tried to sound casual.

"It isn't classified although it is a private study, so I guess I'm free to talk about it." Ralph ran his fork over his plate. "If the rest of the meal is up to this I think we'd better walk home. That is, if we can move."

"What about that paper?"

"It's fascinating. I think it's the most penetrating, clear appraisal I've ever read of an economic, social and political area. But what appeals to me most of all is the solution. It's one thing to pose questions and to criticize. It's another to come up with the answer."

"And this one does?" I asked.

"It has shrewd psychology. It is designed to get all the people in that area, down to the poorest, and they can be poor, to join a program of self and mutual assistance. It's coupled with a splendid philosophic concept that verges on religion, which would make every individual feel he belongs and can do something not only for himself but for his neighbor and his country."

Ralph went into a breakdown of the entire Pan-African Movement. I listened hypnotized to a play-back of the study I had written for Mr Johnson. Ralph broke off when the main course was served. I asked what had prompted him to talk about this subject at this time.

A puzzled expression came over his face. "I don't exactly know. There's something about the whole concept, the ideology along with the practicality that made me think you'd be interested in the Pan-African Movement."

"I am," I agreed. "Is that what it's being called?"

"That was the heading on the study. Whoever the guy or guys are who did it, they deserve a medal."

"I'd like to know who they are too. And how the paper got to the Department."

"Why? What difference does it make?" Ralph asked.

"Oh, I might want to hire them or recommend them to some clients sometime."

"It has no names on it. It came to me as a private study," Ralph said.

The food looked superb. I congratulated the patron. Dutifully I took a few mouthfuls. I couldn't manage more than that. Mildred ate with enthusiasm and even took some of mine. I explained that I'd had a late lunch.

"What happens to this paper now?" I asked Ralph.

"If the others who've been asked to read and comment

are as enthusiastic about it as I am, I imagine the Department will help implement it or at least give its blessings. Basically it is the sort of project that should be started by the combined countries themselves primed by a foundation. Perhaps one of the big foundations will help. They're undoubtedly studying the paper too." He finished the wine in his glass. I poured some more. Turning to Mildred he asked: "How'd you like to go to Central Africa for a few years?"

"Wouldn't mind at all if we can bring the owner here along as chef," she smiled too sweetly. "I thought we had a year or two in Washington before going out again."

"Yes we have. I wouldn't mind going on the Central African desk."

I passed up the dessert. My mind was racing like an engine on a test-block and getting about as far. I couldn't decide why Ralph had talked in such detail. Why had he brought it up? Was he needling me? Was there something in the writing of the report which he subconsciously recognized as my style? I found that difficult to believe. How had the paper gotten to the State Department? I had to acknowledge that it was not a bad idea to have it passed around to the best people for comments and suggestions. But who had done this? Undoubtedly it was Mr Johnson. I had no comeback: I'd been paid to do the job. If Mr Johnson wanted to hand it around that was his business.

I heard Ralph saying that the major difficulty was getting the right man to lead the movement. Once he was selected the rest would fall into place. The leader had to be a native African of the highest possible repute who was divorced from his country's politics. "It has to be a figure of enormous charisma," Ralph concluded. "A man like your friend, President Joseph Nokato, would have been perfect."

"Yes, from what you've told me, he does sound ideal," I agreed.

"I'm afraid he's going to miss the bus, as the British say." Ralph went on: "He's still in prison in Algiers. I have a feeling that the Pan-African Movement is going to be underway very soon. Things can't continue the way they are. This is the best solution."

After we'd had a brandy with the patron and I'd paid the bill we walked to the nearest taxi rank. I let them off in front of their apartment and drove away with Mildred's words in my ears; to make it up with Françoise. There was another echo in my ears and that was, how did I make it up with President Nokato stewing in jail?

I had the taxi drop me at Le Town House. If I couldn't talk to Nokato I could at least talk to someone as concerned about him as I was. There was a new group on the bandstand, every instrument wired into an amplifier. The noise seemed tangible, coming in blasts like waves of water. The place was jammed. Stan, the maître d'hôtel, signalled me to go through to Archie's usual table. I found him there with a party of Africans who were wearing their native robes and bright caps. I couldn't catch the names when Archie introduced us. It wasn't important. I sat with them watching the dancers and wondered how they looked to the other guests at the table. I was certain it was done better at their tribal gatherings; at least it had a meaning. I refused a cigarette: all you had to do was just breathe and your lungs were filled with smoke.

Eventually the band stopped playing, the records came on and the noise tapered off. I learned that the gentlemen at the table were a trade commission from a country next to Nokato's. They were on their way home after a trip to the United States. I wondered what they were going to trade. The major product was peanuts. A survey I'd read revealed they could grow tea, there was a considerable amount of timber and every indication of uranium and other metals but those were neglected. Meanwhile the country was running up a huge debt. The people were on a starvation diet, but not the people sitting with Archie and me.

When they got up to leave, I rose too and shook hands with them. Archie took them to the door. He didn't return immediately. I knew he was busy with his establishment so I waited, watched and thought. I didn't hear the deafening music because I was straining to hear something I could not quite distinguish. For some strange reason French cows give sourish cream: I put some into the coffee and watched it curdle. It looked like my thoughts.

"Come on, I'll run you home," Archie shouted in my ear. We went out the back way through the small, now quiet kitchen. It was almost three a.m. in the morning. We got into his British sportscar and roared away.

Chapter Twenty-One

"Those four jokers you met tonight aren't really a trade commission," Archie said while I turned on some more lights in the living room of my apartment.

"What are they?" Now that I thought about it, they had looked more like four jacks in a poker hand.

"Oh, they're representing their government all right. They've just come back from the United Nations in New York. They were trying to do something about getting Joe out of Algiers."

"That was your idea?"

"Sure. I've been to the Red Cross, the International Free Jurists, Amnesty International and I've had other representatives try the UN. This group did their best in New York. They're very co-operative. We were going to launch the revolt from their country. The landing fields were set, camps ready, supply dumps, everything when –"

"When Joe and I took our little airplane ride," I finished.

Archie nodded. "That cost those jokers a lot of dough. We were going to pay them well for the use of their facilities. It was planned that when Joe took over the presidency there would be economic integration between the two countries."

I got some beer from the kitchen. Archie was sprawled out in a chair. He waved aside the glass and drank from the can.

"I was out-thought," I said reflectively. "When I listed the specifications for the head of the Movement only Joe Nokato had the qualifications. I wanted Mr Johnson to go through the list of people and name Joe and then I could agree. It's an old ploy. Only I was out-ployed. Mr Johnson was reluctant about Joe – or at least pretended to be. Besides Richard informed me that Joe was heavily involved in something. It was up to me to sell the Movement to him."

It was my first visit to Majorca. As soon as I was in my hotel room I asked the operator to get me President Nokato. His booming bass voice forced me to hold the receiver a foot from my ear. I found myself grinning at the exuberance of his greeting.

"Are my boys all right in school?" A note of worry came into his voice.

This was an ideal cover for anyone who wanted to

184

know why I was here. I assured him that his boys were all right but some problems had arisen about their curriculum and some decisions had to be made quickly. I filled in with some nonsense about examinations.

"We were up late last night playing poker and I got a late start with my appointments," Nokato said. "I'll tell you what; you come up and have lunch. After that we can have a private chat."

One of the two Spanish policemen assigned as bodyguards was on duty outside the corridor door. Inside the suite I was greeted by a hawk-faced youth. He introduced himself as the President's secretary. Another man was also waiting; I was introduced to him. The general was a middle-aged man with Arabic features. Nokato entered from another room. He greeted me. In a moment we were all drawn into his orbit.

We had a large circular table in a corner of the hotel dining room overlooking the sea on one side and the swimming pool on the other. There were four other men at lunch. Sitting next to me was a balding chubby American in his late thirties. He wore heavy tortoise-shell glasses with thick lenses magnifying his gray eyes, giving him the expression of a blow-fish. In his mid-western twang he told me that he lived and operated out of Monte Carlo. Beside him was a Czech, exceedingly reserved, who watched everything, as though he wasn't quite certain which fork or knife to use. I learned later that he was in the same business as the American. There was a Britisher whose weather-beaten face and old-fashioned, double-breasted, suit clearly marked him as a retired naval officer. The fourth man was a tall, tow-haired German with intense blue eyes in his deeply tanned face. He moved with a swift animal grace. He was referred to as "Colonel" although he seemed too young for that title.

President Nokato and the general kept the conversation

going effortlessly. Joe Nokato always had amusing comments to make about things he had read and observed. He talked about last night's poker game and about poker in general. He was an ardent player. He had learned the game watching the American airmen on the emergency airfield near his village when he was a youth. He related poker to the conduct of business and to life itself, in a witty and enlightening manner.

After cigars and brandy had been passed President Nokato excused himself and me, explaining that I'd come to talk about his sons at school in the States. One of the bodyguards rose from his table in a far corner and followed us. We passed through the lobby, the patio and across to the swimming pool. There was no one else there.

"Will the sun bother you?" he asked.

"No."

Pulling two beach chairs together he placed them so that we sat with our backs to the hotel. "Better to sit this way," he said. "No one can read our lips."

The sun burned through my shirt. I removed my jacket and tie, the President did the same. In general terms I explained that I had been engaged – I did not identify by whom, but let him assume that it was a philanthropic foundation – to develop a plan designed to bring peace and prosperity to Central Africa.

"I'm for anything that will bring peace and prosperity," he said.

"Enough to be interested in heading the movement?"

He frowned. "You've come at the wrong time. Come and see me in about six months. I won't be able to head your movement, but if it's all you say it is, you'll have the full co-operation of my country and its government."

I was puzzled and said so. He studied me for a moment. "I can trust you, Ben. I know that. What I'm going to tell you is secret, although most people who want to know what I'm up to, have an inkling; through informers on my staff."

"An inkling of what?"

"I take it that Archie told you nothing."

"I had a hard time getting him to tell me that you were here."

"Do you know who those men were with whom we had lunch?" When I shook my head he said: "The American who lives in Monte Carlo is one of the biggest private salesmen of arms and munitions. There have been newspaper articles about him. The little quiet gentleman –"

"The Czech?"

President Nokato nodded. "He's here representing his company, which virtually means his country. They make the most advanced type guns. I'm naturally not only trying to get the best prices but also the best equipment for the money. The Britisher has a clandestine air cargo service that'll deliver virtually anything short of a Sherman tank anywhere in the world and will provide bills of lading so that no questions are asked."

"And the German colonel is a mercenary," I concluded.

Nokato threw me his big grin and nodded emphatically. "He's probably the best in the world. He came up through the Foreign Legion. He has been fighting all over Africa for the past seven years. He's got a fully trained outfit. It isn't an army but it's a lot better than most in Central Africa."

"And the general?"

"We went to school together. He was head of my army when I was President. He was exiled during the military coup. He's my chief of staff."

"Then you're not interested in my idea?"

"I'm very much interested. I want peace in every country."

Nokato did not seem to find it incongruous that he was

about to launch a civil war in his own country: what's more, neither did I.

The sweat was rolling down my face, my shirt was soaking. I suggested moving into the shade. I indicated a large green and yellow beach umbrella with chairs under it. Joe agreed. Before sitting down he examined the inside of the umbrella to make certain there were no wires or hidden microphone. Behind us the shutters were drawn on the bedroom windows. It was siesta time, the guests were sleeping off their meal and getting ready for the next one.

"Much better this way," President Nokato explained when I asked why he didn't get rid of the spies in his entourage. "I know which ones they are. I feed them unimportant information. That keeps them happy. The really important things I do keep secret. If I got rid of them there'd only be new ones. It would take a while to sort them out. They might get hold of the wrong information and cause confusion."

He wanted to hear more about my project. He thought he might be able to help, at least with advice. I was certain he could. I wanted his comments and criticism. My approach had been theoretical, his would be pragmatic. I explained it in more detail, including the religious element and how the Movement was to avoid nationalism and Chauvinism.

There was a light cough behind us. We turned. The young secretary with the manicured beard was standing a few paces away. He asked our pardon but the President had appointments and people were waiting.

I had to almost trot to keep up with his long strides. "We have been talking about my sons in America," he winked down at me. "I have already sent Mrs Nokato to New York. It is better for her to be there during this period."

The Spanish bodyguard who had been watching from the terrace had joined us in the elevator. Nokato asked him in Spanish what time it was and was told it was ten minutes after five. Nokato thanked him and turned to me. "Suppose we meet in your room at ten tonight."

The elevator stopped at his floor and he and the bodyguard got out. I pushed the button. The elevator went down to my floor but my spirits went up.

Later, President Nokato and I sat with the doors closed and the air conditioning on, because the terraces of the other rooms adjoined and we could have been overheard. I had a bottle of Don Perignon 1961 sent up along with a platter of smoked salmon and a jar of caviar.

"Looks like you're expecting a dame," he laughed when I lifted the champagne from the ice bucket and began freeing the wire around the cork.

"Well, I am trying to seduce you," I smiled back. "I'm trying to make you the father of Africa. The modern Africa, united in peace and progress."

I could see this register, the pop of the cork punctuated it. We picked up the discussion where we had left off. He never forgot anything. He had the power of absolute concentration. He could turn abruptly from one subject to another as though a steel door divided them.

"You're asking me to throw in a good poker hand when I know I've got the others beaten," he said.

"You're being dealt a better hand. It's a bigger game. The sky's the limit."

"I've got to know who else is playing so I can get the feel of the game."

I kept on with my sales pitch. I pointed out that if he went ahead with the revolt he would never be known as a man of peace. "Is it so urgent that you overthrow the present regime?" I asked.

"My word is at stake. When our country began its

independence there were several ways to go economically. We could pull in our belts – hardly anyone even owned a belt – and try to be self-sufficient. That would have meant years, probably generations, of hardship, virtual starvation. We haven't the natural resources and enough trained, educated people to get industries started. Or we could invite international companies to invest and help us become economically sound. The big companies want tax concessions and other benefits. Big companies are without soul: they're not doing it to help us but to get dividends for their share holders and bigger salaries for their officials. I understand the game. They're out to squeeze every concession and advantage they can get. I'm out to get everything I can. We made bargains and agreements. There was give and take on both sides. It benefited them and us. On my guarantee those international companies sunk money into mines and other developments. Now the little men who took over from me are threatening to change those agreements, demanding a larger percentage. If the companies don't agree they'll throw them out and bring in others."

"Isn't there any other way to get the present government to reconsider? Can't you bluff them into leaving things alone and not start a revolt?"

Nokato's eyes narrowed. There was no humor in his expression now. "You can't bluff unless the others know there's the possibility that you've got the cards to beat them. I can't threaten them with a revolt just by talking, anymore than they can threaten the big companies by just making speeches in Parliament. And the companies have their cards to play too by shutting down the mines, closing the refineries, cutting off the loans. Except that if you've put a lot of chips into the pot, as they've done by building all those installations, you can't pull them back, you've either got to put in more chips to bluff the other guy or stick along and see if you've got the strongest hand and can take the whole pot."

"I never thought of it in those terms," I said.

"Well do. I've got a strong hand and I'm not bluffing about that revolt. The military will come right over to me," he interrupted. "There are just a few of the younger officers who might be against me. The whole thing could be over in a matter of days or weeks."

"The country will be in a turmoil. The world will view it as another civil war in a new nation. Can't you keep the pressure on? Right up to the point of launching the revolt but without doing it. It's a terrific story for the whole world when it's known that you were about to lead an armed revolt but that you decided that peace was more important. You'll capture everyone's imagination and good will. You'll be an international figure. The number one African man of peace."

I went on in this vein. The ice melted in the bucket. The champagne went untouched except for the glass I'd poured. Absent-mindedly, President Nokato put a spoonful of caviar on a slice of toast. He slid back the glass doors and stepped out on the small terrace. Black figures were outlined against the low underwater lights of the swimming pool. We could hear the voices in German of two girls and a man splashing back and forth. The night air was soft and fragrant. The sound of a small orchestra wafted upwards from the dining room along with the tinkle of dishes and silver. The adjoining terraces were dark. Still Nokato said nothing. He re-entered my room and sat down. He motioned for me to close the glass doors.

"You should have come sooner," he said. "It's too late."

"Why? Your revolt hasn't started."

"It's going to within the next two to three weeks. My

tribe is already up in arms. I've committed myself for the munitions, the planes, the landing sites and for the mercenaries. So that's that." He grinned up at me with his white teeth and warm black eyes. "It's a marvelous idea, Ben. I wish you luck. And I think it'll work."

"It'll work with you as the leader." When he shook his head I went on: "If invasions can be called off and plans changed I don't know why yours can't?" I swung a straight back chair around to face him and straddled it.

"Because I've pushed all my chips in. I've committed virtually all my money. Contrary to what you might have heard I'm not that rich a man. I didn't milk my country. I didn't walk off with the treasury and deposit it in numbered accounts in Switzerland, Lebanon and America. I'd be broke. Arms, airplanes, facilities and fighting men are not furnished on credit."

"I can't make any commitments," I said. "But supposing the foundation" – that was how I had explained it – "agreed to compensate you for the money you've laid out. How much is it in round figures?"

He did not reply at once; he was figuring out the sum in his head. "Quite a lot," he replied slowly. "I'd say in the neighborhood of three million dollars. That's quite a lot for me personally. For a revolt to take over a country it's peanuts. That's because I've been very careful and made thorough plans."

"If the people who are interested repaid you the three million dollars would you give up the revolt and accept the position as head of the Pan-African Movement?"

"Yes, provided I can force them not to abnegate those agreements."

At four in the morning I telephoned the George V in Paris and the Excelsior in Rome, but Maurice Richard was not at either hotel. I caught the first plane back to Paris. I went directly to my office to see if there was any

192

message from Richard. In the mail was a long critique from Oliver and Hardt on the financial plans for the Pan-African Movement. I telephoned the bank in Zurich and talked briefly to Hardt. I told him I agreed with his suggestions. I wanted urgently to reach Maurice Richard. Hardt did not know where Richard was but expected to hear from him and would pass on my message.

"Also tell him," I had said, "That 'Barkus' is willing. He'll understand."

That was how Dickens's character from *David Copperfield* became our code name for Nokato. Two days later Richard got in touch with me. He cut short my protests by explaining that he had already taken up the matter with Mr Johnson and just had word from him to explore it further. I blew a fuse at this. The telephone lines must have burned to whatever city Richard was in: I never knew where he was.

" 'Barkus' is on the verge of going home," I said cryptically. "I can't say more than that."

"I understand. I'm talking to Mr Johnson later today. Suppose the two of us go to see 'Barkus'. I'll have full instructions by then."

Richard had got back to me the next day. Mr Johnson approved of our going to see Joe immediately. "I phoned you," I said.

Archie was rolling the empty can of beer between the palms of his hands. He refused another one. "I remember," he said. "By then Joe had returned to Madrid. Everything was picking up speed for the revolt. I was running the operation from here. The Spanish government are very touchy about such things. That's when they assigned the two additional bodyguards. They were there to watch as well as to protect Joe."

Chapter Twenty-Two

In that stillness before dawn that occurs even in a city, Archie and I stared at each other across my living room. Without it being said we knew that Nokato had believed that his imminent revolt was his ace in the hole. Neither he nor we had realized that the cards were stacked and that I had been slipped into the pack as the joker.

I slid off the moccasins I was wearing. The nap of Persian carpet was warm through my socks. It was getting light, the silhouettes of the city were a darker gray against the sky. Archie joined me at the window. "Are you going back to practicing law in New York?"

"I've got an offer to join a good, small, liberal firm. One that wouldn't handle Mr Johnson. I mean Gary, John Gary. Now, why did I say Johnson?"

"Is that John Gary, the oil man?"

"Yes. A prime son of a bitch."

"I know the type. They make the John Birchers seem like cub scouts."

"Yes. John Gary set me on the road and Mr Johnson sped me on my way."

"Have you a place to live in New York?" Archie asked.

"I'll find one. Housing's not as tough there as it is in Paris." I glanced about at the room. "I was lucky to get this. I hate to give it up."

"It'll be waiting."

"What do you mean?"

"Just what I said. You can have it any time."

Getting up I turned around to face him. "You mean you own this flat? I thought it belonged to some woman who lives in South America."

"It belongs to Joe Nokato. Joe had it fixed up for Lola but she only lived here about a month before he shifted his base to Madrid."

"Then why the real estate agent and all that crap?"

"Don't get your ass in an uproar. Joe wanted to do something for you. You wouldn't take anything. You were looking for a place. This was empty."

There was some logic in this but it irked me to learn how much I'd been manipulated again. Everyone seemed to be using me.

"I understand how you feel." Archie had read my face.

"Do you," I snapped.

"Cut out the belly-aching and feeling sorry for yourself."

"All right, I'll feel sorry for you. How's that?" I asked.

The first barges were floating into view on the steel water. In the distance came the banging of garbage cans being emptied. The city was coming to life but I wasn't.

"Very considerate of you but not necessary," Archie said. "Everyone lives with a dream. You've just informed me that mine's not been punctured. It's just been badly dented."

"How did I tell you that?"

"The Pan-African Movement is going ahead. That's the main thing."

"You believe in it!" I didn't try to hide my astonishment.

"I have to believe in it. What else is there? The Black Panthers, the Black Muslims? The battles for the cities?"

"This won't stop that."

"Nothing is going to stop that. They're our pogroms. The Jews proved that the way to survive is to emigrate to a national homeland."

"And Joe Nokato's country will be the equivalent of Israel?"

"It's my country too. I renounced my American citizenship. But we're going to have more than one small country. We're too numerous. We're going to be decimated too, although it won't be in gas chambers. It'll be in civil strife. There's no way of stopping the Black Panthers and the other militants."

"You envisage a mass emigration to Central Africa after the Pan-African Movement has started," I said. "Well, I don't."

"I agree with you there. I'm a great admirer of what the Jews have accomplished. A Jew in America isn't an Israeli; he's an American. But it is important that Israel exists as a haven and as a point of identification. It'll be the same way with the Pan-African Movement. Few will leave America. Why should they? They were born there. They might have come from Africa generations ago just as others came from Italy, Germany or Scotland. The opportunities are greater in America than they are in Central Africa but the Movement will change that. There'll be a demand for skilled labor, professional men and the likes in Africa. They'll come from America. And it will happen in one generation."

A low shaft of light from the rising sun gave a red tint to the buildings across the river.

"The converts are the greatest zealots," I said.

"I have nothing else. Should I return to America to live the way my aunt does? If I was there I'd be in the streets screaming and shooting at Whitey. But I know that's not the solution. This plan is. Sure it has ulterior motives but the main thing is that it will work. You try to act cynical about it, but you believe in it too."

"I believe in peace and freedom and the dignity of man. But I've had a hard time retaining that philosophy."

"Fair enough. You've done your part. I'm going to do

mine for the simple reason that there isn't anything else for me to do," Archie said.

"I don't know how you go about joining a movement that hasn't started," I reminded him.

"It seems to be moving. You said your friend had seen your paper. And others have too. If Joe was freed right now it would be a front-page story. He'd be the logical choice to head it. Especially since he would be an escaped martyr who was determined to bring peace to his part of the world."

It was like hearing myself except that Archie did have some practical ideas about the way the Movement should function on a lower level. We did agree on one immediate item: we were hungry. We left the apartment, walked down the street and turned into the boulevard. The sidewalks were filling with hurrying people on their way to work. There were queues at the bus stops. In the distance they were diving into the Metro like ants into a burrow. The shops were still closed but shutters were banging open in the flats above. The bars were crowded with people having brandy, coffee and croissant.

I steered Archie into a café that specialized in American style ham and eggs. While we ate we continued talking. I was like a physicist who postulates that certain unseen and unknown elements exist. Archie was determined to prove that I was right. Only it wasn't to be. Someone else had the formula as well as the equipment. We were not going to have the satisfaction of proving we were right. Much worse was the realization that my work, designed as egalitarian, could produce the opposite result in the unscrupulous hands of Mr Johnson.

I explained to Archie how the controls which protected Mr Johnson's investment could be used to pervert the Pan-African Peace Movement. My mistake was that I had always envisaged Joseph Nokato as head. The first leader would shape the Movement just as the first head of a new country shaped the destiny of that nation; there were many examples of that in Central Africa.

"I'm talking as though this whole thing will succeed," I interrupted myself. "The Movement could be a complete failure."

There were cold beads of sweat on Archie's forehead and upper lip although it was not warm in the corner of the café where we sat, the food neglected on our plates.

"It won't fail. Men like Mr Johnson only bet on sure things. Guys like your pal at the Embassy know what they're talking about. The trouble is that it is going to work. It's going to work only too well."

The future was a great question mark; this problem was the oval shape inside the loop of the question mark. I asked: "What's the solution?"

"There are two," Archie said slowly. "Before they name anyone we get Joe Nokato out of Algiers."

"Suppose we don't get him out or get crossed up. What's your other alternative?"

"Kill Mr Johnson before the Movement can get under way."

For a moment there was a lull in the café, as though a film had stopped and the frame was frozen on the screen. It seemed incredible to hear this statement from Archie Smith. It was a repudiation of everything in which he believed.

"How do we go about getting Joe out of prison?"

"He isn't in prison. He's under house arrest."

"What about Maurice Richard?"

"I don't know anything about him. He must still be in jail." Archie glanced meaningfully about the café. It was not full. People were still standing at the bar having either wine or coffee; some were having both. He turned back to me. I nodded. We got up.

We continued talking while we walked across the small bridge and then along the bank of the Seine. We stopped and leaned over the stone parapet while Archie explained why he could not get into Algeria openly. He had been asked to leave after the hi-jacking when he'd rushed there. After getting nowhere with the government officials he had made contact with a number of tough characters who had fought against the French. Word had leaked out that he was going to try to spring Nokato. The government put him on a plane and sent him back to France.

"The guys I had lined up are still available. They guarantee they'll get Joe out now. They know the country. They smuggled arms and terrorists into Algeria from Morocco, Libya and Tunisia in the fight against the French. Joe is up in the mountains, in the eastern part, not far from Tunisia." Archie added: "He told me he's not really guarded."

"He told you!"

"He's rigged up a clandestine amateur radio station and is using fake call letters. I talked to him through a Parisian ham operator who lives in the sixteenth arrondissement. Joe had him telephone me. Early in the morning, we reached him. This only happened the other night."

I knew enough about wireless to see how Nokato could get away with this. As long as the Algerians were not trying to locate the station – and there was probably no reason why they should – it was an ideal method of keeping in touch, issuing instructions and making plans to escape. He wanted me to come to Algiers as part of the plan.

"I'm willing if it'll accomplish the first of your alternatives," I said. "The Algerians were very polite when they released me. But what happens if I don't get a visa? Do I go in illegally with you?"

"Yes."

After we parted I picked up my passport at my apartment. At the Algerian Consulate I saw a swarthy, sharp-featured man in his thirties. His straight back spoke of years of army discipline. Glancing up from the visa form I had filled out he said: "You were recently released from prison in Algiers, Mr Clancy. We are not in the habit of granting visas to people who have been in our jails and deported."

"I wasn't under the impression I'd been deported. Your minister apologized for my having been held in jail." I told him which minister. It did not impress him. It only made him more skeptical.

"I shall communicate with Algiers and let you know about your request for a visa."

"How long will that take?"

"A month. Perhaps longer."

"I want to know right away. Would you please send a cable. I'll pay for it," I added.

At the office, Coquette reported that the London operator was trying to reach me. I went into my almost empty office to take the call.

After I had assured the operator that I was Ben Clancy I heard a familiar voice say: "How are you, my lad?"

"P.K.! It's good to hear from you."

"Delighted to talk to you. When are you coming to New York?"

"I don't exactly know."

"I saw Sally just before I left. She said she'd been in touch with you. She's hoping you'll take the opening in her firm."

"That's very good of her." I realized that it was only natural that Sally would have talked to him about this.

"She said you did a good job straightening out the chancery case."

"That sort of settled itself while I was held in Algiers. But what brings you to London, P.K.?"

"I was in the Middle East on business and then had to come here to move things along and at the same time touch base with another client. I'd like to see you."

"Hop over to Paris," I suggested.

"I was thinking of doing just that. I might be able to finish here in time to fly over tomorrow night, if not, first thing the next morning. Why don't you meet me at the hotel for late breakfast morning after next?"

"That'll be great. Anything I can do for you here? Hotel reservation?"

"No, thanks. I'll be at the Lancaster. I've got a bit of business I can do in Paris but mainly I'm coming to see you. We'll talk."

While I absent-mindedly finished going through the last of my old files I pondered on P.K.'s sudden appearance. I dismissed it while I concentrated on what Archie had told me and what lay ahead.

Chapter Twenty-Three

Sitting in still another hotel suite I tried to determine where P. K. Esty fitted into all of this. Was his sudden appearance a coincidence? I had enough insight to realize that if I got caught in the rain, I'd consider it part of the plot against me. P.K. had put on weight. With his balding head, strong chin and well cut clothes he looked exactly what he was: a successful Wall Street Corporation lawyer. He also looked weary to the point of exhaustion. His skin had a green pallor as though his heart was not pumping enough blood. Still he was charged with nervous energy, talking rapidly and decisively as if he'd been given an injection of adrenalin. We were pleased to see each other and got caught up asking about mutual friends and business acquaintances.

"How's John Gary?" I asked.

P.K. looked surprised. "Fine. What makes you ask about him?"

"Without his assistance I wouldn't be in Paris."

P.K.'s brow cleared. "Oh, all that fuss he kicked up."

"He got me canned. Otherwise I'd never have come here."

"You don't appear to have done too badly from what I've heard."

"That hi-jacking tied another can to my tail."

"You're returning to New York, aren't you, Ben?"

"Are you offering me my old job?"

P.K. had the grace to stammer: "I think you'll find Sally Dalton's firm an even more congenial place to work."

"I liked where I was." I was not going to let him off easily. "It's just that Mr Gary didn't like my being there."

"If I was given a choice as a young lawyer, between my firm and Sally's I'd opt for hers," P.K. said.

It was not fair to needle him except that there was a frozen unrelenting core of revenge in me against whoever had set me up as bait: it could be P.K. as well as anyone else.

"Have you ever heard of a Mr Johnson?" I asked.

"Certainly. He's the ex-President of the United States."

"The man I'm referring to operates out of New York. He's head of a syndicate representing a lot of money."

"Oh, you must mean Johnny Johnson." P.K. held the Spode china pot over my empty cup. "How about some more coffee?"

"No thanks."

"I'd better have some. I've got two appointments before getting to the airport. I'll sleep on the plane to New York."

"You know him, then?" I asked eagerly. P.K.'s expression was blank as he lifted the cup to his lips. "Mr Johnson. Johnny Johnson."

"Sure. You've met him, too."

"Met him? How would I have met him?"

"Through John Gary."

"John Gary!" I echoed.

"Come to think of it you probably didn't." P.K. put down the cup on the table and rolled the table out of the way. "He wasn't in the same area as the things on which you were working for John Gary. You were involved in the domestic side."

"Mr Johnson works for John Gary?" I was stunned.

"Not exactly. Johnny Johnson is a finder."

"A finder?"

"A middle man. A 'Mr Five Percent,' like old man Gulbenkian was. And a lot of other operators are. He has great connections in Africa and the Middle East."

"Africa and the Middle East!" I realized I sounded stupid repeating what P.K. said. I couldn't help myself. Saying the key words helped me to assimilate them; more important, their meaning.

"Johnny Johnson puts deals together and collects a finder's fee. If you have a big company like John Gary and want to acquire another one, or merge, or get concessions in a foreign country, you don't generally do it directly. You work through an emissary like Johnson. He's an honest broker. He represents both sides. Recently he arranged for an American airline to buy a chain of European hotels."

I just stopped myself from repeating: "European

hotels." Instead I asked: "What was he doing for John Gary?"

"Gary wanted to obtain mineral concessions in one of the Central African countries. He had Johnson front for him."

"Did he get the concessions?"

"Yes. Not all he wanted. He's had to share them with a smaller company that was in there before him. He got the potash and some oil rights. It cost a lot."

"But it'll be worth it."

"Yes, John Gary doesn't go in for anything unless it's worth it. He figures this is a foot in the door. He's excited about the potential in Central Africa."

There was the rap of a key on the door and a rattle in the lock. The room waiter asked if he could remove the table. P.K. nodded. The waiter folded the sides and wheeled it out of the room.

"You've just come from that area, I take it." I kept control of myself as I mustered my thoughts.

"Yes, Gary and a number of other big companies are putting up a sizeable sum to get rolling on a long term basis. The big American foundations like the Ford Foundation and others are going into it, too."

"I didn't realize that Gary was a philanthropist," I said. "When I last saw him I had the impression that the last people he would help were the blacks."

"That was on a personal basis and in America. This is business and it's Africa. He's dealing with the heads of state for huge concessions. And it isn't philanthropy." Some color other than green was coming into P.K.'s face. "As you know I shouldn't be discussing a client's interests, Ben. But it's different talking to you."

"It sure as hell is." I was on my feet. My voice wasn't under control. "How much are you involved in all of this, P.K.?"

"I'm just writing the agreements. Johnny Johnson did the negotiating and still is, for both sides. What's this all about, Ben?"

"It's about everything. I don't know how much you know. If you know everything then it doesn't make any difference if I spill my guts. If you don't, if you're as innocent as you say you are, then it's time you heard."

The big square jaw was sticking out. P.K.'s eyes didn't appear to be bloodshot: they were as cold as ice. He stared up at me from the chair in which he was sitting and said: "You know I'm on your side."

"Someone. Johnny Johnson. The CIA. Had their finger on me. I was employed by Mr Johnson through Maurice Richard. I was manoeuvered to get Joseph Nokato interested and keep him interested until Johnson and his associates decided whether they wanted Nokato's revolt to go ahead or to be stopped. Mr Johnson got John Gary his concessions from the present government. If Nokato had gone ahead he would have taken over the country and cancelled those concessions. Johnson stopped the revolt by having Nokato hi-jacked."

"I don't believe the CIA would be involved in something like that."

"Why not? They've been involved in a lot of things. And don't tell me you don't think Mr Johnson wouldn't be. Because I know he was."

For a moment P.K. stared at me. "I don't know whether he was or wasn't." By putting it that way P.K. was saying that he did not put it past Johnson and Gary. He was willing to consider my premise. "Our office has nothing to do with Gary's operations. You know what our legal work consists of. We stay clear of anything like this. If a client asks us for advice we give it. If he wants contracts written we do that. And if he gets into trouble we try to bail him out. But we have nothing to do with obtaining franchises nor are we involved in the managerial aspects."

"Johnson and Gary wrecked Nokato. They damned near finished me. But it's condoned because it's all under the heading of business," I said.

"What do you want me to do about it, Ben?"

"A lot. A hell of a lot."

"Why don't you face Johnson and tell him what you just told me. And Gary, too. I'll stand up for you."

I realized what that statement meant. You don't just throw out a multi-million dollar account. But P.K. was willing to do it. It calmed me. I had learned that it wasn't P. K. Esty who had set me up for this disaster.

"Thanks. I'll face Mr Johnson and Mr Gary later. When I can call the shots. That shouldn't be long."

"Wouldn't it be better, Ben, to forget the whole thing? Come to New York and work in Sally's law firm. That's where you belong. Gary and Johnson are tough and powerful men to come up against."

"At least I've finally found them out. For the first time I know who I'm facing. And why. Now it's my turn to do something."

"All right, Ben. I know you well enough to realize you can't be persuaded."

"Thank Sally for me. Tell her I might be along eventually." I added: "I don't have to ask you to please not say anything about all of this."

"I'll not be seeing Johnson or Gary. I just left them in London. Apparently something big is about to start."

"I'll say there is."

That night I caught up with Archie at Le Town House. I told him what I had learned. He didn't immediately explode as I had, but I could see the fury building up in him the way static does before discharging in a bolt of lightning.

206

"When you get to Algiers ask the minister if you can see Joe."

"What if he says I can't?" I asked.

"Get out of Algiers. Don't hang around trying to do something. You'll only get thrown into jail again."

"How can I help?"

"Confront Mr Johnson and Gary in New York or London, or wherever they are. Expose them."

"That was my initial reaction. I realize now they couldn't care less what I have to say. It'd be like slapping their wrists and telling them they've been naughty boys."

"Go to the newspapers, radio, television."

"And do what? Say that John Gary, his companies and associates have been smart enough to get concessions in Central Africa? It'll just make his company's stock go up."

"I guess if you can't beat them then you kill them," Archie grinned without humor.

"We'll discuss that alternative later." I tried to calm him down. "What do I do if I don't get the visa to Algeria?"

Archie told me to fly to Tunis and to check in at a certain hotel where I'd be contacted. Archie was going to talk on the radio to Nokato either tonight or tomorrow night. And then he would disappear. The next time we'd meet would be in Algeria or Tunisia.

The following day I was informed by the Algerian Consulate that not only was the visa granted but I was the guest of the government. If I wished my flight was arranged for the following morning. I wished.

Early the next morning I was closing my suitcase when the telephone rang. It was Françoise. "Ben, did you listen to the news this morning?" she asked.

"No, should I?"

"It's Archie! Le Town House! He's been killed."

"Archie! Killed! He can't be."

"Le Town House was *plastiqued* – bombed – last night. Early this morning. It caught fire. *Les Pompiers* could not put it out. When they finally got inside they found two bodies. They believe one is Archie. Oh, chéri, I am sorry. It is terrible." She began sobbing.

"It might not be Archie." I tried to console both of us. "What else did they say on the news?"

"It happened about 4.30 this morning. All the people and staff had left. There was an explosion. Several explosions. Police found *plastiques* and also incendiary bombs inside. That is why the fire could not be put out quickly. The police reached Stan, the maître d'hôtel. He had left Archie with the bartender and several others to close up. Stan went with the police to Archie's apartment. He was not there."

"Couldn't he identify the bodies?" I asked.

"No, they were too badly burned. Oh, chéri, he was such a wonderful man. And a good friend."

The doorbell was ringing. I knew that it was André to say that the taxi was waiting. I told Françoise I was all right, I appreciated her phoning and that it was kind of her to be at home if I wanted to come by. Right now I had to rush.

I had the taxi take me as close as the police would permit, to what was left of Le Town House. Firemen were still hacking the ruins to bits while a crowd at each end of the narrow street watched. I managed to get hold of a gendarme who told me that only two bodies had been found: that of the patron and of the bartender. I stumbled through the people and eventually found my waiting taxi.

The driver clucked disapprovingly and said that it was not possible to get to Orly a half hour before my flight time. I told him to try anyway and sank back into a daze. I might as well be driving to the airfield and back as be sitting in my apartment trying to decide what to do. The heavy traffic was coming in the opposite direction towards Paris. Once we got on the autoroute the driver tore along as though we were on the Le Mans race track.

At the ticket counter the girl said the flight was closed. Hearing my name, an Air Algeria representative snatched my bag, grabbed the ticket and rushed me through the baggage section. The waiting room at the gate was empty. We hurried across the tarmac and up the steps. He handed me and my bag to the steward and the door rolled down on the Caravelle.

I was in too much of a shock to do anything but stare unseeingly out of the window. The buildings flashed by and we lifted over Paris and settled into the flight pattern that turned on a southerly course. I took the newspapers the steward offered, refused coffee but said I'd like a brandy. Quickly I flicked through the Paris newspapers. There was nothing about the explosion and fire: these editions had gone to press before it happened.

The sting of the brandy in my gullet helped to clear my head. I realized that it was just as well I'd caught the plane. If it was Archie who had been killed there was nothing I could do for him except what I was doing. If it wasn't Archie then we would meet in Algeria or in Tunis. I tried to calm myself by asking what I would have done if Françoise had not telephoned. I would be on this flight and not knowing anything about the gutting of Le Town House and the two bodies. It was a neat intellectual exercise but the emotional content was too great. I could not pretend that it had not happened.

Another brandy helped. I unfastened the seat belt, tilted back the seat and picked up *The Times*. I skimmed through a libel case in the well-written, under-stated Law Reports. I turned the page and saw the headline: "Start of Pan-African Peace Movement".

Date-lined London, yesterday, the long article called

for an end to the civil strife in Central African countries. Internecine war was being fostered by ambitious native politicians. The countries were sinking to a standard lower than before they were colonized. Instead of freedom, prosperity and health, the reverse was occurring. There could be no investment by hard-headed international companies until there was stability. Nor could there be more self-aid schemes from the United Nations and individual countries. There was need for a belief in the humanity of man, in mutual assistance on the basic level of one person for another, a code of ethics. Such a program was now evolving through a Peace Movement sponsored by a foundation.

It was a neat paraphrase of my document. *The Times* had an editorial calling for the support of the Movement. I went through *The International Herald-Tribune* and found another similar report. I picked up the French newspapers. All had articles on the same subject. This full scale information offensive could only have been launched by an international public relations firm, as I had recommended in my report to Mr Johnson.

The noise of the air brakes blended with the memory of a metal pail on my head being hit with a hammer. The brown coast of Africa was approaching. Algiers rose from the sea hugging the line of the bay like the side of a cup. The multitude of white dots became buildings. Broad boulevards ran along the shore and criss-crossed the city. One led upwards to a green expanse with large buildings which the stewardess informed me was the university, the Free France headquarters during the war.

When I'd landed the previous time I'd not been aware of the scenery: I'd been too busy watching Maurice Richard's revolver. As we turned off the runway I saw the Handley Page Jetstream parked in a bay. The wheel-chocks and wing-locks with red tabs were in position.

There were no guards. The plane was sitting in the same place where it had stopped more than three months ago.

As I came down the steps an airline attendant saluted me. He insisted on carrying my briefcase to the passenger building. Involuntarily I looked over my shoulder across the airfield, remembering the armed soldiers who had lined us up, our outstretched hands pressed against the fuselage of the plane. After being searched we had been pushed into trucks and driven off to prison. It was quite a contrast being ushered to the head of the line where an official stamped a visa into my passport. The customs official waved my suitcase through and hoped I'd have a pleasant stay. The chauffeur put the bag into the trunk of the black Citroën. After another salute from my escort the car drove away from Maison Blanche, the unlikely name of the Algiers airport. The driver, an ex-fat man whose flesh hung loose like a bloodhound, apologized for the cloudy weather.

I tried to absorb the local geography, it might prove useful later. All the while the weight of sadness, verging on despair, was pressing down on me. I went through the motions of normality, trying to present a façade of alertness, while part of me cried that it was useless, to throw in my hand and leave the game: my luck had long since run out.

We wound up Avenue de L'Independence into the grounds of the Hotel St George. I was told for the first, but not the last time, that this was General Eisenhower's headquarters during the North African invasion in 1942. The lobby of the hotel with its arches, mosaics, tiled floor and brass chandeliers resembled the interior of a mosque. I signed the registration card. The manager took my passport to fill in the rest of the information. Leading me to the gilded elevator which resembled an exotic birdcage, he showed me to a suite overlooking the city and harbor.

After he left I checked my watch with the telephone operator. I had an hour and thirty-eight minutes. While I unpacked, two thoughts ran through my mind. Mr Johnson and his cohorts must have intercepted the radio messages and taken this direct means to stop Archie. Why didn't they stop me? It would have been simple to *plastique* my apartment, or have me run over, or shot, or a dozen other methods of assassination. What was I being saved for? I didn't like the answer that I arrived at but it was a better answer than being dead. Perhaps not much better for it only meant a slight delay. I glanced at my watch again, picked up the newspaper, turned it to the front page and left the suite.

There were a few people in the clusters of couches and chairs in the lobby. I had spotted him as I came in but I did not look in his direction until I had been served tea and pretended to drink some. When he caught my eye he tucked his handkerchief inside his left sleeve and smiled shyly. He was a big, round man with a reddish complexion and sandy hair. Pushing himself up from the divan he came over to me.

"I wonder if you'd mind if I ask to have a look at your newspaper?" I knew his voice would have the broad British "a". "It is today's, is it not?"

"It is. You're welcome to it."

Wearing a tweed suit and a regimental tie he was perfect type-casting for the typical Britisher. Everyone appeared to be type-cast in this Moorish setting. I wondered into which category I fitted.

"I just want to glance at it. I'll return it immediately." He accepted the folded newspaper.

"Please keep it. I've finished with it."

He hesitated. "I trust I'm not being rude. You are Mr Ben Clancy, are you not?" I admitted that I was. He went on: "My name is Harvey Owen. I'm a journalist."

"Glad to meet you." We shook hands.

"If you're not busy might I join you?" He sat down.
"Actually I've been waiting for you." He spoke loudly so
that the few guests and all the waiters could hear. "I
checked the arrivals today, as I generally do at the hotels,
and saw your name. I filed a number of stories about you
when you were here before."

"Sorry I didn't see them. I wasn't reading newspapers
in those days."

He smiled knowingly. "So I understand. I'm a stringer
for some of the British newspapers. Actually I'm a writer.
This helps keep me going."

"Have I read anything you've written?"

"I doubt it. I don't write under my own name. They're
paperbacks, thrillers. It's a living. Added to my pension
I manage quite nicely here."

I wondered what had happened to the traditional
reticent Englishman. There was such an air of a sheepish
clown about Harvey Owen that you could not help but
like him. One would accept him for what he said he was,
except that I knew who and what he was. It was only
evident in the shrewd eyes above the almost foolish grin.
Later, when I complimented him on his cover, he explained that he really was an amateur. I discounted that:
from meeting British lawyers and bankers I knew their
tradition of pretending to be dilettantes operating on an
ad hoc basis, while actually they are the most professional
of professionals. Their self-disparagement was part of the
disguise.

I did not know for which intelligence service Harvey
Owen was working. He was the contact Inspector Albert
Giraud had given me. Probably Albert, not wanting to
get me involved any more than I was in the French
intelligence net, had gotten Harvey Owen from some
other source. All I wanted was reputable inside informa-

tion. I could only hope that he was not also working for Mr Johnson. His cover was legitimate. He wanted to file a story on me for his newspapers.

"I'm not news," I said.

"Yes, you are. Anything connected with President Nokato is news. I'm continually being queried by my papers for information about him."

"I'd rather not have anything written about me." Harvey Owen looked disappointed. I needed his help. This was an easy coin with which to repay him. "Suppose we agree that you'll have an exclusive story when I leave?"

"That'll be fine."

"There's one other thing I wonder if you can do for me," I continued when he nodded: "Something happened in Paris this morning. It's not in today's newspapers. How late are the papers getting here?"

"Quite late. Days sometimes. That's why I'm so pleased to see yours."

"Do you have any source to news from Paris?"

"My newspapers are British." I could see the wariness in his eyes, warning me against continuing the conversation. Pointedly he invited me to have dinner with him tonight.

Chapter Twenty-Four

We drove out of the hotel grounds and down into Algiers. I turned in my seat to watch out of the back window while talking to Harvey Owen. He shook his head at the story of the bombing and destruction of Le Town House. He understood why I wanted to know if the bodies had been positively identified. He agreed that his London newspaper could query Paris and cable him, but he would not do it.

"The Algerian government threw Archie Smith out of here," Harvey explained. "They knew he was trying to arrange an escape for President Nokato. If I send such an inquiry it'll mark me and also you."

"I'm already marked. I'll send the cable."

"I wouldn't advise it. What is your primary purpose in coming here?"

"To get Nokato out of here."

"That's not the reason you put down on your request for a visa."

"I'm here as a guest of the Algerian government. They invited me. They're picking up the tab for the whole thing."

Harvey shot me a quick glance and turned back to driving the car. "The men running the country have given up the old Arab tradition of hospitality. If anything they suffer from xenophobia. You have your reason for being here. But just remember they have theirs. If I were you I'd find out quickly why they invited you, before it's too late."

I mulled this over. When we stopped for a traffic light I glanced again through the rear window.

"No one's following us," Harvey said.

"How can you be so sure? I figure they want to know where I go and who I see."

The signal changed. The car pulled away, pinging at the low octane gasoline.

"They do. Everyone saw you leave the hotel with me. Tomorrow I'll get a phone call. I'll tell the police where we were – if they don't already know."

"That's nice of you," I snorted.

"No harm done. Shows we've nothing to hide. In turn

I'll pick up a few items. For my newspapers, of course," he added significantly.

"You haven't happened to pick up any information about Maurice Richard?" I asked.

"He's still in jail."

"And Nokato?"

"He's not in jail. But the Algerian censor won't let me send that out. He's under house arrest in the east part of the country, near Constance. On a big estate formerly owned by a wealthy French family."

There were very few women on the street. Many of the men wore the traditional Arab robes: oddly, they had small cases slung over their shoulders. I could not figure out what they were until we stopped at another signal and I heard the din of music coming from the transistors.

"Are you planning to see Nokato?" Harvey asked when the signal changed and we moved away from the background noise.

"I don't want to get you involved in this." I was not certain how far I could trust my new friend and I also didn't know if he wanted to be trusted. This gave him a polite way out.

"I'm in the clear to see you. I got off a cable to my Sunday newspaper that I was getting an exclusive story from you. What are your immediate plans?"

"I have an appointment tomorrow morning with the minister."

Harvey slowed the car and pulled it in towards the curb in front of a restaurant. A robed figure detached itself from the door.

"Be careful," Harvey spoke rapidly. "The Algerians are a new brand of Arab. You can't predict how they'll react or what they'll do. I've been here for years and they keep surprising me."

The white-gowned figure was trying to open the car

door. Harvey reached across me and unlocked it. In the restaurant a gloom fell over me despite Harvey's bright chatter. I wondered what the Algerians had done to Nokato and if it wouldn't have been better if I'd missed the plane. I probably should have headed for Tunis and taken Archie's place, only I didn't know what he had planned to do there. Harvey caught my attention when he mentioned that the women in Algeria were still virtually in purdah and that both his wives were Algerian.

"I wasn't married to them at the same time," he answered my look of surprise. "My first wife was seventeen when we met. She was fighting with the Algerians. Still her family had arranged her marriage to a seventy year old Algerian."

"Did you elope?"

"I didn't feel like having my balls cut off first and then my head. No, I just paid a larger dowry. She died at childbirth and so did the baby." Harvey stopped piling couscous onto his fork. His eyes revealed that the hurt was still there. "I didn't know about it until it was all over. Midwives handle those things here. They never called a doctor. But mind you, this is a very modern country. They even have a birth control clinic. It's only for mothers with four children or more."

I took another drink of the dark red wine. "You remarried?"

"To another Arab girl. Perhaps I'm addicted. There is something fascinating and beautiful about them. But I can't take her out to dinner here even though she's a university graduate. Her parents wouldn't approve. We live with her family."

He returned to his food as though eating it was a duty. Abruptly he said: "I'll show you Algerian night life. Such as it is. We can have coffee or tea there."

There was little traffic on the streets. Harvey steered his

small car into a wide avenue. Most of the lighted shops sold radios and television sets.

"Where are we going?" I asked.

"To the Casbah, the old native quarter."

"It sounds familiar."

"The natives will try to be familiar. Just keep shaking your head politely no matter what they say or try to sell you. And be sure that your wallet is buttoned tightly in an inside pocket."

Harvey turned the car into another street and pulled over to the curb. He led me across the road to a red stone arch, the entrance to a narrow, cobble-stone street that curved upward. Bright illumination came from pressure lamps in minute shops that were more like caves. The usual smell of the Middle East of urine and excretion, dust and sweat was overlaid with a mixture of leather, spices, the fat of meat grilling, tobacco and roasting coffee. Sound poured from the windows above and around. It was bedlam. It was life.

"We're almost there," Harvey shouted. As the alley narrowed we were pressed on all sides. We burst through the bottle-neck into a wider steeper passageway and took several more turns. I had lost my sense of direction, the shops and passing faces looked like others we'd just passed.

Abruptly Harvey ducked into a doorway. A pressure lamp hissed a white glare on the white walls where a dozen Arabs were sitting at small tables. The room smelled of coffee, mint and Turkish tobacco. Harvey said something to the man behind the bar who wore pants and a short sleeved white shirt. One side of his face had been burned or blasted, the other side revealed that he was in his thirties and had been handsome. The moveable part registered doubt. Harvey said something else as he slid some money across the counter. The man palmed it and gestured for us to wait. He disappeared through the back door.

"He's going to see if there's room. Don't worry, we'll get in."

"Aren't these places legal?"

"The government officials are very strait-laced and fanatically religious. However, dancing girls are ingrained in the culture and tradition so they haven't closed these places although they keep them under wraps."

None of the customers appeared to be paying attention to us but I had a feeling we were being watched. Several of them had small rubber tubes in their mouths connected to water pipes gurgling on the floor.

Our scout returned. Keeping the working side of his face towards us he jerked his chin at the open door. It closed behind us. Harvey led the way down a narrow, stone passageway. As we got closer to another door we heard the whine of music. When he opened the door the blast of shrill discordant sound hit me with the smoke and heat. A dwarf in white robes materialized to lead us stumbling through the audience, sitting cross-legged on cushions, to a corner beside a pillar. Either there were no more cushions or as foreigners we were given stools against the back wall. We were in an oblong enclosure of about thirty feet by forty feet.

I deduced we must be in the inner roofed courtyard of an elaborate town house. Above, running along the four sides, supported by the pillars, was a gallery filled with spectators. In the opposite back corner I noticed one of the audience, the hood of the burnoose about his head, settle further back on his cushion, while leaning against the wall. I did the same on the stool. At Harvey's suggestion I had mint tea. It was too sweet but I soon forgot that.

A hush and atmosphere of expectation seemed to stop

the smoke from swirling about the beams of colored spot lights as the next entertainer came onto the stage. The music never stopped. She flowed into the dance, the way a bather walks into the water of a lake, keeping time with her hip movement. Later I was not convinced that what I was seeing was not an optical illusion caused by the swirling lights and the gauze and long hair undulating about the dancer. Still as I watched I would have sworn that it was happening.

She was not beautiful by western standards. She was plump. Her face was broad. The large heavily mascaraed brown eyes were bovine, lips a swollen oval, eyebrows heavy and masculine, meeting across the bridge of her large curved nose. Even at this distance I could see the heavy down of a moustache on her long upper lip. Her black hair coming to her waist glistened with a natural wave. She was barefooted. Transparent black gauze pantaloons were tight at her ankles and just below her hips. Her arms and shoulders were also covered with the same material. Everything else was exposed.

In rhythm with the music she was slowly turning and twisting. Barely discernible, the swaying became more of a gyration. To my ears the music became less obnoxious and almost melodic. The girl swayed back and forth, hair flying one way, then another, momentarily covering her. Gradually the tempo of the instruments became more insistent. Without taking any steps she was dancing, and the action increased. Her hips gyrated, pelvis thrust forward while her torso bent backwards. Every bit of her was in movement except her feet. Slowly, gradually, heaving sinuously she was sinking towards the floor, all of her was vibrating as she mounted the invisible lover.

And then it was happening. Tilted forward and upward her breasts jumped and twisted. Each rotated back and forth in a different direction. At the same time her belly vibrated, twirled and then oscillated pulsating with the gyrations of her loins. Her mouth stretched open in an unheard scream. Her head was still. Her eyes closed, her face contorted at joy that was too great. All the while her belly quivered, heaved and jumped with a life of its own. Her breasts became rigid, turning upwards at the enlarged red nipples. Then her breasts quivered and twitched as though the muscles had been shocked by an electric wire. She sank onto the floor. Her head abruptly jerked forward. Her hair fell in front, covering her. The music ended in a caterwaul.

There was a moan from the audience. As though coming out of a trance the men started to yell and scream. The girl stood up. Sweat was pouring down her face, body and legs. She smiled vapidly at the audience.

"How did you like it?" Harvey turned to me.

"I don't believe it." I shook my head. "It was all done with mirrors."

"Or something," he grinned.

The girl was bowing. Money was thrown onto the platform. The audience was shouting something insistently. Then it was taken up as though a chant. Although she shook her head she continued smiling.

"I guess there isn't enough money," Harvey said. "She won't do it tonight."

"Do what? There isn't anything left for her to do."

"She picks up the money without using her hands."

"With her mouth," I said.

Harvey glanced at me knowingly. "Well, it's sort of a mouth."

I didn't attempt to hide my surprise. "You're kidding."

"I've seen her do it. And pick up a bottle. Imagine what she can do to a man."

"I'd rather not, thank you."

Out of the corner of my eye I saw the man with the

hood dart a glance towards me and quickly move towards the door. I was still thinking of what Harvey had described when I turned. The door was open. The light hit the features of the man in the burnoose. Then the door closed and he was gone. I was on my feet.

"Where are you going?" Harvey held me.

"That man!" I gasped. "It's Richard!"

The hubbub of the audience's excitement was dying down. My voice sounded above it. I started towards the door. A waiter carrying drinks on a tray was blocking my path.

"Are you sure?" Harvey asked.

"I'm sure."

I must have stepped on one of the audience for I heard a man yell and then I was past the waiter and at the door. I dashed into the corridor, Harvey behind. Three men filled the passageway, coming from the café. We managed to get past them, through the café and out into the narrow alley. The glaring shop lights showed the passing throng. All were in native dress, some had hoods turned up. None was Maurice Richard.

After we had pushed our way through the maze of alleys Harvey suggested we stop. He was as lost as I was. He pulled me into an identical café.

"You're sure it was Maurice Richard?"

"Positive. There was something familiar when I first spotted him but I didn't realize it. He carries his head inclined towards his right shoulder. Then I caught a glimpse of his face as he went through the door."

"My information is that Richard is still in the same prison," Harvey said under his breath.

"I hate to call your source a liar."

"They said that Richard isn't under close confinement, nor is he being interrogated any more." There was nothing stupid about Harvey's face now. "It isn't unusual to give prisoners parole for the night, to see their wives or –" He gestured.

"What's to prevent his escaping?"

"Maybe Richard doesn't want to escape," Harvey answered for me. "If he tried he wouldn't get very far unless he had careful plans and moved quickly to get out of the country. But those days are over when wanted men could hole up here in the Casbah. If an important international criminal like Richard broke his parole the authorities would put their hands on him immediately."

I did not ask Harvey how he knew that Maurice Richard was an international criminal. The fact that I had contacted him through Albert Giraud of Interpol answered that.

"Can you find out from your source if Richard does get out at night?" I asked.

"I can ask but I won't get the answer. The prison authorities wouldn't admit it."

"I'll ask the minister when I see him tomorrow."

"I wouldn't if I were you," Harvey warned. "He'll have to deny it. It might start an investigation and hot things up again. There could be repercussions for your friend, Nokato."

I was envying those two elderly men sucking away contentedly on the hookahs with their only problem seemingly to keep the water-pipe lit. I had the opposite problem: I wanted to put out the fire inside me.

Chapter Twenty-Five

With its graceful, marble staircases, high vaulted dome, wide corridors and spacious rooms, the government building was a relic of French colonial days. The spartan furnishings of battered desks, bare walls and floors gave the tenor of the present regime. The huge chandeliers were the exception, probably too heavy to be removed. Monsieur Petit was not the minister I had seen previously; I never did find out what happened to him. Monsieur Petit was massive and gnarled like an oak. His neck was the width of his head and his chin appeared to grow out of his chest.

Monsieur Petit neither got up, nor greeted me. He said: "This is yours, I believe."

With a pencil he pushed the barrette across the desk, as though to touch it would contaminate him. I examined it with undisguised pleasure, and placed it in my wallet.

"The prison official who failed to return it to you has been punished." His voice was a deep rasp. "I hope it caused you no inconvenience."

"I'm wearing my hair shorter this season," I replied. The minister took this literally so I added: "However, I'm glad to have it back. It is a good-luck piece."

Monsieur Petit was staring at the folders on the desk. I could read my name on one, Nokato's on another, and Richard's on the third. When I glanced up he was staring at me.

"I take it those are the files and interrogations," I said. He nodded. "I'd like to read Maurice Richard's. I want to know who told him to kidnap President Nokato and why."

"Richard insists it was his own idea."

"That doesn't make sense. I'd like to see him."

"That will not be possible."

It was on the tip of my tongue to say that I already had, but I remembered Harvey Owen's warning. I put an expression of resignation on my face.

"From these interrogations and from our embassies, Mr Clancy, we know that you have made studies and recommendations for large investments in other countries. We would like you to consider our country."

Harvey Owen was proved correct. And I began to understand Archie's instructions.

"I did make certain surveys and recommendations for investments for property developments in Spain," I replied guardedly. "I am not certain if the people for whom I did them are still interested."

"President Nokato is. He trusts your opinion. He would be guided by your recommendations and your legal advice."

"My recommendation didn't guide him very well last time. He ended in prison here."

"He is no longer in prison."

I pretended to be surprised. "Where is he?"

"He's at an estate he bought. It is his initial investment."

"That proves he has faith in Algeria," was the most polite thing I could manage to say.

"We have reason to expect that he is about to make a sizeable investment here."

I had my cue. "If you will forgive my saying this, Mr Minister, I would like to take instructions directly from my client. I would then know exactly what he has in mind."

"Of course." Monsieur Petit handed me a thick folder. "These are drafts of agreements which our legal department has drawn up. You may have some points you wish to raise with them before you see your client, President Nokato."

I ran my eyes over the pages of type. "I'm glad it's translated into English," I said. "My French isn't really that good."

"The translation is from Arabic. That is the official language."

"When I finish going through the documents and have talked to your legal people about them I shall get to see President Nokato?" I asked.

"Of course."

I was in the government building another hour meeting the Algerian government lawyers. Briefly they explained differences between English law and Algerian law, which was basically the French Napoleonic Code with Moslem embellishments. The next day, after studying the documents, I asked the basic question: in the event of a dispute would the matter be resolved before an international tribunal? The answer was that it would be settled by the Algerian courts.

The writing between the lines I understood only too well: coercion and ransom. I wondered what sort of a deal Maurice Richard or his master had made with the Algerian government. It was conceivable that Richard was back at his old trade. It could even be given a polite name: he was a finder, like Mr Johnson, and would receive a percentage of the deal.

All of this I could understand. Also why Nokato had agreed to it. Construed solely as an investment it could even be profitable; the terms were fair. But there was one hole large enough for a camel to pass through: where was all the initial money coming from? Perhaps Nokato's plan was to escape without signing the documents and depositing the money.

For two days I spent my time between the government buildings and the hotel attempting to get better terms for my client. All the while I pleaded that I had to see him. It did not help my frame of mind to receive an envelope from Harvey Owen containing a clipping from a Paris newspaper dated the day after my departure. The headline announced that two were dead in a nightclub fire after a bombing. One victim was positively identified by his French dentist as the bartender. The other was believed to be the owner, Archie Smith, the former American athlete and Olympic team member. The police had requested X-rays of his teeth from America. There was thought to be a political motive in the bombing. The nightclub had been a haunt of Central African refugees and dissidents. The police were working on several leads to solve the crime.

I couldn't sleep. All the usual tricks to switch my mind into a calm backwater failed. The turbulence was too great. My fortitude was breaking up under the frustration and injustice of what had happened. I lost control as suspicions and alarms broke over me. Unable to lie in this storm I got out of bed, turned on the light and looked gratefully at the reality of the walls, the heavily lined curtains and the figured carpet.

"Ask him to wait, please. I'll be right down," I told the concierge into the telephone.

"You aren't disturbing me," I assured Harvey. "I'm glad of the excuse to get out of my room."

"You look pale," Harvey said. "A walk in the garden will do you good."

As we left the lobby I apologized for not having seen him. Harvey nodded and said he knew how busy I'd been. We took a path that wound gently upward through the beautifully kept gardens.

"Sorry I couldn't get you more information about your

friend. There may be something in the next newspapers from Paris."

"There won't be," I said. "It'll take several days or a week for the X-rays to get to the authorities."

"That's true," Harvey agreed. "By then it'll be a dead story – pardon the pun, it wasn't intentional – and they won't print anything."

"I'll just keep hoping and praying it wasn't him," I said. "They're finally letting me see Nokato. I leave tomorrow."

"It's not a long flight."

"They insist I go by car."

"That's a very long trip but it's not bad along the coast."

"I'm not going that way. I'm going the long way through the mountains."

"Those are difficult and even dangerous roads." Harvey looked worried.

"It's Monsieur Petit's idea. It'll take two days. He insists I must see the interior to get an idea of the great tourist potential. He's all for my going into the Sahara Desert and spending some time visiting the different oases. I told him I'd do that after I'd seen Nokato. That was about the only concession he did make," I concluded grimly.

We reached a prominence overlooking Algiers and the curve of the bay. Two ships were moving into the harbor leaving a lighter gray-blue wake. Far out on the curved expanse of sea the stack and the smoke of another ship was slipping below the horizon.

"I wanted to see you to tell you that I've got to leave tomorrow for a few days. My newspaper in London sent word that there's a big story about to break in Tunis. I have to cover it."

"We'll meet when you come back and I can tell you how I found Nokato."

"I don't like going off." I couldn't see Harvey's eyes, only myself and the gardens reflected in the dark glasses. "I won't be able to keep an eye on you."

"I didn't know you were."

"Interpol is concerned that nothing happen to you. But I can't ignore my newspaper's cable. The Algerians would get suspicious if I didn't go."

"Nothing's going to happen to mc." I was feeling warmed as I silently blessed Albert Giraud.

"I'm not so certain." Harvey had dropped the droll manner of speech and was talking rapidly as he did when serious. "Something's up. I haven't bcen able to find out what it is. All I've been able to learn is that it does concern Nokato. And that you fit into it some way."

"What do you suggest I do?"

"Get out of here."

"I can't."

"Stall them. Don't leave the city until I get back. I don't like the idea of that drive."

I shook my head. Harvey jerked his head in warning. I turned around. A gardener wearing the usual white robe was coming up the path pushing a wheelbarrow. We moved off in another direction towards a bank of flaming hibiscus.

"I asked to see Maurice Richard," Harvey said. "This time I wasn't turned down."

I stopped but Harvey's arm slipped through mine and pulled me around the turn where a magnificent blue-green fir tree stood sentinel.

"What did Richard say?" I asked.

"I haven't seen him yet. I get the impression he'll be released next week. But the Algerians don't believe he'll talk."

"I don't think he will, either. Someone's still pulling the strings on him."

"Well, they're not on you. Tell them you're too sick to travel."

The sun was hot but I could barely stop myself from shivering. "I'm not so sure they're not," I said.

"What?"

"Pulling strings on me, too."

"They won't be if you don't go to see Nokato tomorrow," Harvey urged.

"Maybe that's what they want me to do, not to go to see him. To stay here."

We stopped walking. We stood in the shade of an old olive tree. The smell of newly cut grass came sweet and nostalgically reminding me of times when life was simpler.

"I don't mean to confuse you," Harvey said. "Yet I know I am. It's just that I get the distinct feeling that I may never see you again after today."

"Want to make a bet?" I asked.

"Only if I'm sure I'll lose," he replied.

Chapter Twenty-Six

The hills rose from the green sea. The car passed villages perched on top of hills. We reached a fertile plateau in the midst of towering mountains. Beyond the southern range lay most of Algeria in the Great Sahara Desert. At the end of the two-day trip we left the main road, passed over a ridge overlooking a small lush valley. On the other side stood barns and farm houses. Workers in white robes were in the fields. Through a double row of cypresses we approached a rambling house. Oleanders grew in profusion. The car stopped in front of a new wing which held a second floor and terrace. I told the driver I did not know how long I would remain: probably until some time tomorrow.

"*Malesh*," he replied. I had learned that this was the equivalent of "it doesn't matter". He had been here before and would wait at the farm buildings. The car disappeared around the house and I went up the four stone steps to the portico. I lifted the oval brass knocker and let it drop. I glanced about and noticed the carriage stone and the hitching post. The door was opened by an elderly man wearing long pleated, black bloomers and white mess jacket. I told him I wished to see President Nokato and gave my name. The black tassel of the skull cap gyrated, just missing his pince-nez glasses. He led the way across a large foyer, opened a door and indicated that I should go up. At the top of the marble steps I found a heavy door. There was a muffled response to my knock. I stepped into a room blinding with the late afternoon sun.

As my vision cleared I made out a man's legs suspended in mid-air. The head rested on the floor, cradled in his arms. I twisted my neck to look upside down. It was Joseph Nokato. I mumbled apologies and walked out onto the terrace.

Above the greens of the trees the sky was becoming salmon pink. Behind the houses stood cassia trees, their long pods hanging like earrings from the branches. The air was crystalline with an ozone that made me breathe in and out rapidly. I heard footsteps and turned to be embraced and pounded on my back.

"Forgive me. I learned in prison that yoga was the best way to relax. I've been excited, expecting you." Nokato held me at arm's length to study my face.

"What's happened to Archie?" I blurted out.

231

"What do you mean?"

"You haven't heard about the nightclub?"

"What about the nightclub?"

"It was bombed. Two bodies were found. One of them probably Archie."

"It wasn't. He's here."

My legs started to give way. Black dots sprang before my eyes. Nokato guided me back into the room and I sank onto a divan.

"Are you all right, Ben? What happened?"

I rolled my head against the back of the divan. I didn't open my eyes as I told him.

"That's terrible. Archie doesn't know anything about it."

"Where is he?"

"He's here. In the back bedroom sleeping. He slipped in late last night." I heard Nokato's footsteps and the click of glass. "Let me get you something to drink."

I opened my eyes. "What are you having?" I asked.

"Nothing. I've given up drinking and smoking."

Nokato was wearing white, tight-fitting pants, resembling jodhpurs; a matching jacket that buttoned to a round standing collar; a white cap, pointed in front and back, wide in the middle.

"I like the outfit," I said. "You look like Nehru."

"Thank you." Abruptly the old grin lit his face. "I can't tell you how glad I am to see you, Ben."

"Likewise, as we say in New York," I smiled back. "You've lost a lot of weight."

"I was getting too fat and soft."

"You've overdone it." I studied him. I couldn't get over the change. He didn't appear haggard as much as he seemed fined down to the point of looking ascetic. This was a different Joseph Nokato. "You must have had a rough time in prison."

"Others have had it worse." He lowered himself onto a black cushion on the floor. "It gave me an opportunity to do a lot of hard thinking."

He cut off my apologies about the hi-jacking and told me to forget Maurice Richard. I explained that I couldn't; that I'd caught a glimpse of Richard and felt haunted by him, as though at any moment he would appear and wreck everything. Nokato sat motionless as a buddha.

"He won't bother us again. I've given a lot of thought about how to untangle this and how to get it back on the right track."

"I've noticed that already," I said. "By the way you used that business agreement to get me here." When he nodded I added: "I wasn't able to get any concessions from the Algerians on the contract. All I could do was to clarify some minor points."

"I didn't expect you to do more than that. They're dealing the cards. But I managed to slip in a joker."

"I wouldn't advise escaping without signing that agreement. Things like the Ben Bella affair, the way the Algerians have pushed around the French and the Israelis, are proof that they wouldn't let you get away with it."

"I'm signing the agreement."

The setting sun was reflected on the glazed diamond-shaped tiles on the walls. It lit up the Moorish decor, the small carpets laid on top of heavy rugs. There was the faint stirring of air but it did little to cool me. Still I was able to follow Nokato's example and sit quietly. I waited for him to speak.

"The Algerians hold the winning hand. When someone has you beaten you throw in your cards. You get set for the next deal where you can raise the bets."

"I was never much of a poker player," I said.

"I make up for you. The Pan-African Movement is the

233

big pot. What the Algerians don't realize is that I would have paid even more to get out of here. Now we've got to turn that, and every disadvantage, into a plus."

"How do you mean?"

"You undoubtedly feel that for the amount I'm investing, they should immediately fly me out. But you forget that the Algerians can't release me without causing a big diplomatic row. However, if I escape, it isn't their fault. And that's the only way they'll let me go. That's why I'm not really guarded. All right, Ben, how do we turn this escape to our advantage?"

I was getting the drift. "It's a big news story. The whole world will be sympathetic. Especially when they see how you've changed while in prison."

The gleam in his eyes acknowledged that I was right. "I wanted you here, Ben, to help plan the moves we make when I'm free. Top priority are statements to the press. They've got to be designed so that I'm actually talking about the aims of the Movement."

"So that once the Movement is announced you're the logical man to head it," I added.

"And don't worry about my losing the money. It's in a blocked account in Beirut."

"Where did it come from?" I asked.

"It was raised. I look at it as an investment. Eventually we'll have the Movement here too. When we do, we'll get it back and more with it."

"Do you think Mr Johnson and his associates are going to sit back and let you walk away with their Movement?"

"They will if they have no choice. After all they approached me first about it."

"The stakes are higher now. You're playing against them and not with them. They're going ahead because they feel certain the Movement will accomplish what they want."

234

"So am I," he said firmly. "But it will accomplish what we want."

Quickly he explained the escape plan. Although it was a mock escape, the Algerians insisted it must appear to be genuine. Nokato led me to the back section of this upstairs apartment. He kept the servants out of here. No one was aware that Archie was in the house. We went to a little room scarcely larger than a cupboard. It was filled with wireless apparatus.

"Equipment has improved since the days in the bush when I learned from the air force. But like bicycle riding, you don't forget," Nokato said over his shoulder after he'd given the call letters and thrown the switch. "I'm letting them know we're moving out tonight."

A hand fell on my shoulder. I turned to look into Archie's sleepy face. We gripped each other's hand. He stood with his arm across my shoulders watching Nokato slowly turn the dials, waiting for the reply to his call letters. Finally I told him that we'd be in the other room. In the dusk I stumbled over some cushions before finding the divan. Archie lowered himself onto the couch next to me.

"When did you leave Paris?" I asked.

"The very night we talked."

"It's a lucky thing you did."

I told Archie what had happened. The muscles tightened along his jaw and his eyes lost their softness. I would not like to be the culprits when Archie found them. I was glad when he started to speak. It was not good to have that much hate and vengeance building up inside him. Talk was a safety valve. I encouraged him by throwing in questions.

Archie kept coming back to the death of his two employees, innocent bystanders in the attempt to kill him. Mr Johnson's people must have been monitoring the radio for that was the only way they could have known that Archie was leaving and what he was going to do. Nokato had told him to start the next day. It was Archie's eagerness to get moving quickly that had saved him.

"Something good comes out of bad," I said. "I'm not trying to be the perennial optimist. Mr Johnson and his bunch think you're dead. No one knows that you're here."

"If they knew about me leaving, they must have known about your plans," Archie said. "Why didn't they try to stop you, Ben?"

I could hear Archie fumbling for something. A light went on beside him in a brass lamp, the shade was made of bits of colored glass. I was bathed in purple, Archie in green. We stared at each other.

"I don't know," I replied. "I've been trying to come up with the answer to that. Right now I just want to get Joe out and take the play away from them before they make the formal announcement about the Movement. They've already laid the ground work."

"Joe told me. He was listening to radio commentators in Europe and America last night when I slipped in. I sure startled him."

"I can see you would." Archie was wearing green and brown camouflage combat uniform, jumpboots, a holster belt strapped about his waist. "Did you have trouble getting here?"

"It took a little time finding some Algerians to smuggle me over the border from Tunisia. From then on it was nothing. They'd done it so often fighting against the French that it's practically a highway. They stuck me in a burnoose and drove me to the forest overlooking the house. And you?"

"I just followed your instructions."

"I didn't have more than that to give you. Apparently you picked up the trail."

I realized that I'd picked it up all right. I realized too that there were a number of paths leading off it which I had not yet explored. We both fell silent. When I looked at him I knew what he was thinking.

"I've assembled something which I thought we could control for the good of everyone," I said. "Suddenly when I'm not looking, it's moving. It has a life of its own. It can become a monster, not a force for good, as I'd planned."

"We have to control and guide it or kill it before it gets out of hand."

"Suppose our plans don't work? Suppose Joe doesn't become head of the Movement? How do we stop it?" I asked.

"The same way we're forcing changes in America."

"I thought you were against violence."

"I thought I was too."

The door opened. The white figure of Nokato emerged into the soft patches of multi-coloured light. "Why are you sitting in that light?" he asked. Swiftly he moved to the windows and began closing the shutters.

"We were scaring each other with the bogey-man." I helped him with the shutters. Anyone looking from outside would see only Nokato and me.

"Who's the bogey-man?" Nokato asked.

"Mr Johnson," Archie replied.

"And the people behind him. Those are the ones who count," I added.

"I figure that our first face card has to be so strong – an ace – that it forces them to throw in their hand right then and there," Nokato said. He closed the last shutter and turned on the centre lights.

"What do you mean?" Archie asked.

"President Nokato's sudden appearance will be so dramatic that it will capture headlines and photos throughout the world," I replied. "He has to say something powerful, something so clear and strong that from then on, whenever people think of the Pan-African Movement they'll automatically associate it with him."

"That's it," Nokato agreed. "The very first statement is the key to the entire thing."

"It's got to sound spontaneous. After that, the next day or so, you can make a more detailed statement and the world will pay attention to that. By then everyone will have noticed how much your appearance has changed. That you suffered in prison. You'll show that you're not vindictive. In fact that prison was your time of wandering in the wilderness." I was getting caught up in the idea. The gleam in Nokato's eyes and the expression of approval in Archie's spurred me on: "You're no longer seeking power or political prestige. If you do return to your own country it'll be as a private citizen, not seeking office. The world is too small for civil strife. Just as Gandhi did for India, so you are trying to do for your people. You are devoting yourself to the cause of peace among the African states. These new countries must prove to the world that not only can they govern themselves, but they can stand together and can work for each other."

It all poured out of me and a lot more. We passed slogans back and forth, refined statements, tried to get away from rhetoric, and, most of all, from clichés.

Nokato glanced at his watch and disappeared into the back of the apartment for a short time. When he returned I was surrounded by crumpled balls of discarded paper as I wrote and rewrote the statement. Nokato said that he had received coded confirmation on the radio that the newspapermen and television people were alerted in Tunisia to a big story. They were being brought to the border to meet us. Only they had not been told what the story was or who was coming across.

I didn't like it. It was too late for me to protest. It had

moved too quickly and too swiftly to be halted. I could not conceive that Mr Johnson, John Gary and associates would let the whole thing be snatched from them after they had worked everything out. Up until now they had thought of every contingency. Why would they slip up now? It did not seem logical that they would not hear that something was going to happen on the Algerian-Tunisian border early tomorrow morning that would affect the Pan-African Movement.

"What's bothering you, Ben?" Archie asked.

I just shook my head and didn't explain that everything was churning inside me. That I felt I was on the verge of being able to put it all together. And that it was essential I do so before we crossed that border. Instead I said: "I'm just hung up on the first statement. It's got to be very short."

"It's got to be like a telegram," Nokato said, "so that it can hit the headlines."

"Like, 'Lafayette, we are here'. Or 'I have nothing to offer but blood, toil, tears and sweat'," Archie said.

I tore another scribbled sheet from the pad, wadded it into a ball and dropped it to the floor. I thought of others: "Dictators ride to and fro upon tigers which they dare not dismount". Yet I kept coming back to: "Power tends to corrupt and absolute power corrupts absolutely".

Chapter Twenty-Seven

Archie slept. I marveled at his ability to relax. I sat and stewed and rewrote the statements: the longer one was no problem. When I woke Archie he looked at me with concern.

"You should have gotten some rest, Ben."

"You get nothing but that when you're dead," I said.

"There are those who think otherwise."

I wasn't going to argue theology at this moment. I had Nokato sign the document I had brought from Algiers. Archie and I witnessed it. I put it in a large envelope on which was printed Monsieur Petit's name and official title and left it on the desk. I stuffed the duplicate copy in my jacket.

"You realize," I told Nokato, "that the money is now irrevocably blocked in the Beirut bank."

"I'm not worried about it. I get a very high rate of interest. It'll never be turned over to the Algerians."

"That's not what they think."

"It'll take years to draw up plans, have estimates and get all the interested parties to agree, especially me. You went through that in Spain," Nokato said. "Long before that the Movement will take over the obligation."

I didn't argue. Nokato knew what he was doing and exactly how he wanted it done. Every detail had been thought out. I remembered Albert Giraud's comment about men in prison making elaborate schemes to be executed when they are released.

We slipped out of the house. In the distance the sound of a flute rose and fell. A dog barked. A horse whinnied. Under the incandescent glow of the full moon we moved with a rustle through the grain field. Archie led the way; he was wearing a holster with a .45 automatic. The stepping stones were black in the silver rush of the small stream. The air was cool and aromatic of moss and rotting wood. At the top of the forest I glanced back at the valley. The villa stood below, dark and silent. A light came from one of the windows of a distant farm building. I touched the breast pocket of my shirt and felt Evy's barrette.

The small car was hidden in a grove of trees on the other side of the road, too far from the valley for anyone to hear it start. The moon was so bright that Archie drove the car with only the small lights. Nokato sat next to him. The roads were deserted. It was miles before we passed a village on a nearby hill.

Above the throb of the motor Nokato rehearsed the vital first statement he would make to the press. He read it several ways. I had him change a few words.

"You're getting it, Ben. It hits the right note," Archie said. "It's the modern equivalent of 'Liberty! Equality! Fraternity!', for all Africans throughout the world."

Nokato grinned at me over his shoulder. "We've got it."

"Let me try to improve the long statement," I said.

The car went slower on the mountain roads. Moonlight washed away the color. We were out of the wooded area. The landscape was harsher. I stopped mumbling phrases to myself when Archie asked Nokato where he thought the headquarters of the Movement should be located.

"Well, the Organization of African Unity is in Ethiopia," Nokato replied tentatively.

"The OAU is powerless and ineffectual. We'd get tainted by their image," Archie said.

"Nkrumah built a huge assembly hall at Accra. Only one congress met there."

"Ghana's having its problems," Archie said.

"So is the United States. Yet the United Nations functions in New York," I said.

"Paris would be my choice. But it wouldn't do. It has to be in Africa," Nokato said.

"It should be an enclave like Liechtenstein or Tangiers," I said. "Created for the Movement. Ideally it should be on the borders, between two or three countries, with each nation giving a bit of land for it."

"That might be difficult to sell to the countries concerned," Nokato said.

"I don't think so, not if you also make it an international settlement and a free port. What modern Africa needs is an international banking haven where the young merging countries can get quick credit and preferred terms instead of being dependent on Switzerland, New York or Beirut."

"Ben, that's an excellent idea. That gives the Movement the last important facet. It ties the whole thing together in a tight package," Nokato exclaimed. "Why didn't I think of that?"

"You would have, I'm sure."

"Perhaps, but it would have been later. Maybe too late. You have to anticipate these things. I'm really glad you're here."

"Actually I've been wondering why you wanted Archie and me here."

"To help me to escape."

"Signing the agreement and putting up the money did that. There's no trick to this faked escape. There are plenty of Algerians around who would take you across the border."

"I wanted both of you with me. You're the two most important people. Without you I wouldn't be in this situation."

"That's true," I accepted the veiled accusation. With this, the key piece fell into place. I had been so obsessed with rectifying what had happened that I had not seen what was in front of me all the time. "I owe you a great deal."

"You've done more than I ever expected," Nokato said.

"No matter what you've told him, Ben has always felt responsible for your being held here," Archie said.

"The whole slate is clean now." The white, double-peaked cap turned. The teeth gleamed at me. "Especially with this new idea."

"Thanks. I realize it's been bothering you to move a large amount of money out of Switzerland. From your own bank," I said.

"That's true." Nokato did not face the front of the car. He was staring at me.

"When the Algerians insisted, Oliver and Hardt probably got good interest rates from the Lebanese bank where the money is held."

"I wasn't in a position to handle those details. I leave things like that to the experts."

"The ham radio station was a swift improvization when you discovered that you'd miscalculated the Algerians. It kept you in touch everywhere."

He regarded me the way an overfed lion stares at an unarmed man, wondering if it's worth the trouble: knowing he is the master of the situation. Slowly he said: "You have it all figured out, haven't you?"

"Not quite. I still don't understand why Archie and I are here."

"I knew you could help with the final things. And you have: with the statements and the other ideas. They're excellent."

"What's eating you, Ben?" Archie asked as he shifted the car into low gear. He turned onto a narrower, dirt road and put on the headlights. He steered carefully to avoid trees and huge rocks.

"My stupidity. I don't know why it took me so long to put it all together."

"I don't either," Nokato said.

"You didn't slip anywhere. You really are a great executive. Your choice of men is impeccable."

"Especially picking you and Archie," Nokato nodded.

"Yes. You're a terrific psychologist. You anticipated

my thoughts and reactions every step of the way. When I was about to give up you got me angry by going after Françoise. After I took the bait again you kept me on the string."

"Right from the beginning you did more than I ever anticipated."

"You mean in working out the Pan-African Movement?"

"Yes, I was only exploring that idea."

"You'd won the pot when Maurice Richard hi-jacked the plane. But you had a lot of time to think when the Algerians crossed you up and held you. The more you thought about it, the better the Movement seemed. Especially when you had Mr Johnson distribute my report and got back favorable comments from everyone. And besides I was still around; I hadn't been killed."

The road had become a cart trail. Big boulders made solid shadows on the silver earth. The car whined in first gear. When the wheels hit crevices we had to hang on. There was a silence in the car but an atmosphere was building. A fuse had been touched off and the spark was running along the string.

"What the hell is this all about?" Archie finally said.

"How are we for time?" Nokato asked.

Archie shot a quick glance at his chronometer. He looked up just in time to avoid another rock. "We're on schedule. Almost there."

"Good."

"I want to hear your side of this, Joe," Archie grunted.

"Ben's correct. It took him much longer to figure it out than I thought it would."

"Put it down to stupidity," I said.

"I wasn't bluffing about the revolt." Nokato went on: "If I'd gone through with it I'd have taken over the government quickly. The oil wells would have been cut off, the mines shut down, all construction work stopped."

"General Moki realized that. In exchange for calling off the revolt he agreed to revise the agreements and cut John Gary and others in."

"How did you pick that up?" Nokato asked.

"John Gary! You were doing business with that bastard!" Archie exclaimed.

"Like music, money is an international language," I said. "Probably John Gary didn't know who he was doing business with. Everything was handled by that honest broker, Mr Johnny Johnson. But even if Gary knew, it wouldn't have made any difference to him."

"That's true," Nokato said. "This is the biggest game. I'd pushed in a lot of chips with the revolt."

"You still had a lot left in New York and in that swell Swiss bank you bought two years ago. When you were President you sold those franchises. When Moki discovered that the country was bankrupt you started your revolt. That way you shook down the original companies again – you had them over a barrel – and you also cut in John Gary. When you got everything into line the only way you could stop the revolt without losing face, without loss of reputation, was to have yourself hi-jacked. You had that figured out long in advance. You set me in the pipeline to do exactly that."

"Apart from being held in Algiers you haven't been badly treated or paid," Nokato said. "If you weren't such an idealist you would have put it together earlier. Still only an idealist would have grasped the idea and developed the Movement."

"You're still going ahead with the Movement?" Archie asked.

"I am the Movement. This is a fresh deal and I've got all the aces. John Gary and the other interests are putting up big money for concessions in other countries. The large American foundations have already earmarked grants. The United Nations will ask member countries for volunteers like the Peace Corps. Central Africa will be at peace and be prosperous."

"Like a graveyard," Archie snapped.

"No, they'll be alive and live longer because there won't be strife. They'll have a creed as strong as a religion. It will take hold and it'll expand until it takes over the entire continent."

"Today Central Africa. Tomorrow the world," I muttered.

"I'm not Hitler." Nokato turned to me. "I'm not putting people in gas chambers or starting wars."

"What are you doing?" Archie demanded.

"I'm doing what needs to be done. Africans can't run their own countries. They can't run anything. Don't you think I tried the first year I was in power? I had factories, machines, boats, vehicles, and spare parts brought in. In America they may turn in cars when the ashtrays are filled but here they walk away from a tractor when it runs out of gas. Sure, they'll learn, but not in this century. Take a look at the civil wars. What are they about? They're about who gets the biggest share of the spoils and percentages on the concessions. The market here is too big, the land too fertile, the opportunities too great. It's a vacuum sucking in investment and commerce. I'm in first. I'll call the cards as they turn up. And they'll turn up the way I call them because I'm dealing."

The car was running along the edge of a precipice. Far below I caught the glint of light reflected by a stream. I wondered why Archie didn't turn the wheel. The car would bounce down the ravine until we ended, smashed, thousands of feet below. To my mind that was preferable to what was being prophesied and it was going to happen just as surely as the sun was now about to rise. Everything fitted together: Joseph Nokato was going to be dictator of Central Africa; the despot of his race. He would sell his fellow man's birthright to the same foreigners who had held them in bondage since the continent was discovered.

Again Nokato proved that he knew his men. Archie kept the car to the side of the wall. It inched about the turns of the cliff. Finally he swung it into an indentation. The motor and lights went out.

"We're a few minutes early, aren't we?" Nokato glanced at his watch.

There was no time for Archie to reply. Three white gowned figures materialized in the distance, seemingly moving without effort as though on wheels. We got out of the car. The Arabs stood out in the clear moonlight as they came down the mountain trail. They had been hiding in a place where they could watch us approach. Each wore a *gangourah*, a white gown, over it, white burnooses.

"The only one who knew everything was Mr Johnson," I said. "He was your façade, your ventriloquist's dummy."

"I don't think he'd like being referred to that way. I was his client just like John Gary and others are. He was negotiating for me, doing what I requested."

"Including instructing Maurice Richard and the Swiss bank."

"Everything."

I did not have an opportunity to continue, not that there was anything more to go on about. The three Algerians were alongside. After greeting us, the leader talked rapidly in French. I got most of it. What I did not get I read on Archie's face. Nokato was replying to them when I said in a low voice: "I take it they're not happy about the soldiers in the area."

"They report that there's a large contingent of the Algerian border patrol," Archie replied.

Nokato turned to us: "There's nothing to worry about. The Algerian troops are going to pretend they tried to stop us. But they were too late. You've got that, about my escape, in the long statement."

"I'd write it differently now," I answered.

"You and Archie aren't realists." Nokato spoke sadly, with resignation.

I glanced towards Archie. His emotions were as clear on his face as words on a blackboard. There was the dazed expression in his eyes of an animal who has been betrayed by his master.

The cart track was a trail, winding, leading upward towards the overhanging peaks which were flat cutouts against the graying sky. The three Arabs moved quickly up the path. The last one beckoned to us before taking the turn and disappearing. We started after them. The trail led through a ravine. We could hear and feel the cool rush of a stream below. Against the brown of the earth and the gray of the rocks it was easy to pick out the guides ahead: their white robes stood out as did Nokato's. Archie, in camouflaged battle dress, and I, wearing dark slacks and blue-black blazer, blended into the background.

The path widened. Nokato dropped back to walk beside me. Archie continued in front. I knew Nokato was waiting for me to ask questions so that he could justify his actions. I refused to give him the opportunity. We were all aware that this would be the last time we would ever walk together. Crossing the border from Algiers into Tunisia was our Rubicon.

"You said that I'd misjudged the Algerians. That I never expected them to jail me." Nokato could not contain himself any longer. He spoke in a low tone. I did not know if Archie heard him. "You're right. But the Algerians weren't the only ones I misjudged. It was the world and world opinion. I figured the Algerians would hold me for a short time. They would be forced to let me go because of the outcry. That there would be so much pressure from various countries and influential people for my release that I'd immediately be set free. I should have known better. I relearned an old lesson. The world couldn't care less. Because I'm black."

I had to speak. "That's not true. People and organizations tried to get you out. They protested to the Algerians."

"What organizations? A lot of do-gooders who have no influence, no force," he said scornfully. "If I'd been white I'd have been released immediately. The whole western world from the Pope to the heads of states would have screamed at the injustice and demanded that I be freed. But I'm black, even though I'm only the founder and first President of a country. So I rot in jail until I figure how to buy myself out."

The path narrowed and turned. We had to walk single file. Nokato was between Archie and me, in the rear. I could not see our guides. The multitude of stars had disappeared. The moon hung lower on the horizon. There was a stillness, the hush that always comes before dawn. The loosened stones rolled noisily over the precipice. After five minutes of rapid climbing the path broadened and leveled, Nokato slowed so that I caught up with him.

"Don't think I'm bitter," Nokato continued. "I'm not, I learned my lesson years ago. I learned it repeatedly at every step I took. This is a white man's world. If you're going to win you have to play it according to his rules."

"And the name of the game is wealth and power," I said.

"That's right. I've heard it said that if you had a place to stand, a leverage point and a fulcrum, you could move the earth. Well, I'll stand in Central Africa, money is the fulcrum and the Movement is going to be the leverage. I'm going to move the world in the direction I want it moved."

"Why can't it move in the direction Archie wants?"

"Because that's a dream. The Africans won't be ready for freedom or democracy in my generation or the next one. I'm not interested in what happens a hundred years from now. I'm only interested in right now and in me."

I was glad when the path narrowed again. Nokato glanced at his watch. He hurried ahead of me. I stared at the back of his white jacket. We continued in silence. At the next level place Nokato increased his pace to come abreast of Archie. They were several hundred yards ahead of me. I saw Nokato glance at Archie. He said something to him but there was no response. Nokato moved in front.

I remembered his credo: "There are not good men and bad men: there are only strong men and weak men." Although I knew that he was wrong still he was proving that he was right.

We had turned away from the stream and could no longer hear the rush of water. The path, though narrow, was easy to follow. I had not seen the guides for almost an hour. The eastern sky warmed to a rose color. The dark blue was becoming paler in the west. In the diffused light the rocks and shrubs stood out without shadows.

The sweat ran down my back and beaded my face. I pulled off my jacket. I took the next turn. There was no one in sight. I hurried. The tops of the mountains were washed in the first rays of the hidden sun. I thought I saw something move on top of a peak. The path narrowed, then rose abruptly, passing through a split in a high rock to extend upward over a hundred feet.

I emerged from the defile; I was on the threshold of a small plateau. About a third of a mile away, rocks rose on the other side. At the far end I saw the white figure of Nokato. In the middle of the bare expanse was Archie in his camouflaged uniform. In the brighter light he stood out almost as clearly as Nokato. I started to run to catch up. As I did a puff of dirt rose beside me. I heard the ricochet of the bullet before the report of the rifle.

It was happening fast. Yet it seemed as clear as a series of individual snapshots. Rifle shots rang out. I zigzagged sharply. I felt the rush of wind as the bullets tore around me. I threw myself under a huge boulder. I saw Nokato running for the end of the ravine. The white suit marked him as the one who was not a target. Archie jerked forward. He stumbled, fell to his knees. And then he was up, he ran, turned, twisted, breaking his stride, eluding phantom tacklers. Puffs of dirt hit all about him. I have never seen a man run that fast. He disappeared at the end of the plateau.

I glanced up slowly, so that my movement was not detected, I saw our three guides above, rifles in hand. I inched back behind the boulder where I could not see them; more important, they could not see me. Suddenly I heard more firing. It did not come from above, but from ahead. I looked up. There were only the rocks and the tops of the mountains. The guide-executioners were gone. Another shot rang out.

I sprinted across the expanse. The hairs on the back of my scalp tingled with fear. I saw myself in the sights of the rifles above me. I dived into the shelter of an over-hanging rock. I was out of the ambush of that plateau. I kept running. The path turned and headed down. There was a large printed sign in Arabic. I realized this was the border. I tore around another sharp turn. I stopped running.

The trail was a road again. Archie sprawled in the middle of it. He was face down, right hand extended, holding the .45 automatic. A hundred yards ahead of him lay a figure in white. As I rushed towards Archie I was conscious that the sun had reached us.

A new color was staining the brown and green of Archie's shirt. Kneeling I turned him over. He moaned. A trickle of blood ran from the corner of his mouth. His eyes opened. He recognized me.

I was saying a lot of words: assuring him that he was okay; that he must not move; that I'd get a doctor; that he really wasn't badly hurt. I could see that he knew better. The lost expression in his eyes was a contrast to the strain of his corded neck, clenched jaw and bunched muscles.

"Nokato?" Archie gasped.

Getting up I ran to the white figure. The air was becoming hot. There was a glare. In a few minutes I was back beside Archie. A spasm of pain shook his body. I tried to still it by holding him tightly. Blood bubbled over his lips. I wiped it away.

"Is he dead?"

"Yes, he's dead."

From the distance I heard the approaching sounds of vehicles. It was the correspondents coming for their big story. They were not going to be disappointed. I took the automatic from Archie's hand and slipped it back into the holster. Let the newspapermen write the obvious story. The Algerian government could not deny that Nokato had been a prisoner, had tried to escape and that their soldiers had prevented this.

I felt Archie stir in my arms. His eyes were staring at me, asking a question. I read his lips: "Did Joe say anything?"

I hesitated. I realized that Nokato's words could ring down through the years with the force that only a man dying for his beliefs can give to them. What would

Nokato have said? What would Archie have wanted him to say?

And so I repeated to Archie and later to the newspapermen the short statement we had prepared. And thus began the legend of Joseph Nokato.

Knowledge and Understanding of the World in the Early Years Foundation Stage

Knowledge and Understanding of the World cuts across all of the EYFS guiding themes and this book will encourage practitioners to think about and develop their own understanding of the implications for inclusion, respect for oneself and for others irrespective of ethnicity, culture or religion, home language, family background, learning difficulties, gender, disabilities or abilities.

Stella Louis works as an Early Years consultant for Southwark where she specialises in promoting effective teaching and learning in the Early Years Foundation Stage. She is a visiting lecturer at London Metropolitan University.

Practical Guidance in the EYFS
Series Editor: Sandy Green

The *Practical Guidance in the EYFS* series will assist practitioners in the smooth and successful implementation of the Early Years Foundation Stage.

Each book gives clear and detailed explanations of each aspect of learning and development and encourages readers to consider each area within its broadest context to expand and develop their own knowledge and good practice.

Practical ideas and activities for all age groups are offered along with a wealth of expertise of how elements from the practice guidance can be implemented within all early years' settings. The books include suggestions for the innovative use of everyday resources, popular books and stories.

Titles in this series include:

Personal, Social and Emotional Development in the Early Years Foundation Stage
Sue Sheppy

Communication, Language and Literacy in the Early Years Foundation Stage
Helen Bradford

Knowledge and Understanding of the World in the Early Years Foundation Stage
Stella Louis

Creative Development in the Early Years Foundation Stage
Pamela May

Problem Solving, Reasoning and Numeracy in the Early Years Foundation Stage
Anita M. Hughes

Physical Development in the Early Years Foundation Stage
Angela D. Nurse

Planning for the Early Years Foundation Stage
Sandra Smidt

Knowledge and Understanding of the World in the Early Years Foundation Stage

Stella Louis

Routledge
Taylor & Francis Group

LONDON AND NEW YORK

First published 2009
by Routledge
2 Park Square, Milton Park, Abingdon, Oxon OX14 4RN

Simultaneously published in the USA and Canada
by Routledge
270 Madison Avenue, New York, NY 10016

Routledge is an imprint of the Taylor & Francis Group, an informa business

© 2009 Stella Louis

Typeset in Optima by
Taylor & Francis Books
Printed and bound in Great Britain by
TJ International Ltd, Padstow, Cornwall

British Library Cataloguing in Publication Data
A catalogue record for this book is available from the British Library

Library of Congress Cataloging in Publication Data
Louis, Stella.
  Knowledge and understanding of the world in the early years foundation stage / Stella Louis.
    p. cm. – (Practical guidance in the EYFS)
  1. Early childhood education–Activity programs. 2. Early childhood education–Social aspects. 3. Child development. 4. Socialization. I. Title.
  LB1139.35.A37L68 2008
372.21–dc22   2008038525

ISBN 978-0-415-47837-3 (hbk)
ISBN 978-0-415-47304-0 (pbk)

To my beautiful daughter Hannah Louise Ram,
with love and appreciation,
and my friends, David and Joy Crookes

Contents

Acknowledgements

I would like acknowledge and thank my parents Vincent and Mary Louis for encouraging me to believe in myself. I would like to acknowledge Alexander Fairtlough and Charlotte Wise for their practical support and constructive feedback. I also want to thank Pauline France, Professor Tina Bruce and Julia Manning-Morton for their reviews. Thank you to Sandy Green for her patience and inspiring feedback. Also I would like to acknowledge and thank Dr Monika Lee, Sophie Thomson and Liz O'Donnell. Thank you to Laura Henry for suggesting that I should write this book. Finally I would like to thank all of the children and practitioners for sharing their learning stories.

Introduction

Since 1997 we have seen a number of national initiatives aimed at reducing child poverty, tackling social exclusion and raising educational achievements and progression within the early years. The Ten Year Strategy for Childcare, 'Choice for Parents', the Best Start for Children, and the Childcare Act (2006) provide the context for the implementation and the delivery of the Early Years Foundation Stage (EYFS). The central aim of the EYFS is to put the individual child at the centre of our thinking. The EYFS incorporates the five Every Child Matters outcomes of staying safe, being healthy, enjoying and achieving, making a positive contribution, and achieving economic well-being. It provides a regulatory framework aimed at raising standards and ensuring consistency in all early years care and educational settings. This includes independent schools and reception classes in primary schools so that all children get the best start to life. All early years settings will have the quality of their provision monitored by Ofsted, whose role is in part to ensure that all children have access to individual care and education. From September 2008, the EYFS became statutory. It is the first single framework for children from birth to five years and will mark a transformation of early years provision as we currently know it. Based on research, it provides practical guidance (DfES 2007b) on the delivery of an early years play-based framework. Much emphasis is placed on practitioners' existing good practice; this book will help practitioners implement the EYFS principles in their everyday work with children. Practitioners are challenged to reflect and evaluate their own knowledge and understanding of development matters. They will also be asked to reflect on how they build upon children's previous learning, experience and interest. This book will support practitioners to plan appropriate developmental learning that builds on previous experiences and interests where play and exploration have high priority.

The role parents play and their contributions to their children's development and learning is recognised as being central to 'Knowledge and Understanding of the World.'

The EYFS places emphasis on the role adults play as key in babies' and young children's development and learning processes. We now know that for babies and young children interaction with other people has a direct impact on how their brain develops. Learning through play and exploration supports babies and young children to make connections, through explorations and experiments as well as through cooperation and relationships with others around them. This book will help practitioners to further understand how young children learn and how adults can support them through developing genuine partnerships with parents. Practitioners' ongoing observations and assessments of babies and young children underpin the successful delivery of the EYFS. This book incorporates all aspects of development and learning in the areas of knowledge and understanding of the world. It will support practitioners to provide children with encounters and experiences that will challenge their existing capabilities. Children's ability to organise their thoughts logically is fundamental to how they interact with and develop a knowledge and understanding of themselves and the world around them.

The EYFS integrates the curriculum guidance for the *Foundation Stage* (2000) and *Birth to Three Matters* (2003) and provides practitioners with a new practice guidance (DfES 2007d). Six areas of learning and development are covered. This book introduces practical activities that link to the practice guidance. Practitioners will find this book of great use as a resource to help them through the most challenging areas of learning and development.

This book incorporates:

- a theoretical framework in which to reflect on practitioners' attitudes to the learning process for children;
- examples of children's self-directed and exploratory play;
- a guide for practitioners to help them understand the diverse ways in which children develop and learn;
- strategies for responding to the individuality of each child;
- advice for practitioners on how to create stimulating and enabling environments;
- activities and ideas for offering age-appropriate experiences for development and learning.

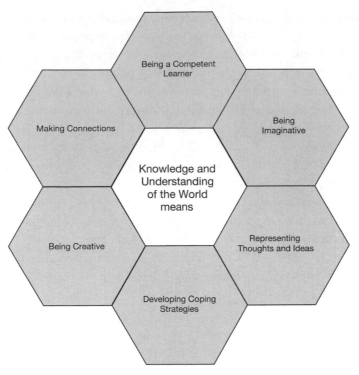

Figure 1
What knowledge and understanding of the world means for children
Source: DfES 2007d

Four themes guide the statutory framework and these are grouped into categories of:

1   a unique child;
2   positive relationships;
3   enabling environments;
4   learning and development.

This book uses the main headings from the practice guidance and keeps as close as possible to its format. The activities are closely linked to the EYFS framework so that learning outcomes can be easily monitored and evaluated. It provides reading lists about nature study, exploration and investigation, cultural aspects and key vocabulary throughout each chapter. It follows the series format which includes a substantial summary of all relevant theories at the beginning; in this case, the focus will be on research into how babies

and young children develop a knowledge and understanding of the world. It provides ideas and activities to support development throughout the EYFS, making links to early learning goals where appropriate and encouraging reflective practice. The chapter headings follow the sections of learning and development set out in the practice guidance (see Figure 2).

Each chapter relates to the full age range and incorporates the early learning goals (see Figure 3).

Each developmental aspect has six learning stories allocated across the age range, recognising the fact that children do not follow a linear pattern of development. The focus is on effective practice, teaching and learning and how practitioners provide real first-hand experiences for children. The role the practitioners play in supporting, sustaining and extending children's play features in each story. Play and learning focuses on applying the EYFS themes to everyday practice. All of this is closely related to the other three categories in the learning and development sections in the practice guidance,

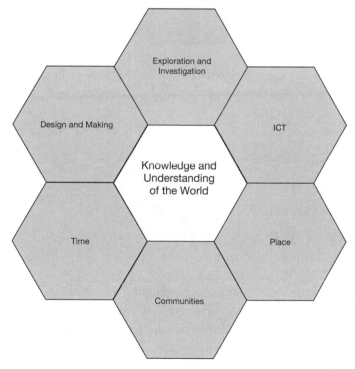

Figure 2
Areas of learning and development
Source: DfES 2007d

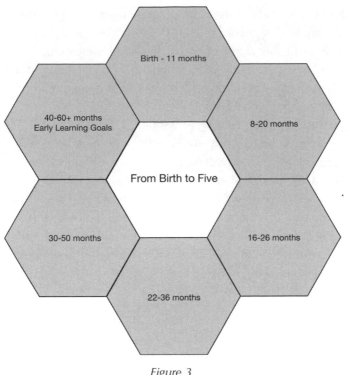

Figure 3
EYFS age ranges
Source: DfES 2007d

where practitioners are encouraged to look, listen and note, to be effective in their practice and to scrutinise the appropriateness of their planning and resourcing. Each chapter will build on how children develop their knowledge and understanding of the world.

A theoretical basis

Knowledge and understanding of the world is one of the most challenging areas of development and learning to assess. It is an incredibly wide subject area and covers play, exploration and investigation, memory, thinking skill, ability to think abstractly, problem-solving, reasoning, nature, science, history, geography and cultural diversity. The emphasis in research on 'how' babies and young children acquire and construct knowledge and understanding of their world has changed to 'what' ideas and concepts they are exploring through their play and explorations. We know that babies and

young children learn about the world through their available movement and all of their senses. The theory of Jean Piaget (1896–1980) has proven to be very influential in the world of early childhood education. His ideas and contribution have given early years practitioners a theoretical framework on which to base their understanding of how children acquire knowledge and understanding of the world around them.

Piaget saw children as active learners. He believed that knowledge should not merely be verbally transmitted but must be constructed and reconstructed by learners. Piaget asserted that for children to know and gain knowledge of the world, they must first experience objects through their available senses, and it is this process that provides knowledge. Piaget's main interest was in children's intellectual development and, most especially, in concepts which constitute the building blocks of thinking. The concept of cognitive structure is central to his theory. Piaget outlined several principles for building cognitive structures, which he defined as schemas:

- assimilation
- adaptation
- accommodation.

Piaget believed that cognitive structures change through the process of assimilation, adaptation and accommodation and that during play and exploration babies and young children would experience their environment using whatever mental maps they have so far constructed from previous experiences.

Assimilation occurs when children come across an experience or object of which they have no knowledge, for example a toy which they need to press for it to squeak. Through trial and error, children approach the problem from many different angles, until they work out how a thing works.

Accommodation occurs when children fit a new idea into their cognitive structure, which alters their old way of approaching a problem. Accommodation enables babies and young children to modify their cognitive structure to make sense of their world as well as developing an understanding of cause and effect.

Adaptation relates to how babies and young children develop new ways of thinking based on previous experiences. In this way, children can be seen organising their perceptions and linking them to previous experiences. These theories are echoed in the research findings of Rima Shore (1997) into early brain development. Her research on the young brain found that early interaction and experiences had an influence on how the brain is wired in

early childhood. Shore found that babies were born with approximately 100 billion brain cells or neurons that they would need for development and learning in childhood. These cells are not yet linked up as a complex network, which is needed for later developments in early childhood such as symbolic representation or pretend play. Shore goes on to describe how the cells become connected when babies and young children begin to develop synapses: 'A synapse is a connection between two brain cells, formed when the axon of one neuron hooks up with the dendrite of another neuron' (1997). Her research suggests that babies need to create electrical activity in the brain in order for it to develop. Catherwood (1999) and Shonkoff and Phillips (2000) equally recognised early experience as being fundamental to development as it directly affects the strengthening of the synapses in the brain. Early interactions and experience with parents and practitioners will have an impact on the way the brain is wired and how babies and young children develop an understanding of their immediate and cultural environment. Her research suggests that babies's emotional well-being is crucial to development and learning and points out that secure relationships with primary carers create a favourable context for early learning and development as this directly affects the way the brain is 'wired'. Shore's finding is based on a considerable body of neuro-scientific evidence and is further reinforced by the work of Alison Gopnik, Andrew Meltzott and Patricia Kuhl.

> In the early years, children's brains form twice as many synapses as they eventually need. If these synapses are used repeatedly in a child's day-to-day life, they are reinforced and become a part of the brain's permanent circuitry. If they are not used repeatedly or often enough, they are eliminated. In this way, experience plays a crucial role in 'wiring' a young child's brain.
>
> (Shore 1997: 17)

The work of Gopnik et al. (1999) is also significant and important as it suggests that babies arrive knowing much more than was previously recognised. Babies were found to imitate facial expressions and manual gestures right from birth. This intuitive mirroring is not random, even though babies do not always respond instantly. This delay in reaction may cause one to think that there is no direct correlation.

> At first glance this ability to imitate might seem curious and cute but not deeply significant. But if you think about it for a minute, it is

actually amazing that there are no mirrors in the womb, newborns have never seen their own face, so how do they know whether their tongue is inside or outside their mouth.

(Gopnik et al. 1999: 30)

The work of Gopnik et al. considers the whole child in context and provides fascinating insight into the development of the young brain as it examines how babies make assumptions and predications in their play and explorations, how they recognise that they are different from adults and how they discriminate between what is familiar and what is not. Gopnik et al. suggest that babies are born sociable and intuitively know a great deal. They found that movement and action are important as they enable babies and young children to explore and learn new things about their world. The development of language reveals intelligence in their actions. Gopnik et al. found that babies and young children understand words which are related to their actions. For example, babies would show an understanding of 'up' and 'down' by going up and down a low step repeatedly. Interaction through gesturing, talk and communication gives babies the means not only to be sociable but also to influence others through their actions, sounds and gestures. Gopnik et al. describe the importance of self awareness and point to significant changes in their understanding of their psychological and physical awareness of themselves by the time babies are one year old. They point out that by the time babies are eighteen months old, they understand quite complicated things about how objects affect each other: 'Children and scientists are the best learners in the world, and they both seem to operate in very similar even identical ways, ways that are unlike even our best computer. They never start from scratch, instead they modify and change what they already know to gain new knowledge' (Gopnik et al. 1999: 156–7).

Imitating the actions and sounds of others is of crucial importance in babies' and young children's search for knowledge and understanding of the world. Gopnik et al. discuss babies' love of stripes and edges. Repeated first-hand experiences allow babies to plan and predict and draw their own conclusions based on what they already know and can do. Much emphasis is placed on the importance of repeating play and interaction with other children: 'We can see how our knowledge emerges from the ideas we start out with, our ability to learn, and our interactions with other people' (Gopnik et al. 1999).

What Gopnik et al.'s work does is to highlight that interaction with other people during the first years of development and that learning is crucial to the development of the young brain. This resonates well with the theory

of Vygotsky (1896–1934) who similarly recognised that knowledge was passed on from one person to another. Vygotsky saw the child as an active learner and placed much emphasis on communication and instruction, the role of others and the importance of society and culture. He believed that language was not only a cognitive tool of communication and put forward the notion that children's learning is shaped by their social influences. He emphasised the importance of the context or situations in which learning takes place and believed that through interaction with more capable members of a society that children can do things that they would not do on their own (sharing books, singing songs and rhymes, and painting and drawing). According to Vygotsky, development and learning occur through the internalisation of social processes and interacting with others. The learning process was not a solitary exploration by a child of the environment. Children are only as cognitively developed as the cultures in which they live allow. The culture and environment in which the child grows overrides the mental cognitive schemas outlined by Piaget.

Learning according to Vygotsky depends on development but development is not dependent on learning. Development can be furthered by effective instruction. Vygotsky identified the 'zone of proximal development' as the difference between children's capacity to solve problems on their own and the capacity to solve problems with assistance. In this, Vygotsky included all functions and activities that children can perform only with the assistance of someone else. The person who intervenes could be a parent, practitioner, sibling or peer who has already mastered that particular function. He believed that the role of adults was to be attuned to what children already know, in order to support and extend development and learning. Wood and Bennett (1997) point out that practitioners need to understand how play develops in early childhood and how development can be enhanced as a result of their previous experiences. Solomon (1994) and Newton and Newton (2000) suggest that the quality of education a child receives is affected by how knowledgeable teaching staff are about children's early knowledge and ability to understand. In a similar way to Vygotsky's theory, they suggest that children benefit from shared interactions with adults whom they are familiar with and who can relate to what they already know and can do. Vygotsky was concerned with what children could do. He believed that educators need to know just how much the child already knows in order to take the development and learning forward, enabling children to benefit from play. Vygotsky put forward the notion that the child's learning is shaped by their interaction and their cultural and social influences.

Margaret McMillan had a deep appreciation of the early experiences that young children got from the home and parents. Like Vygotsky, she realised that the child's social and cultural environment had a profound impact on learning. She believed in supporting parents by encouraging them to become involved in their children's development and learning (McMillan 1930: 131–3).

Evidence-based research carried out in Oxford has definitively shown that the quality of early learning environments may have a positive or detrimental impact on children's brain development and how they develop a knowledge and understanding of the world. The Effective Provision of Pre-School Educational (EPPE) Longitudinal study found that children benefit significantly from good quality pre-school experiences giving them an advantage by the end of Key Stage 1. The study found that babies and young children need:

- emotional support, stimulation and challenge;
- opportunities to play with other children;
- a learning environment that stimulates development and learning;
- practitioners who are well versed in children's play and exploration and who place importance on the process and not the end product.

The study suggests that good-quality early pre-school experiences have a positive effect on how children develop a knowledge and understanding of the world. This is further advanced where parents are involved and engaged with their child's learning. The study concluded that a number of factors were necessary to support high-quality play and learning experiences:

- adult involvement, engagement and reflection;
- environment in which children can take risks, be creative and imaginative and develop their ideas;
- opportunities for children to explore and investigate both indoors and outdoors;
- practitioners using observation and assessment to structure the learning environment and to inform them on planning and resourcing.

The findings of the EPPE project provide further confirmation as to what we know about young children's early learning. Much emphasis is placed on the quality of the environment and the role of the practitioner in supporting and extending development and learning. This is in line with the theory of

Vygotsky and Wood and Bennett (1997). In addition, the Reggio Emilia approach, which is world renowned, in many of its approaches to education, particularly in relation to listening to children and in its promotion of continuous staff reflection, has been integrated into the sixteen commitments that underpin the EYFS. Loris Malaguzzi was the first head of the Reggio Emilia pre-schools in 1965. Influenced by the work of both Piaget and Vygotsky, he pioneered a new approach to working with children. He believed that children learn through 100 different languages, not just the spoken word. Children learn through art, drama, theatre, animation and auditory sources. As a result, a space for expression was created in Reggio pre-schools called the 'atelier room' where professional artists were available to teach the children specialised forms of expression using various means such as music, dance and art.

Malaguzzi believed that knowledge was not predetermined. Each person approaches knowledge in different ways, that is, we all learn in different ways. We need to work with others because we need others to help us develop our knowledge. We therefore need to reflect on ourselves in order to review (what we've learned, how we've learned, how did we arrive at that conclusion). Malaguzzi believed that there was a strong interrelationship between learning, teaching and the environment: 'What children learn does not follow as an automatic result from what is taught. Rather it is in large part to the children's own doing, as a consequence of their activities and our resources' (Nutbrown 1996: 61).

A competent learner

Moyles (2005) suggests that play and exploration help young children to be competent learners, who make connections between the different parts of their lives, who can imagine, create and transform ideas and knowledge, represent their ideas imaginatively and expressively. Competent learning is about how children use all of their available senses to find out about things around them. All the sub-headings in this section interlink as they involve different types of play, exploration and investigation. Where children are apt to learn from first-hand experience, through exploring and testing out their ideas, they make discoveries, experiment with different materials and adapt or transform knowledge, attitude and skills. In essence, children's competences are developed through their play and exploration. As they begin to organise and link their previous experiences, working out what will happen

next, they develop a knowledge and understanding of the world by inter-acting with it. It is only through becoming fascinated by objects and activities that hold their interest that babies and young children begin:

- making connections;
- being imaginative;
- being creative;
- representing.

Making connections

Babies are naturally curious about people and their immediate environ-ments and will want to make connections between the different parts of their lives and themselves. Their sensory exploration is important to their all-round development and learning as it helps them to make vital connections in their brain. Research indicates that babies and young children learn through repeated play patterns. Bruce and Meggitt (2005) suggest that repeated play patterns help children to organise their thoughts and experi-ences thus making meaningful connections with previous knowledge, experi-ence and understanding. Shore (1997) suggests that the mental images and patterns of understanding are laid down in the brain so connections begin to form between them if the experience is a repeated one. The EYFS acknowl-edges the significance and importance of schemas in children's play and explorations and suggests that practitioners 'provide materials that support particular schemas, for example, things to throw, for a child who is exploring trajectory' (DfES 2007a: 77).

As children begin to connect objects and ideas between the different parts of their lives, they start to develop an interest in the world in which they live. Becoming mobile aids their exploration and investigations – find-ing out about things through trial and error is a key element of discovery, for example, the thrill and adventure for children of going for a walk, experi-encing their local environment for perhaps the first time, stumbling on a slope, being able to use their own ideas and imagination to make sense of this puzzling situation. Older children will make connections with symbols, numbers, counting, space and the world around them in a variety of different ways. Holt (1989) suggests that 'Learning means making sense of the world around us and being able to do things in it' (1989: xvi).

Being imaginative

Interaction and experience is fundamental for brain development; cells not only respond to the environment, they begin to record it, forming memory. Babies love to imitate. This is an imaginative way in which they direct their play and interactions with others. As they imitate, babies are demonstrating their knowledge of the physical self and making connections between all that they see. They begin to put reality into the middle of their first-hand experiences. Their imagination starts to form concepts that fit in with their understanding. They form memories about what has happened to them and will imaginatively recreate what they see and hear around them through their actions and intonations. Singer and Singer (1990) suggest that the imagination is 'a miracle of human experience opening up the concept of "what might be" or what is possible' (1990: 19).

Babies and young children need fragments of memory to create ideas; they need to draw from experiences to imagine. It is important that practitioners understand that they cannot just draw these from thin air. Parents can offer practitioners useful insights into the imitative games that their babies enjoy. The emergence of self primarily enables babies to perform meaningful actions for themselves as they become gradually intrigued or interested in everyday objects, materials and people. Emotions give babies something to manipulate as well as a channel to express their thoughts and feelings.

Steiner (1996) believed that education was an art and could only be built on the acquisition of real knowledge. He was concerned with the whole child: mind, body, spirit and soul. He believed in the seriousness of children's play. According to Steiner, play and exploration of the natural surroundings help children to create and recreate powerful images which are not present to the senses. For Steiner, imaginative play was fundamental to all development and learning. He believed that the development of memory through interaction and experience in a natural home environment aids concentrated periods of imaginative play where children try to make sense through their play of things and events that they have experienced: 'As the muscles and hands grow firm and strong in performing work for which they are fitted, so the brain and other organs of the physical body are guided along the right lines of development if they receive the right impressions from the environment' (Steiner 1996: 19).

Meek (1985) similarly suggests that imaginative play helps children to develop a deep meaningful understanding of their world. She places much

emphasis on the development of memory from direct hands-on experience and interaction as forming the roots of imagination. She makes the point that creativity and imagination are the 'basis' in learning to read and write. Children need to be free to select recourses and roles that they encounter: 'The most strenuous period of imaginative activity is the time in childhood when we play with boundaries of our views of the world: sense and nonsense. The real and the fictive the actual and the possible, all within the cultural domains we inhabit' (Meek 1985: 53).

Early experience not only develops children's imagination and creative thinking, it also enables them to develop, consolidate and apply skills, theories and ideas to new and different situations. The transforming schema involves changing things by mixing different substances, for example by adding water or other liquids and melting or freezing them. This schema requires children to use their imagination to make one thing stand for another, such as a leaf as money or a stick as a gun.

Babies who, for example, may be exploring how to put their thumbs or fingers into their mouths and repeatedly going through these motions may often be observed to persevere when faced with difficulties in mastering this goal. As babies begin to consciously coordinate their hand and eye movements, they develop an awareness of their fingers when holding objects. They start to develop an interest in sounds, light and movement. They will begin to show an awareness of different sounds and light sources and will follow movement around them.

At this stage, they may also enjoy interacting with others and objects and will have probably gained some knowledge of cause-and-effect toys. For example, they now know that if they shake a rattle it will make a noise. Babies will start to explore the space around them using imagination in their movements and may move about in a variety of ways from lying on their backs to rolling over on to their stomachs, by turning around in circles or moving backward and forward.

The experience of movement helps babies to develop an understanding of physical sensation and its effects. As babies gain more control of their limbs, their exploration becomes more active and purposeful, and they may develop a strong preference for one object over another, such as a favourite toy. They now begin to explore using for example, their fingers. At six months, babies may be observed concentrating by using both hands to explore a block before putting it into their mouths. This simple exploration enables babies to integrate physical movements through gaining control of their bodies and making mental connections through exploring objects and

finding out what they can about them. Gopnik et al. suggest that more attention should be paid to these explorations: 'When babies are around a year old, they begin to point to things that other people point to. Like imitation, pointing is something that is so familiar we take it for granted. But also like imitation, pointing implies a deep understanding of yourself and of other people' (1999: 32).

Being creative

Babies and young children will have their own unique way of creating and transforming their ideas, knowledge and understanding of the world. In order to create ideas, children must have previous first-hand experiences, which they can make connections with, then reproduce and imagine. For example, toddler Sam had spent some time in the garden watching intently the movements and characteristics of a slug. A few weeks later, at bath time, Sam was seen to be hiding underneath his towel. When he was asked what he was doing, he replied that he was being a slug.

The EPPE research confirmed that the process of exploration and investigation has deep roots in development and learning. It found that when practitioners work together with children, through their creative self-directed activities children begin to engage in progressive periods of creative and sustained shared thinking. The research highlights the importance for practitioners of creating a warm and affectionate environment which is conducive for children to engage with their learning positively and for them to develop self-respect. Much emphasis is placed on the practitioner's ability to ask open questions indicating that this will either help or hinder children's ability to think creatively. Siraj-Blatchford (2000) suggests that practitioners need to know the aim or purpose of extending children's play, knowledge of what problems they are trying to solve and what ideas or concepts they may need to have clarified for them. Practitioners need to consider what questions they will ask children and how they will support and encourage creativity based on what the child is ready to learn. Duffy (2005) similarly makes the point that practitioners need to understand the values of creativity in play. She believes that play for a child is a form of learning and that play gives children a voice. She emphasises the importance of the creative process as being central to broadening young children's knowledge and understanding of the world.

> Being creative is important to all of us. It supports us in exploring the full range of human potential and improves our capacity for thought and action. It enables us to respond to a rapidly changing world by reappraising our values and ways of working. The creative process helps us to deal with the unexpected by extending our current knowledge to new situations and using information in new ways. It encourages us to take risks, think flexibly, be innovative, play with ideas and respond imaginatively.
>
> (Duffy 2005: 152)

Babies often display their creativity in their enjoyment of finger play or on hearing familiar rhymes and songs. They will quickly make sense of the play or song and respond through their senses and movements. Manning-Morton and Thorp (2003) suggest that for babies 'Creativity develops as a direct result of babies' and toddlers' growing agility and dexterity. Once new tools or materials have been thoroughly investigated to see what they can do, they are played with imaginatively and incorporated into a game' (Manning-Morton and Thorp 2003: 41).

As children develop, they begin to express their creativity through the sounds and actions they make. Children will explore materials creatively as they wrap themselves up in layers of material and clothing, are intrigued by opening and closing lids or exploring in and out, play games such as peek-a boo, turn objects round and drop things. This play and exploration are fundamental to how children develop a meaningful knowledge and understanding of the world. Bruce (1987) suggests that while many children's interests reflect developing schemas such as 'enveloping' and 'transporting', others seem to reflect the children's experiences and encounters with the world.

Babies and young children use their first-hand experiences and interactions as a database for deepening their knowledge and understanding of the world. Bruce (2001) points out that

> Children at play are able to stay flexible, respond to events and changing situations, be sensitive to people, to adapt, to think on their feet, and keep altering what they do in fast-moving scenes. When the process of play is rich it can lead to children creating rich products in their stories, paintings, dance, music, constructions, or in the solving of scientific or mathematical problems.
>
> (Bruce 2001: 46)

For babies and young children, it is the process of creating which is important, not necessarily the end product. Children need to be able to make choices, decisions and to use their skills and techniques with a range of different materials. For example, during a 'sticking' activity some children may know what to do and will create symbols for which they will give names: 'This is my mummy.' Others at the same activity may watch what other children are creating and ask practitioners for help. Children under two may not yet be ready to glue and stick pieces of fabric on to their paper but may just want to dip fingers or glue stick into the glue watching it dribble on to their paper without any desire to spread it. Children are all individuals and will learn in ways that are appropriate and meaningful to them. Their ideas, feelings, relationships, physical and creative development need to be nurtured by practitioners. Edgington (2003) urges practitioners to recognise that without hands-on experience the process is meaningless, as without experience 'the constraints on time seriously affect children's opportunities to engage in-depth in the process of exploring ideas, materials and feelings for themselves without any requirement to produce an end product or piece of work' (Edgington 2003: 38).

Children need to be given choices and allowed to make decisions. They also must be given space and time in which to create and recreate their experiences. Children begin to imitate roles which they have observed, learnt and experienced. They begin to create situations for themselves in which they rehearse over again and again through their physical actions. As children develop more skills and techniques they begin to experiment with different media such as dance and two- and three-dimensional art. They become more skilful as communicators and use language as they talk and listen to each other.

Representing thought and ideas

Symbolic play starts to emerge where children make one thing stand in for another. When children have the ability to symbolically represent their ideas, they are able to apply their thinking to a wide range of events, feelings, roles and relationships. Vygotsky (1978) identified symbols as being products of human beings, developed in various ways by different and diverse cultures over historical times. He recognised that babies use signs and gestures to communicate and interact with others before they use their voices. By the age of two, they begin to use language symbols. Vygotsky believed

that once children begin to use one thing to stand for another they begin to understand the symbolic function of language. He believed that language helps children to form ideas and to think. According to Vygotsky (1978) thought and speech have different roots in humankind, thought being non-verbal and language being non-intellectual in early stages of development. But their development lines are not parallel; they cross over again and again. At a certain moment around the age of two, the curves of development of thought and speech, until then separate, meet and join to initiate a new form of behaviour. This is when thought becomes verbal and speech becomes rational. For example, a child at first will use language for superficial social interactions but at some point the language goes underground to become the structure of the child's thinking.

> For children some objects can readily denote others, replacing them and becoming signs, and the degree of similarity between playthings and the object denoted is unimportant. What is important is the utilization of the plaything and the possibility of executing a representational gesture with it. This is key to the entire symbolic function of children's play. For this point of view, therefore, children's symbolic play can be understood as a complex system of 'speech' through gestures that communicates and indicates the meaning of playthings.
>
> (Vygotsky 1978b: 108)

Vygotsky believed that when children reach the age of about four years of age, the language itself helps the child to form ideas and children are able to describe both what they are doing and what they are going to do. This he called 'inner speech'.

The purpose of inner speech according to Vygotsky is to control, to plan, to recall and to predict. This Vygotsky believed enabled children to become aware or conscious of what they were thinking. According to Vygotsky, as children mature, their inner speech becomes shorter and shorter. He argued that children need to be aware of their own thought processes in order to learn and suggested that children need both social speech, talking to others and inner speech for intellectual development. 'The structure of speech does not simply mirror the structure of thought; that is why words cannot be put on by thought like a ready garment. Thought undergoes many changes as it turns into speech' (Vygotsky 1986: 219).

Children will begin to demonstrate their knowledge and understanding by following simple instructions such as 'Where is the doggy?' Young

children's symbolic representations will be varied, sophisticated and diverse depending on their experience and quality of interaction with the world around them. This is an important and significant step in their development, as children begin to use objects symbolically to represent what they know. Children will use their experiences and existing knowledge to further develop their understanding of the world. Similarly, Matthews (2003) picks up on Vygotsky's theory suggesting that play has a direct impact on learning.

> The concept of play is implicated in the child's understanding and use of symbols, signs and representation. Children need opportunities to temporarily encouple means from ends in tasks, allowing them the opportunity to investigate processes as entities of interest in themselves and worthy of repetition. In Vygotskian terms, play allows the child to separate words from objects, and actions from meaning.
>
> (Matthews 2003: 27)

As an example of this concept, a child comes across a hose displayed in a DIY store and interacts with it, turning it as if it were a steering wheel. The child is not using the hose for its usual function but is able to detect a similar characteristic that enables them to investigate, experiment and solve problems. The research of Athey (1990) and Nutbrown (1999) indicates that children are capable of developing purposeful play and learning experiences. Toddlers may be observed using equipment for a purpose, for example talking on the telephone and dialling numbers. They may push an empty buggy or operate a push-along car or bike. Children will use symbolic representation to help them make connections with what they already know about, and this puts them in charge of their own learning. Isaacs (1981) suggests that symbolic and imaginative play is vital, as not only does it help children to solve intellectual difficulties, it also helps them to achieve inner balance and harmony through expressing themselves actively. This contrasts with Montessori (1912) who only saw the value symbolically although she did place some importance on domestic play where children carried out adult roles making beds, putting clothes in drawers, etc. This type of play gave adults an opening to interact with children under Montessori methods. Montessori placed very little value on the benefits of imaginative play, believing that it gave children a false picture of reality.

Symbolic play helps children to express their developing ideas and concepts actively through their explorations as well as helping them to make sense of their experiences. Symbolic play helps children to develop

an understanding of real and imaginary worlds. Smilansky (1968) describes the benefits of symbolic play for children:

- The child learns to gather scattered experiences and to create out of them a new combination.
- The child learns to draw on his experiences and knowledge selectively, according to some fixed frame of reference.
- The playing of role demands intellectual discipline. He can include only the behaviour that characterises the role he is enacting. He must judge and select.

(Smilansky 1968: 12)

Symbolic play is important as it helps children to know what they want and learn about making choices.

Children will also begin to express their thoughts, feelings and ideas through the use of artistic creation, for example making representations of ideas through painting. This experience and exposure to paints and other diverse materials such as chalk, crayons, sponges, etc., will help develop children's general understanding and of the different mark-making and writing tools.

Teaching and learning

The EYFS places much emphasis on developing practitioners into 'teachers and learners'. Practitioners' own understanding of development matters will affect how aspects of 'knowledge and understanding of the world' are interpreted, assessed and planned for within the EYFS. The importance of learning and reflection is highlighted throughout the document. The EYFS statutory framework and practice guidance are accessible to all practitioners whatever their level of qualification and experience. The practice guidance starts with what practitioners already know and provides them with appropriate challenges to become more effective. The practice guidance also offers practitioners:

- clear guidance based on theory;
- a range of practical activities;
- opportunities for practitioners to reflect on how they provide age-appropriate developmental and learning experiences;
- assess and plan for 'learning and development'.

The theory of child development is central to knowledge and understanding of the child's world. Recent theories on brain development in early years show that babies are not passive but are constantly seeking meaning from their experiences, which influence how they come to develop an understanding of the world. Theories are useful as they encourage practitioners to reflect on their own knowledge, understanding, experiences, values and attitudes towards play and exploration and how these affect the quality of development and learning experiences. The practitioner's own knowledge and experience of childcare and education theory will influence how they navigate their way through the EYFS practice guidance. The theories of both Jean Piaget and Lev Vygotsky have well-established roots in early childhood education. They provide practitioners with a theoretical framework for deepening their understanding of knowledge and understanding of the world. The EYFS sets out its clear intention to improve the quality of children's self-directed play and exploration. The principles are put into practice as they cut across all of the EYFS guiding themes. Children's self-image is recognised as important for them to develop a sense of identity, confidence and independence.

Wood and Bennett (1997) suggest that practitioners often underestimate the extent of children's early knowledge and understanding. They found that young children's knowledge and understanding would increase with age as they gradually modified their concepts and theories replacing them with scientific and abstract knowledge. The diversity and complexity of development and learning cannot be underestimated. Our society is made up of many different cultural groups who may have differing perceptions and beliefs based on what they know and understand about play, development and learning. It is important that practitioners involve parents in the process of their child's learning. Easen et al. (1992) suggest that the roles of practitioner and parent should in practice complement each other when they say: 'Through talking together both partners engage in a process of sharing and exploring different perspectives on their observation rather than transplanting the parent's perspective with a "better" professional one' (Easen et al. 1992: 288).

Alongside 'Every Child Matters' comes another document 'Every Parent Matters' which states that 'parents and the home environment they create are the single most important factor in shaping their children's well-being, achievements and prospects. Parents and carers are a crucial influence on what their children experience and achieve' (DfES 2007c).

Emerging evidence in early years has indicated that early learning in partnership with home learning has a significant impact on the child's social, emotional and cognitive development. However, research indicates

that although high-quality early learning adds value, the quality of the workforce is of fundamental importance. The DfES practice guidance (2007c) provides the following headings:

- development matters;
- look, listen and note;
- effective practice;
- planning and resourcing.

The broad development phases are introduced to help practitioners to see babies and young children as individuals at different points of development. The broad stages of development overlap because children develop at different speeds in different areas and some need more support, or more challenge, than others. Development matters supports practitioners in tracking children's development and progress across six areas of learning and development.

1   personal, social and emotion development;
2   communication, language and literacy;
3   problem-solving, reasoning and numeracy;
4   knowledge and understanding of the world;
5   creative development;
6   physical development.

'Look, listen and note' requires practitioners to make ongoing observations of children. This will help practitioners

- to find out about children's interests and needs;
- to assess the progress which children are making;
- to plan the next steps in development and learning;
- to identify any concerns about the child's development and to develop practitioners' own understanding of development and learning.

Effective practice is dependent on practitioners who are able to provide babies and young children with play experiences, which will help them construct knowledge and understanding of the world around them based on what they already know and can do.

Planning and resourcing is central to making children's development and learning experiences meaningful, exciting, varied and progressive. Practitioners

need to be able to have an understanding about how individual children learn and develop. Planning should respond to self-initiated play explorations by groups or individuals by providing babies and young children with materials and resources which are open-ended, for example a box, a chiffon scarf or a piece of fabric, to support or extend their exploration. Practitioners need to also consider planning for and providing some activities again and again and again:

> Children must be supported in developing the knowledge and skills and understanding that help them make sense of the world. Their learning must be supported through offering opportunities for them to use a range of tools safely; encounter creatures, people, plants and objects in their natural environments and in real life situations; undertake practical 'experiments' and work with a range of materials.
>
> (DfES 2007a: 14)

For children to develop a knowledge and understanding of the world they need adults who are knowledgeable and able to respond to their interests. Children have a natural curiosity and openness. They need practitioners to respond to them with excitement and enthusiasm by following their lead in their self-initiated play and explorations. Children need resources, demonstrations and explanations in order to further develop their understanding, for example, what causes the magnet to pull objects made from metal. An important part of the Ten-Year Childcare Strategy is the commitment made to reform the early years workforce. A group of experts from the Department for Children, Schools and Families (DCSF), health, justice and sports departments have been brought together to develop a single flexible, affordable and integrated workforce for children. The intention is to build a world-class early years service by improving early years care and education through raising the bar of the qualifications of the workforce. The vision is that a graduate will lead in every early years setting by 2015. Carlina Rinaldi reminds us of the importance of continuous learning and development, taking the view that practitioners are teachers and learners:

> Good staff development is not something that is undertaken every now and then, reflecting only on the words of someone else. Instead, it is a vital and daily aspect of our work, of our personal and professional identities. Staff development is seen above all as an indispensable vehicle by which to make stronger the quality of our interaction with children and among ourselves.
>
> (Rinaldi 2005)

Exploration and investigation

Exploration and investigation is about how children investigate objects and materials and their properties, learn about change and patterns, similarities and differences, and question how and why things work.

(DfES 2007a)

Learning by doing using real tools

Exploration and investigation begin as soon as a baby is born and have to do with how babies and young children explore objects and materials. Initially their exploratory drive is driven by their sensory motor system and their first-hand experiences of interaction with objects, materials and others. Exploration and investigation emerge into self-directed play as babies and young children progress through the different developmental phases. Different types of play begin to emerge. Babies will find a variety of ways to try out new things, which will help them to develop an understanding of their own limits – what they can manage alone and what they need help with.

Gopnik et al. (1999: 56) point out the connections that babies begin to make through their play and explorations: 'They make predictions, they do experiments, they try to explain what they see and they formulate new theories based on what they already know.'

Children will show their curiosity by exploring different areas in their immediate environment. They will share talk and conversations with practitioners about things that they do with their families and places which they have visited.

Design and making

Designing and Making is about the way in which children learn about the construction process and the tools and techniques that can be used to assemble materials creatively and safely.

(DfES 2007a)

Showing someone younger how to use tools and develop new techniques

The construction process is important for children, as the experience of constructing with different materials will develop their knowledge and understanding of weight, stability, balance, patterns and systems. Practitioners' own knowledge and the quality of interaction during children's exploration are key to how children understand the construction process. Children need to learn to understand and experience this construction process, using tools, materials and a range of skills and techniques. They need practitioners who will not only support and guide them to use tools and equipment appropriately but also encourage their explorations and thinking. The Froebel Blockplay Research Project (Gura 1992) found that construction using blocks has its own unique stages, which will often be seen when children are involved in 'block play':

Stage 1   Children may be observed carrying blocks around or mouthing them. They are exploring the weight and properties of the block.

Stage 2   Children may explore blocks by stacking two or three vertically or placing them in a horizontal row on the floor.

Stage 3   Children may use three blocks (this is called bridging), when two blocks are connected by a third.

Stage 4   Children may create enclosed spaces, which may be square or circular enclosures.

Stage 5   Children will recreate buildings using blocks. The children may explore symmetry, schematic patterns and balance.

Stage 6   Children may name buildings as part of the play but will be dependent on the practitioner to explain the purpose of the building – for example, children constructing their own block of flats and the car park below.

Stage 7   Children's constructions are often recreations that symbolise actual buildings that they will bring into their play.

Lindon (2001) suggests that schemas are not only developmental but also are a child's way, often their favourite way, of exploring the world at a given time. Schematic patterns can often be observed in block play (see EYFS CD-ROM Learning and development 4.2 block play video).

The DfES has produced the EYFS, which is made up of a statutory framework, practice guidance, principles-into-practice cards, a wall poster and a CD-ROM.

Children will observe different materials and techniques being used at home or in their immediate environment. They may have parents or family members who are in the construction industry and may have already explored and investigated a range of materials. The EYFS encourages practitioners to use a parent's knowledge of their child to extend children's unique experiences of the world. This information will need able practitioners to plan more opportunities for children to practise what they know, understand and can do. For example, children who have recently had builders at their home putting in a new kitchen might develop a fascination towards hammering things using nails and other connecting materials. It is the experience of doing that allows children to imagine and recreate, thus expressing their ideas through play and construction. Children need to be able to explore natural materials in their environment. Practitioners should encourage children to explore and select materials and equipment that allow them to practise skills such as cutting, sawing, joining, folding and building for a variety of purposes and to use materials and adhesives such as nails, tape, staples, threads and screws, using real screw drivers, hammers and saws.

Practitioners must develop a positive attitude towards children using tools and equipment. This may mean dealing with your own attitudes and perceptions of children using real tools. Children are unique and individual and will have varying knowledge about materials depending on attitudes and interaction with tools. It is only from hands-on experience of trial and error that children discover the forces and properties of materials using tools. This exploration also supports children in developing self-assurance in their own abilities and their confidence to try out and practise their new emerging skills. Duffy (2002: 16) reinforces the point when she says 'The experiences we offer children in their earliest years are crucial in their future development. The richer the experiences are, the more opportunity children will have to develop the disposition and understanding that they need now and in the future.'

Children's creativity will be seen in the structures which they construct and base their imaginative play around. Duffy (2002) links creativity and play suggesting that they both involve

- an attitude and a process;
- a state of mind and disposition;
- the ability to cope with uncertainty;
- the ability to explore new ideas;

- divergent thinking, which is the ability to look at a problem in a variety of ways;
- a lack of constraint;
- the existence of choice;
- creating and recreating.

When practitioners model how to use tools and equipment safely, children will, with time, experience and encouragement learn how to use tools and equipment correctly for themselves. It is important that practitioners recognise that for younger children in particular there is much repetition. For example, young children may not want to cut paper with the scissors but may just want to put their fingers through the holes and practise opening and closing the levers. Alternatively, children may not know how to use scissors, as these have always been kept away from them at home. The children will require demonstration and explanation from the practitioner about how to operate a pair of scissors. The learning environment is key. Children need access to natural resources that excite and sustain their interest both indoors and outdoors. The learning environment must support and encourage children's critical thinking, curiosity, interests and choices. Observation of children's exploration will give practitioners information that will support them in providing opportunities for developing meaningful experiences in which children can practise what they know, in a stimulating way, until they know it.

Information and communication technology (ICT)

ICT is about how children find out about and learn to use appropriate information technology [IT] such as computers and programmable toys that support their learning.

(DfES 2007a)

We are living in a highly technological world in which children are interacting with remote control and communication systems. Isaacs (1930) suggests that children's worlds are full of exciting and interesting technical explorations, which practitioners sometimes take for granted. This resonates well with research studies carried out by Solomon (1994) and Newton and Newton (2000), which also suggest that practitioners often misjudge babies' and young children's early knowledge and understanding of the world.

Children enjoying ICT

This, I believe, is in part due to the fact that babies and young children will be experiencing varying degrees of exposure to things being operated by batteries, for example remote controls being used to make things open, such as car doors, or work, such as televisions. Pushing a button at the traffic lights could generate discussions about how to use the stop button, why people use the stop button, the purpose of the stop button at the lights and maybe the consequence of pressing the button when you don't want to cross the road. Accompanying an adult to the cash point machine each week will give children exposure to different types of cause and effect. Information from parents about their child's knowledge of ICT and the range of toys and programmable equipment (camera, tape recorder, iPod or computer, etc.) which children can operate independently at home can be used to contribute to practitioners' long- and short-term strategies to effectively support and extend development and learning based on what children already know. Children's Knowledge of Communication Systems and IT awareness will increase as children interact and explore the wider world around them.

ICT is about more than just computers, machines and programmable toys. It is also about language and knowledge of signs and written symbols. Children on a computer may recognise signs and symbols and use pictures and symbols to communicate meaning by following patterns or sequencing.

ICT has a direct impact on children's language, literacy and communication. Practitioners also have a key role to play in supporting and extending children's language.

Children will frequently return to a programmable toy or computer programme and follow the sequence of instructions to operate them, thus demonstrating to practitioners what they know. The challenge is for practitioners to support children in developing their skills using a range of tools. When practitioners present children with demonstrations, explanations and resources that support development and learning, children begin to learn the skills and techniques needed for today's technological world.

Learning how to operate new equipment and computer programmes can be challenging at times. However, when practitioners bury their heads in the sand they cannot promote children's development and learning in this area. Practitioners should model being learners if they are to support children making links with their learning.

Babies and young children will have daily exposure to household ICT such as television sets, remote controls, mobile phones, cameras, washing machines, dishwashers and programmable toys. Children work out solutions to problems such as finding out what the television remote actually does and why it may be important in the household. It is only through observation, interaction and trial and error that they begin to work out cause and effect.

Time

> Time – is about how children find out about the past and present events relevant to their own lives or those of their families.
>
> (DfES 2007a)

For babies and young children, time is abstract and non-representational. How then do they begin to interpret time when they cannot see it, touch it, taste it, feel it or smell it? Piaget (1927) depicts the child's sense of time as being indistinguishable to the child's actions, perceptions and feelings. He suggested that babies' and young children's awareness of time is dependent on their individual experiences and on what they are doing. Piaget's findings are further reinforced by studies carried out by Phillips (1969) who suggests that for babies time is about living in the here and now, living in the moment: 'Time is limited to that which encompasses a single event, such as moving a hand from leg to face, feeling the nipple and beginning to suck, or hearing a sound and seeing its source' (Phillips 1969: 20).

Parents and Children spending 'time' together

It is widely agreed amongst early years practitioners that time gives babies and young children information, such as that bedtime follows bath time. Manning-Morton and Thorp (2003: 96) suggest that for a two-year-old particular words or events can trigger a child to recall something that happened a month ago: 'Children appear to want to have the same conversation about this event each time they recall it.'

Knowledge and understanding of time will be built up a layer at a time. Time gives meaning to events which babies and young children experience. The first layer is developed from the experience: children lay down a mental map, forming a memory of their experience. The second layer emerges when children link the experience and the memory. This enables children to not only integrate knowledge and understanding but also develop thinking skills that later on help them to form conceptual ideas. Experience and encounters with people and objects give babies and young children a reference point from which they can begin to predict what is going to happen to them next. Toddlers may anticipate lunchtime by going and getting their bib. The action alone indicates that the toddler understands that it is lunchtime. Young children will show their understanding of time by pre-empting activities, such as closing the curtains at bedtime or going off to put on their shoes or their coat. They understand that it is time for Mummy to

collect them, yet they are unable yet to verbally communicate this event. Children are often concerned with the immediacy of their action, not really wanting to consider time, in the objective way we do as adults. People, places and objects are important as they reinforce in babies how they make connections with time and how they provide meaning to their actions. Young children will already have acquired knowledge about their own lives and those with whom they live. At this stage, they will be inclined to talk to practitioners about their families and interests. Routines, seasons, photographs of past and present events, artefacts from the past, birthdays, days of the week, weekends, weather, cultural and religious festivals, anniversaries, the cycle of life, birth and death will all provide children with information about time and events. For children to recall events they have to understand the basic concept of time, before and after an event. Many more layers start building on their initial grasp of the passage of time as they begin to develop thought, imagination and the ability to think in the abstract. Harner (1981: 503), in a study of conversations with pre-school children relating to time, found that children's perception of time was based on their individual experiences of waiting and being rushed: children 'have mastered some of the rudiments of the ordered system of past, present and future relations. They have a basic understanding of events as preceding or following the present moment in which they are speaking.'

Individual routines and schedules are important for children as they naturally support them in developing a degree of security and a knowledge and understanding of the sequence of time. From this they develop a degree of certainty about what may be going to happen next. Children will be constantly increasing their awareness of time as they explore the world around them. Many more layers in their development will begin to emerge as they start to reason, plan, think ahead and speculate about future events in their lives.

Place

Place is about how children become aware of and interested in the natural world, and find out about their local area, knowing what they like and dislike about it.

(DfES 2007a)

When babies begin to explore and investigate space through movement, they will first show that they have acquired a basic knowledge and understanding by rolling over or moving backwards and forwards. Through these

Reaching out into new places

actions they are developing a perception of their own personal space. Babies and young children are naturally curious. They will be taking in information about the characteristics, natural features and geographical layout of the places and spaces which they encounter. They will make connections with places using their sense of sight, sound and smell:

- identifying places in the world;
- identifying weather conditions in different places.

Children develop a growing understanding of where they live and what has happened to them since they were babies. For example, a trip to see Grandma on the train, or in a car or bus will be full of intrigue for young children. In addition, visits to places in their local environment such as a building site, the train station or bus terminal, market, florist, pet shop or fishmonger by varied means of transport such as car, bus, on foot or by buggy will allow children to develop an awareness and understanding of many things including different locations and how the weather can affect them. They will begin to notice familiar features, which can provide an indication to them of where

they are, for example how near they are to Grandma's house or their school. Children's knowledge of places can only be nourished by their first-hand experiences.

Communities

> Communities is about how children begin to know about their own and other people's cultures in order to understand and celebrate the similarities and differences between them in a diverse society.
>
> (DfES 2007a)

Culture in its broadest terms covers many aspects of our everyday lives. It is too simple to suggest that it is just about race, religion, class and sexuality. It is indeed about identity, diet, attitudes, diversity, language and all that we do, know and understand.

It therefore follows logically that children will use a variety of different ways to express their ideas, based on what they already know and have experience of. Children's play and exploration tends to be about their immediate experiences and interactions with others. In order to understand and celebrate the similarities and differences between different cultures, practitioners

A sense of community at play

need to build on what children already know about themselves, other people and events. Lindon (2003) urges practitioners to reflect on how they built up their own sense of cultural identity as a child. She poses the question, 'What does culture mean to the three year old and how can they connect with the ideas of their own recognised life?' (Lindon 2003: 38).

Lindon also suggests that babies and young children make sense of the culture of their family from meaningful personal experience and interactions. Similarly, Gopnik et al. (1999) suggest that children are developing an understanding of themselves and others through these interactions. This challenges practitioners to provide children with a meaningful context in which their experience and understanding can be both integrated and connected. 'Communities have distinctive ways of thinking and feeling as well as dressing and eating, and children must learn these ways of being from the grown-ups around them' (Gopnik et al. 1999: 24).

Football is a culture; some young children not only are frequent visitors to stadiums but they also gather information through watching the game at home on the television. Whole communities get involved. This is an event which they can experience, and they may have considerable knowledge and understanding of the rules of the game. In seeking to find out about the world, young children will experiment with what they have heard or seen others do and integrate the experience into knowledge and understanding of different people and events. Children's awareness and understanding of other cultures plays an important role in their development. Practitioners should talk to children about various cultural festivals, such as Chinese New Year. This will provide children with a basic understanding of a culture of which many will have had no previous reference point. This basic understanding can be increased by talking to children about the different types of noodles available on the menu at the local Chinese restaurant and having Chinese cooking utensils and chopsticks in their home corner. This will enable them to integrate their knowledge and understanding of similarities and differences in cultures in a meaningful way. Margaret McMillan (1864–1931) saw the home, culture and community as major contributors to the care and education of babies and young children. She was one of the first to appreciate the educational values of the home. She recognised that a gap existed between the middle- and working-class communities in the quality of early experiences and interactions. McMillan promoted working in partnership with parents; some of her ideas are comparable with the principles that underpin the EYFS. The EYFS acknowledges that a gap exists in provision and practice. It challenges practitioners to recognise, welcome, value

and respect the impact of cultural diversity on babies' and young children's development and learning. 'All practitioners will benefit from professional development in diversity, equality and anti-discriminatory practice whatever the ethnic, cultural or social make-up of the setting' (DfES 2007a).

The influence and the impact that the family have on the emergence, development and progression of knowledge and understanding should not be underestimated. Partnerships with parents in part underpin the successful delivery of the EYFS framework. Vygotsky (1978) points out that children develop complex cognitive abilities, which he called 'higher mental functions', as a product of their interactions with more accomplished members of their culture such as parents, educators, siblings and peers. Learning and development occurs through the internalisation of the social process. 'Every function in the child's cultural development appears twice: first between people (interpsychological) and then inside the child (intrapsychological). This applies equally to voluntary attention, to logical memory, and to the formation of ideas. All the higher functions originate as actual relationships between individuals' (Vygotsky 1978: 57).

For Vygotsky, language is a primary form of interaction, which adults transmit to children. As learning progresses, children's own language comes to serve as their primary tool of intellectual adaptation, interacting with the knowledge that exists within the culture. Siraj-Blatchford and Clarke (2000) reinforce Vygotsky's notion of 'higher mental functioning'. They suggest that bilingual children in the early years not only speak two languages but that they also have an understanding of both the cultural and social codes that go with them.

Children need to feel strong and confident in their first language if they are to confidently develop and express their ideas and thinking skills. Language is a fundamental part of a child's cultural identity. Practitioners need to understand that they, along with everyone else who contributes to the development and learning of a child, of, for example, English as a second language, can make a significant difference to the development and long-term life outcomes for that child. Practitioners need to be aware of and adapt to children's growing awareness and confidence in using English. It is important that practitioners plan for the diversity of children's language needs, both to support their understanding of self within the community and to support all aspects of learning about the world in which they live.

Exploration and investigation

From birth–11 months

> ### Development matters
>
> - Babies will use their movement and senses to focus on, reach for and handle objects.
> - Babies will learn from observing others and their effect.
>
> ### Key words
>
> sensory exploration

Learning story

Rahim, aged seven months, is described as being of a passive nature; he enjoys interaction with others. He has a fascination in cause-and-effect toys and is intrigued by opening and closing lids.

Rahim was observed sitting on a blanket with some of his favourite toys which were placed around him in the grassy area of the garden. The childminder sat down next to him and began to walk her fingers up his arm, and then she tickled his nose with a blade of grass. Rahim responded by laughing and bouncing his whole body and waving his arms as he anticipated being tickled. The childminder repeated this several times. Rahim saw a cat and crawled off the blanket on to the grass towards it.

Activities

Play and exploration

Practitioners need to provide a range of resources and materials for babies to touch and listen to so that they can explore different textures and sounds, for example:

- rough
- smooth
- hard
- soft
- loud.

Practitioners can point out sounds of aeroplanes, birds and traffic. Practitioners should also consider everyday and natural objects, for example:

- large wooden and metal spoons
- sieves, both metal and plastic
- whisks
- pots and pans
- plastic containers
- jam-jar lids
- fir cones
- feathers
- brushes
- fabric
- cushions
- purses or wallets.

This exploration will support babies in using all of their senses and it enables them to choose objects for exploration that interest them. Sing songs and rhymes to babies that name parts of the body.

Look, listen and note

- Look out for how babies explore objects by putting them into their mouths.

- Note down the objects which babies choose to explore and the ones which they reject.

- Watch out for what sounds they notice and which ones excite them.

Effective practice

Provide resources and materials that enable babies to make connections with their first ideas and early understanding of the world.

Teaching and learning

- Practitioners need to develop an understanding of how important babies' sensory explorations are when supporting them to develop a conceptual understanding of time, space, sounds, sights, scents and taste.

- Observation of babies' active exploration will enable practitioners to anticipate what babies might need next in their development and learning.

Planning and resourcing

- Babies are initially non-mobile; they need practitioners to provide resources and materials at different levels, for example on the floor and at eye level.

- Babies require space so that they can observe, reach out and roll and somewhere where they can sit up with support.

- Practitioners need to take babies out for walks in the fresh air so that they can experience crawling on the grass or touching flowers.

Home links

- Practitioners should mirror home routines in their practice as much as possible.

- Make connections with the everyday scents, for example: baby wipes at nappy-changing time, air freshener, herbs and spices – both raw and during cooking.

Additional resources

The EPPE research suggests that sharing books with babies is important as it helps to stretch their minds and thinking skills. Below is a list of books that offer babies sensory interaction. Books are available from The Letterbox Library, 71–73 Allen Road, London N16 8RY. Telephone 0207 503 4801 www.letterboxlibrary.com.

- Bowie, C. W. (2003) *Busy Fingers*, illustrated by F. Willingham, Watertown, Mass.: Charlesbridge.

- Bowie, C. W. (1998) *Busy Toes,* illustrated by F. Willingham, Watertown, Mass.: Charlesbridge.

- Birkett., G. (2006) *One, Two Peekaboo*, London: Campbell.

- Birkett., G. (2006) *Peekaboo, Hello You!* London: Campbell.

- Christian, C. (1996) *What Happens Next?* photos by L. Dwight, New York: Starbright.

- Christian, C. (2003) *Where's The Baby?* photos by L. Dwight, New York: Starbright.

More books for babies

📖   Campbell, R. (1997) *Dear Zoo,* London: Campbell Books.

📖   Cousins, L. (1999) *Maisy's Mix-and-Match Mouse Ware,* London: Walker Books.

📖   Hill, E. (1994) *Spot Goes to a Party,* Harmondsworth: Puffin Books.

📖   Hughes, S. (2001) *Noisy,* London: Walker Books.

Further reading

📖   Langston, A. and Abbott, L. (2007) *Playing to Learn, Developing High Quality Experiences for Babies and Toddlers,* Maidenhead: Open University Press.

From 8–20 months

Development matters

- Babies now pull to stand and become more mobile.

- The scope of their investigations widens.

Key words

memory, thought, experience, process, imagination and creativity

Learning story

Isobel is eighteen months old. She has been described by her childminder as demanding and constantly curious about objects that go up and down as well as on and off (except when she is tired).

Isobel was observed in the garden standing by the pond with her childminder. Isobel pointed at the water and said 'tadpole'. The childminder

repeated 'tadpole' and pointed to some tadpoles swimming in the pond. She told Isobel that first they were frogspawn and now they are ..., Isobel replied 'tadpoles'. The childminder continued by saying that the tadpoles were going to grow ... Isobel replied 'legs: one, two.' The childminder continued and then they will turn into ... 'frogs', Isobel replied. Later on that day, the childminder observed Isobel standing at the top of the slide, refusing to slide down, pointing and saying that a ladybird was on the slide.

Activities

Active learning

Some of the ways practitioners can stimulate active learning:

- Sing songs and rhymes and tell stories.

- Sit down with children and talk to them about what they are doing.

- Provide materials for dressing up dolls and teddies, putting on hats and coats and using combs or brushes.

- Provide open-ended resources such as boxes, pots and containers of different sizes.

- Allow children to try on adult shoes and trainers.

- Talk to children about opposites, for example, in and out, up and down, small big, under, over.

- Provide opportunities to talk to other children and adults.

- Make time for walks in the local environment to shops or park or posting letters, etc.

- Encourage young children to explore fallen leaves in the autumn or blossoms in the spring.

- Provide opportunities for children to experience and feel the wind.

- Encourage exploration of insects and other wildlife in the garden.

- Provide young children with stacking containers in circular and square shapes.

- Provide water-play experiences with sprinklers, hoses, taps, watering cans, and buckets.

- Encourage exploration of puddles both natural and artificial.

- Talk to children about the ripples on the water and the effects of rain and of 'getting wet'.

Look, listen and note

- Look out for the types of experiences that children are fascinated by and choose to engage themselves in.

- What can you learn about the children's memory and thought connections from your observation?

- Note down how toddlers use their make-believe play to help them make sense of their world.

Effective practice

Practitioners should use observation to inform practice, based on knowledge of the child. Practitioners must think about ways in which they can begin to develop meaningful play experiences for individual children based on their fascinations and explorations.

Teaching and learning

Vygotsky believed that children's language and actions are part of a process of logical thinking and reasoning. For Vygotsky children need to be aware of their own thought process in order to learn. He considered the context and situations in which learning took place to be vital. Vygotsky placed much emphasis on the interrelations between thought and

language. Vygotsky suggested that language is not merely an expression of the knowledge the child has acquired. There is a fundamental correlation between thought, speech and action in terms of one providing resource for the other. 'A child's speech is as important as the role of action in attaining goals. Children not only speak about what they are doing; their speech and action are part of the same complex psychological function, directed towards the solution of the problem at hand' (Vygotsky 1962: 25). For more information about the thinking of Vygotsky, see p. 17.

Planning and resourcing

Practitioners need to plan experiences that will support children to imagine and recreate the uniqueness of their experiences. This might include adding resources that support a particular schematic interest:

- Consider providing a range of everyday household objects for play and explorations.

- Use opportunities to explore the natural environment for example feeding the ducks at the park.

- Provide opportunities to study the process of the natural world such as a spider spinning a web or watching an ant collect food.

- Provide access to different surfaces such as grass, mud, paths and slopes.

- Provide a variety of accessible resources and tools, so that children can have choice when gardening.

Practitioners need to recognise the importance of being flexible with young children and provide children with routines that respect their interests, relationships and needs.

Home links

Practitioners should encourage parents to provide real everyday opportunities to help children make sense of their world, such as going to the library and sharing books. It is important for children to observe adults and others reading books. Parents should also be encouraged to sing songs and rhymes with babies and toddlers.

Additional resources

Gerhardt, S. (2006) *Why Love Matters: How Affection Shapes a Baby's Brain*, London: Routledge.

Goldschmied, E. and Jackson, S. (2005) *People under Three: Young Children in Day Care*, 2nd edn, London: Routledge.

Woolfson, R. (2006) *What Is My Baby Thinking? Understanding Babies and Toddlers from 0–3 Years*, London: Hamlyn.

Dorman, H. and Dorman, C. (2004) *The Social Toddler: Promoting Positive Behaviour*, Richmond: CP Publishing.

From 16–26 months

Development matters

● Children now sometimes focus their enquiries on particular features or processes.

Key words

observation, exploration, discovery and repetition

Learning story

Daniel, aged sixteen months, has recently started attending the children's centre. He is described as inquisitive, and he likes to explore movement by using transport toys. His play often involves him playing on the floor, the surface of cupboards and dropping toys behind them. Troy, aged eighteen months, is described as being a typical boy, interested in anything that moves. Daniel was observed watching Troy, who was playing with three magnetic trains. Troy squatted over the trains, placed one train in each hand and skilfully linked all three trains. He then proceeded to move the train backwards and forwards. The practitioner offered Daniel two trains. Daniel reached for the trains and moved one of the trains backwards and forwards crashing one into the other. Daniel was observed to be preoccupied as he sat comfortably on the floor, with one finger in his mouth as he moved his train, repeatedly crashing it into the other.

Activities

Active learning

Practitioners need to consider providing everyday resources that support toddlers' understanding of the function of everyday activities, for example by providing resources for water play such as bottles, straws, guttering, funnels, sieves, buckets and jugs.

- Encourage children to fetch water and let it flow down guttering into a bucket.

- Compare water coming out of sieves, straws and funnels.

- Talk to children about the different sounds water makes and the changes to the texture of their skin.

- Add sand to water and talk to children about the change.

- Let the children explore with floating and sinking different objects.

Practitioners must support children in finding out about the environment and other people by helping them to connect their ideas and develop an understanding of the world.

- Encourage children to socialise, interact and communicate with each other.

- Add dolls, brushes or combs to comb a doll's hair.

- Provide toys that toddlers can transport, such as cars, trucks, trains and push-along toys.

- Provide picture books that depict everyday activities.

- Provide empty boxes which they can climb in and out of, push-along toys that they can use to transport.

Practitioners must help children to become engaged and involved through their sense and movements.

- Play listening games with children, for example record different types of transport then ask the children to identify the different sounds made by cars, motorbikes, fire engine or lorry.

- Make connections with the opposite of things such as in and out, big and small, light and dark.

- Help children to identify colours, patterns and shapes.

- Tell stories with props to support development and learning.

Look, listen and note

Look out for children's repeated actions in their play, exploration and mark-making. A pattern may connect these activities showing the practitioner that the child is following a particular way of thinking and exploring. This is called a schema. Further information on schemas can be found on p. 6.

Effective practice

Practitioners need to be able to anticipate what experiences to provide for young children in order to sustain their developing interests.

Teaching and learning

It is important that young children have plenty of opportunities to represent their experiences. Practitioners might observe frequent repetitive patterns in some children's behaviour. Whilst these patterns may seem random, young children are beginning to demonstrate a particular focus and interest and very possibly their preferred way of engaging with the world. This will give practitioners additional insight into what resources and equipment to provide to support and extend development and learning.

Planning and resourcing

Practitioners need to provide a range of opportunities for toddlers to walk and explore their environment with the time to investigate the incidentals that they might discover along the way. For example, a toddler might come across a slope whilst pushing a buggy on a walk to the park. They will need time and understanding from practitioners if they are to help solve the problem at hand. Encourage exploration with cooking utensils, hats, scarves, fabric, empty boxes, handbags, to support imaginative and role-play.

Home links

Involve parents by sharing information about the EYFS and by inviting them to contribute to your long-term and short-term plan for their child's development and learning. Parents can support children by naming and recognising other parts of the body such as 'neck', 'shoulder', 'fingers', 'knees' and 'ankles'.

Additional resources

Louis, S., Beswick, C., Hayes, L., Magraw, L. S. and Featherstone, S. (2008) *Again, Again: An Introduction to Understanding Schemas*, Lutterworth: Featherstone Education.

Lambert, A. (2005) *All Change! Jobs, Astronaut*, Swindon: Child's Play.

Lambert, A. (2005) *All Change! Jobs, Nurse*, Swindon: Child's Play.

Lambert, A. (2005) *All Change! Jobs, Fire Fighter*, Swindon: Child's Play.

Lambert, A. (2005) *All Change! Jobs, Gardener*, Swindon: Child's Play.

Lambert, A. (2005) *All Change! Jobs, Mechanic*, Swindon: Child's Play.

From 22–36 months

Development matters

- Children now explore, play and seek meaning in their experience.
- Children now use others as a source of information and learning.
- Children now show an interest in why things happen.

Key words

the process of learning, children exploring their ideas and interests in depth, making meaning

Learning story

Kai, aged thirty-three months, attends a local pre-school. He is described as having a fascination for Spiderman. He enjoys getting dressed up as Spiderman

and, when involved in role play, will only respond if he is called 'Mr Spiderman'. Kai lives at home with his mother and father and is the youngest of four boys. He is described as a typical boy, happiest when he is outside, climbing, digging and playing superhero games. The practitioner observed Kai in the morning looking at a spider's web in the garden, which had early morning dew on it. The practitioner gave Kai a magnifying glass to aid his exploration and interest. Kai appeared to be intrigued by the patterns made by the tiny drops of water on the web. At times, Kai looked quite confused. He asked the practitioner if it had been raining, and she answered 'no'. Kai examined the spider web through the magnifying glass. Being very careful not to touch it he described to the practitioner what he could see. He pointed out that all of the web was covered with rain but some parts of the web had very large beads of dew and other parts had tiny droplets and that he thought that the spider was going to get wet when he went home later. Later that afternoon, the practitioner encouraged Kai to look at the web again. By this time, the tiny drops of water had disappeared. Kai asked the practitioner 'Where has the rain gone?'

Activities

Transforming understanding

Practitioners can extend children's exploration by encouraging them to make comparisons between insects, reptiles, animals and people. Young children need to engage with the natural world, for example by jumping in puddles, observing patterns of circles made by raindrops and feeling the wind on themselves.

An example of problem-solving through exploration of the natural world could be a focus on the wind. Being able to feel it and not see it and its function in the evaporation process and drying washing will raise lots of questions for young children.

Practitioners need to talk to children about the changes that take place. Theses important conversations will help children to connect their real and imaginary worlds. Practical tasks that will support this process might include:

- making a paper aeroplane

- flying kites

- looking at things that move through the air such as helicopters, jet planes, rockets, air balloons, parachutes and birds.

It is particularly important that practitioners provide activities for development and learning to take place in the garden, for example (to follow up on our example of the wind):

- hanging up different types of fabric and plastic

- moving different fabrics in the wind

- making streamers, bunting, flags and windmills.

Practitioners should also provide a range of climbing apparatus with the scope to jump from different levels and encourage activities such as:

- digging

- planting

- feeding the birds

- playing hide and seek

- running.

Look, listen and note

- Look out for how children respond to new discoveries.

- Listen to the types of questions they ask during play and exploration.

- Encourage children to think out aloud. Listen to them and discuss their developing theories and ideas.

Effective practice

Observe young children involved in imaginative play. What ideas and experiences might children be recreating or exploring?

Teaching and learning

Provide young children with resources and activities that will support their imaginative exploration and growing independence. The garden area is a classroom in its own right, a place in which butterflies, birds, worms and snails come to visit. The learning that might occur outside is often spontaneous and may involve groups of children investigating together. It is well documented in early years development that some boys tend to function at much higher levels of involvement when engaged with play and exploration outside. Ouvry (2005: 17) pointed out that 'boys are generally more interested in action, exploration and the vigorous fantasy associated with superheroes (all interests which require a lot of space for movement) whereas girls, stereotypically, like playing imaginatively in the home corner and working alongside adults.'

All children must be offered opportunities to engage with their natural environment.

Effective practice

Practitioners need to examine their own attitudes and beliefs towards outdoor play and the learning possibilities it provides. Essentially, practitioners need to reflect on their current provision and ask themselves whether their outdoor provisions, resources, routines, schedules and practitioner knowledge allow children to pursue developing interests.

Home links

Invite parents to explore the outdoor play area with their child. Display photos of the children investigating natural and life objects.

Additional resources

Bilton, H., James, K., Marsh, J., Wilson, A. and Woonton, M. (2005) *Learning Outdoors: Improving the Quality of Young Children's Play Outdoors,* London: David Fulton.

Ouvry, M. (2005) *Exercising Muscles and Minds: Outdoor Play and the Early Years Curriculum,* London: National Children's Bureau.

From 30–50 months

Development matters

- Children now show curiosity and interest in the different features of objects and living things.

- Children can now describe and talk about what they see.

- Children now show a curiosity about why things happen and how things work.

- Children now show an understanding of cause and effect relations.

Key words

active learning, first-hand experiences, the process of learning that enables children to learn from each other

Learning story

Joe, aged forty-eight months, and Emma, aged forty-six months, attend a local school and are in the reception class. The children are neighbours and spend a lot of time together in and out of school. Joe and Emma were observed with a large clear plastic container half filled with soil. They were spiking the grass in a grassy area of the garden, using small garden forks. Joe demonstrated to Emma just how to do it as he wiggled the fork in the soil. Within a short time, the worms began to emerge to the surface. Emma then compared the worms to 'spaghetti'. Joe told Emma that he thought that the worms were like small snakes dancing and jumping. Emma noticed that the wiggling sometimes caused the worm's body to form letters of the alphabet and some numbers. They watched in awe and wonder as the worms began to stretch and extend themselves. Joe and Emma began to gently collect the worms and put them into the container. Joe went into the classroom and returned carrying two magnifying glasses and a selection of laminated photographs of insects. They spent some time examining the worms through the magnifying glass, talking about the movements. The practitioner later helped Joe and Emma to return the worms to the soil.

Activities

Context for learning

The EYFS recommends that children have continuous access to outdoor learning. The garden provides many opportunities for nature and scientific studies. Children will show curiosity and interest in the features of natural objects and living things. Practitioners must also provide children with visual illustrations to stimulate their interest. Activities could include:

- games involving identifying a range of sounds made by domestic and wild animals;

- asking children questions that support them in making comparisons;

- organising visits to a local farm, park, pet shop and veterinary hospital.

Look, listen and note

- Note down the different ways in which young children express their understanding of the natural world.

- Look out for how young children react to and handle insects, animals and plants.

Effective practice

Practitioners need to respond to children's interest in insects with interest and enthusiasm by asking them questions about what they see in a range of situations where practitioners' knowledge and participation is required to support and sustain development and learning.

Teaching and learning

The EYFS places much emphasis on children's self-directed play and explorations. It recommends that practitioners should plan for children to have continuous access to outdoor play, learning and exploration. The outdoor learning environment should be at the heart of every early years setting. The DfES (2007) states that 'Children need plenty of space and time to play, both outdoors and indoors.'

Practitioners need to provide children with the opportunity to experience play and exploration in different contexts, indoors and outdoors.

Planning and resourcing

Practitioners need to plan for development to take place outdoors. Provide children with space to dig and to look at rocks and shells with magnifying glasses. Practitioners should plan to study nature, growth and change

with children. The children planting vegetables and plants could further extend the nature study. Practitioners need to provide photographs, resource books, drawing tools and cameras.

Home links

- Link to children's own first-hand experiences of pets, insects and animals by asking them questions such as

  - What does your cat eat?
  - What does your cat feel like?
  - How big is your cat?

- Practitioners must use gestures and actions to support children's feelings, relationships, ideas, words and gestures.

Additional resources

- Campbell, R. (1997) *Dear Zoo,* London: Campbell Books.

- Clarke Chichester, E. (2000) *I Love You Blue Kangaroo!* London: Collins.

- Cooper, H. (1994) *The Bear Under the Stairs,* London: Random House.

- Carle, E. (1987) *The Very Hungry Caterpillar,* London: Puffin Books.

- Foreman, M. (1991) *Mother Goose,* London: Random House.

- James, S. (2003) *The Wild Woods,* London: Walker.

- Kerr, J. (1992) *The Tiger Who Came for Tea,* London: Collins.

- Langley, J. and Andersen, H. C. (1996) *The Ugly Duckling,* London: Collins.

- Lear, E. (2002) *The Owl and the Pussy Cat,* illustrated by L. Voce, London: Walker.

📖 Souhami, J. (1996) *The Leopard's Drum,* London: Frances Lincoln.

📖 Waddell, M. (1992) *Owl Babies,* illustrated by P. Benson, London: Walker.

📖 Waddell, M. and Firth, B. (2000) *Can't You Sleep, Little Bear?* London: Walker.

📖 Whybrow, I. and Reynolds, A. (2003) *Harry and the Bucketful of Dinosaurs,* London: Puffin.

From 40–60 months

Development matters

- Children now notice and comment on patterns.

- Children now show an awareness of change.

- Children now explain their own knowledge and understanding and ask appropriate questions of others.

Early learning goals

- Children now investigate objects and materials by using all their senses as appropriate.

- Children now find out about and identify some features of living things, objects and events they observe.

- Children now look closely at similarities, difference, patterns and change.

- Children now ask questions about why things happen and how things work.

Key words

exploration of self and nature and living things

Learning story

Anastasia, aged forty months, is described as a very talkative and inquisitive girl. At school, the children were delighted when the snow covered the garden. Most of the children went outside and engaged in a range of activities such as making and throwing snowballs at each other, building snowmen, making patterns in the snow with their footprints, and riding their bikes. Anastasia went outside but stayed close to the practitioner; as they walked in the snow, the practitioner asked Anastasia to tell her how the snow felt. She described it as being soft and bouncy. As she picked it up she told the practitioner that it felt cold. The practitioner told Anastasia that if she held on to the snow for a little longer it would feel colder and icier. The practitioner demonstrated how to make snow into a ball and handed it to Anastasia, who held on to it until it started to melt. She rubbed her hands together then proceeded to make herself another and aimed it at the practitioner.

Activities

Adult involvement

Practitioners need to support children in developing an understanding of weather. They can extend children's understanding and encourage them to explore and investigate both the properties and the consequences of weather change. Discussion and talk with young children about the weather, forecasting and the seasons is important as it will support them in developing a meaningful understanding of the changes that occur when there is:

- hot weather
- cold weather
- snow
- fog
- rain and drizzle.

Ways in which practitioners can encourage development and learning include the following.

- Try simple ice experiments such as freezing water in ice-cube containers, making ice lollies, crushing ice, freezing water inside a rubber glove and making ice crystals.

- In sunny weather, encourage children to carry out simple experiments in the sun by exploring their shadows as the sun moves around during the day.

- Painting on concrete with water on a warm day will increase children's knowledge of the properties of air and water. This type of experience helps children develop an understanding of evaporation.

- Support children's understanding of the weather by providing them with weather boxes for the four seasons. For example, in the winter box you may have items such as wellington boots, hats, gloves, scarves and umbrellas.

- Practitioners need to support children to monitor the weather throughout the day.

- Practitioners could further extend children's knowledge and understanding of plants by creating a herb garden where children can grow herbs such as lavender, mint, rosemary, lemon balm, garlic, thyme, sage and chives. Practitioners can encourage children to develop their sense of smell by sniffing and pinching the plants. Activities that involve tasting herbs, cooking and drinking them can also be explored.

Children can use tubs or containers to plant seeds, which they can watch grow, as not all children will live in homes with gardens. It is important that practitioners create an interesting outdoor learning environment where children are able to plant and grow herbs so that they can describe the different smells and make comparisons and connections between the smells, taste and types of plant.

Look, listen and note

- Look out for the many different ways children begin to focus on their immediate environment.

- Listen to what they have to say about where they live and the things that they do.

Effective practice

Children need hands-on experiences of nature's wonders and living things. If children are only shown a photograph of a daffodil and asked to describe it without experiencing it, their responses will be limited. The hands-on experience of the daffodil increases the children's understanding of what it feels like, smells like and looks like. This will give the children information, which they can select, and it will help them to describe and talk about what they see.

Teaching and learning

Practitioners need to encourage and support children to explore together and independently by providing children with resources and materials that reflect the cultural lifestyles of the children attending and the wider community. For some practitioners, this may mean finding out more information about the cultural practice of children and families with whom they are working.

Planning and resourcing

Practitioners should provide children with a range of household utensils to stimulate play and conversations about how things work. For example:

- weighing scales
- garlic press
- cheese grater
- pepper grinder
- tin opener
- rolling pin
- nutcracker.

Materials that support construction play and exploration outdoors are, for example:

- hinges
- nails
- screwdriver
- pliers
- hammers
- saws
- spanners
- axles
- wheels
- cogs and pulleys.

Practitioners need to provide children with a designated area of the garden for nature study. In this space, children can dig, make puddles or mud pies. They can experiment using gardening tools, potting compost, yoghurt pots, etc. Practitioners need to plan for and provide experiences for children to explore and experiment with water. Access to an outdoor tap, hose, watering can and bucket and other measuring containers will aid exploration.

Home links

- Most children will have experience of water at bath time. Talk to parents about adding household objects to the bath to help children explore with floating and sinking, volume and capacity.

- Encourage children and families to take up library membership.

Additional resources

- Practitioners will need to provide children with books and visual illustrations of nature and wildlife.

- Ensure that they have enough equipment for children to explore the garden safely.

- Make wellington boots and other protective clothing available for children.

- Resource books on nature studies and scientific explorations which can be carried out in the garden will assist children to develop a deeper understanding by extending their thinking.

- Practitioners may need to consider holding workshops for parents on the importance of outdoor play and exploration and the learning opportunities that it presents.

The EYFS principles

The EYFS principles are grouped into four themes:

1   a unique child;
2   positive relationships;
3   enabling environment;
4   learning and development.

The themes are concerned with development, relationships, needs and learning of individual children. The early principles can be put into practice when practitioners ensure that babies and young children have appropriate developmental early learning experiences supported by positive relationships and enabling environments. The EYFS principles are woven throughout the section 'Exploration and Investigation' as they relate directly to how practitioners can begin

- building positive relationships through involving parents in their children's early development and learning, in ways that enable parents to support and enrich children's learning at home;
- creating a stimulating learning environment where children have opportunity to explore their interests in depth.

Development in this area relates to children learning through first-hand experiences, interactions and observations. Ironically, learning is a solitary activity for children, in which they must integrate new knowledge and understanding. The role a practitioner plays in helping children to make connections in their learning is crucial. Practitioners must learn to reflect on how they respond to, support and extend learning, as well as encourage children to reflect on what has been learnt.

The learning stories and activities give practitioners a vehicle for teaching and learning through a range of practical activities as well as opportunities to reflect on best practice.

Designing and making

From birth–11 months

Development matters

- Babies now explore objects and materials with their hands and mouths.

Key words

learning through senses, mouthing and touching

Learning story

Rahim, aged seven months, was observed sitting upright on his childminder's lap, using both of his hands to put his foot into his mouth. He appeared to be intrigued and motivated as he persevered with this repeated movement over and over again.

Activities

Active learning

Some of the ways in which practitioners can stimulate active learning and exploration are through:

- providing babies with a variety of skinned fruits to touch, explore and taste, such as oranges, satsumas, lemons, limes, peaches and grapefruits;

- placing familiar toys and objects on a large piece of bubble wrap and letting babies explore and make new discoveries with it;

- playing and exploration using musical instruments, pots, pans and wooden spoons which all create new and interesting sounds;

- playing with a variety of textures, soft, furry, plastic and silky.

Look, listen and note

- Watch out for how babies respond to other babies.

- Look out for how they respond to different tastes, sights, textures and sounds.

- Listen to how babies begin to take part in conversations by making sounds and manual gestures in response to verbal interaction with others.

Effective practice

Practitioners need to understand the importance of sensory exploration and how it all works for different babies.

Teaching and learning

- Practitioners should organise their time, resources and materials so that they are able to take learning forward and offer both flexibility and support.

- Babies will use their five senses to send messages to their brain. The information the baby's brain receives will relate directly to what babies see, smell, taste, feel and hear. Practitioners need to support babies exploration through all of their senses.

Planning and resourcing

Practitioners need to plan for babies to:

- explore different textures such as soft blankets, silk scarves and even a doormat;

- investigate new surroundings such as the garden;

- build time into daily routines to talk to babies and sing them interactive songs or rhymes;

- provide a range of resources and materials for babies to enable them to construct, carry, stack, fill, empty, thread, stir, fasten, push and pull.

Home links

Talk to parents about children's explorations at home and what sort of things interest them.

From 16–26 months

Learning story

Asia, aged twenty-four months old, attends a local children centre and is described as being a typical girl who enjoys play in the role-play area with the dolls. Asia was observed at the centre going to a cupboard. She reached in and pulled everything out. Soon she found a basket filled with small wooden blocks, she took out nineteen bricks which she transported, individually across the room. She stacked nine blocks into a tall tower then pushed them over. Asia repeated this building up and knocking down game for some time.

Activities

Active learning

A schema is a word which practitioners can use to describe a repeated pattern of behaviour in babies and young children. Practitioners should offer a range of activities that support children with rehearsing their particular schema. As well as supporting children to develop their dexterity through manipulation of materials, activities that involve children building and constructing (for those with a schema such as Asia) will provide a number of real challenges. Practitioners will also need to provide activities that support other schemas such as going through a boundary – this is where children put one object through another, for example, posting

a ping-pong ball through a cardboard tube, or pushing their fingers through dough or doing up buttons. Practitioners might consider responding to relevant schemas by providing resources that children can explore with again and again, for example:

- making sandwiches

- sticking paper with glue and sticky tape

- mixing sand and water

- mixing water and washing up liquid

- mixing compost and water or cornflour and water

- freezing ice

- exploring corn flour dry and wet

- playing games that involve parking cars or lining up trains

- creating treasure hunts by hiding objects in sand

- encouraging exploration of natural materials such as twigs, shells, conkers, cones and leaves

- playing with culturally diverse artefacts such as Russian dolls, African baby wrap – Ackra, a range of combs and brushes from different countries

- simple gardening, digging, pulling out weeds in the garden.

Look, listen and note

Look out for repeated patterns of behaviour which babies and toddlers show in their play and explorations.

Effective practice

- Keep talk and conversations with children fluid.

- Keep talk simple but natural, talk to children about what they are doing, show an interest and ask them meaningful questions.

Teaching and learning

- Practitioners need to recognise the importance and significance of interacting, questioning and responding to children's questions.

- A key part of the practitioner's role is to support and extend children's language and communication.

Planning and resourcing

Practitioners should provide babies and toddlers with a range of resources and materials that they can choose from to support early schematic explorations. One of the ways in which practitioners might consider doing this is by adding stimulating resources and materials to the learning environment to ensure a continuous flow of challenging activities:

- objects which children can turn, twist and spin such as cogs and wheels;

- objects for them to carry such as buckets, bags and trolleys so that they can explore filling and emptying;

- a range of solid and fluid materials for babies and toddlers to change things by mixing, adding water and freezing ice;

- construction materials that can be joined and taken apart such as interlocking tracks and simple interlocking grooves;

- materials for babies and toddlers to hide in, wrap and cover themselves, containers and bags for them to put things in;

- materials which babies and toddlers can begin to categorise such as transport toys, farm, and domestic animals.

Home links

- Take photographs of children involved in schematic exploration and share these with parents.

- Find out what schemas babies and toddlers are exploring with at home. Are they different to the schemas being displayed at the setting?

Additional resources

Louis, S., Beswick, C., Hayes, L., Magraw, L. and Featherstone, S. (2008) *Again, Again, Understanding Schemas in Young Children,* Lutterworth: Featherstone Education.

Manning-Morton, J. and Thorp, M. (2003) *Key Times for Play, The First Three Years,* Maidenhead: Open University Press.

Tolstoy, A. (2001) *The Enormous Turnip,* London: Walker Books.

From 22–36 months

Development matters

- Children are now curious and interested in making things happen to see the cause and effect.

Key words

active learning

Learning story

Kai, aged thirty-three months, was observed playing with four large empty boxes outside. He lined them up in a row, got into one and pretended to be driving a train. He made train sounds. After a little while, Kai went off and returned with two long-handled spades. He moved one box on to the grassy area of the garden, got into it and pretended it was a boat using the spades as oars.

Activities

Transforming understanding

Practitioners can build on children's interest by providing them with a range of activities and resources to sustain and extend their exploration. Observation of children in action is necessary if practitioners are to offer a range of experiences to support individual needs. Practitioners can promote every child's development and learning when they provide developmentally appropriate construction materials that children are able to explore.

Simple experiments allow children to explore, discover and make sense of what they see, for example:

- Roll plasticine into balls to explore sinking, then roll it out to flatten it and make it into a boat to see if it will float.

- Drill some holes in some logs and let children explore with real tools such as screwdrivers and different-sized screws.

- Connect chains and objects together using simple interlocking devices, such as Velcro and more complex ones such as padlocks and keys.

Look, listen and note

- Look out for how children use particular materials as they construct.

- Note down the child's preferred way of placing things. Are they placing things on top, in the middle, next to, in between or in front?

Effective practice

It is important that practitioners recognise that some children will need adult intervention and support when exploring with joining construction materials and finding out about what makes things happen.

Teaching and learning

Practitioners should interact with children in ways that support their explorations and styles of learning. Children need to be able to find out for themselves how to use construction materials. They will develop new skills in techniques such as folding, cutting and joining.

Practitioners can talk to children about their designs, paying particular attention to the size, shape and position of materials. Practitioners need to understand what children can do so that they are able to offer appropriate support and identify next steps in development and learning.

Planning and resourcing

Practitioners might consider providing children with construction toys and materials which have a range of features such as nuts and bolts, cogs and wheels, and different shapes – rectangular, square and cylindrical. Construction materials such as wooden bricks, Stickle Bricks, Duplo, Lego, Mobilo, Popoids, sand, clay, dough, plasticine, paper, card and recycled household items and cereal boxes can also be provided. Practitioners should ensure that they have enough materials for children to construct, design and build. It is important that children are offered opportunities to understand the construction process of natural and manufactured goods.

One of the ways in which practitioners can further support children is by selecting a range of appropriate tools and equipment, for example scissors, sticky tape, masking tape, packing tape, Blu-tack, paper clips or fasteners, stapler, PVA glue, Pritt Stick, a hole punch, Velcro, string, thread. It is the experience of using the materials repeatedly and seeing materials being used by others that will support children to develop skills and techniques such as cutting paper with scissors. Add materials such as paper, card, sponges, plastic and metal spoons, plastic lids, wood, wood shavings and polystyrene.

Home links

Encourage parents to tell children about their experiences of making and creating a home, for example, DIY and making clothes and curtains, talking about materials, tools and processes.

Additional resources

Siraj-Blatchford, J. and MacLeod-Brudenell, I. (1999) *Supporting Science, Design and Technology in Early Years,* Buckingham: Open University Press.

📖 Pre-school Playgroups Association (1992) *Technology through Play*.

📖 MacLeod-Brundenell, I. (1998) *The Design and Technology Handbook for Pre-school Providers,* Wellesbourne: Design and Technology Association.

📖 Community Playthings mini hollow blocks (see www.community playthings.co.uk).

From 30–50 months

Development matters

- Children investigate various construction materials.

- Children realise tools can be used for a purpose.

- Children join construction pieces together to build and balance them.

- Children begin to try out a range of tools and techniques safely.

Key words

designing and making things for purpose

Learning story

Oliver, aged forty-eight months, attends a local nursery school. He is described as a boy who spends a lot of time in the construction workshop, connecting pieces of wood. Oliver was observed in the garden area with a long piece of wood. He placed the wood in an angled position against a low wall. He put his foot on the wood, to keep it balanced. He used a large saw to begin with; he then used a smaller saw to complete the task. When he had finished, he went over to the practitioner. He told her that he had made some fire wood for her fire.

Activities

Making connections

Some of the ways in which practitioners might consider providing children with a range of experiences in which they can construct and design include:

● providing activities where children can use real bricks and dissolvable cement to make constructions;

● providing a range of activities where children can use scissors to cut card or paper;

● letting children explore with staplers, paper fasteners, treasury tags, sticky tape, packing and masking tape;

● playing simple games with children describing a repair or an improvement which needs doing in the home such as hanging a picture.

Encourage children to re-enact construction situations, by providing props and resources for play that links with their home.

● Ask children what tools you might need.

● Further extend this game by asking children to think about what tools you might use to hang a picture if you did not have a hammer and nails.

● Involve children in carrying out simple repairs to books and equipment.

● Take photographs of buildings in your local environment.

● Encourage children to look closely at their environment through a magnifying glass and through binoculars.

● Encourage children to look at materials and their purpose in constructions such as tiles, bricks, timber, scaffolding and paving slabs.

- Play games with children using your local environment as a stimulus to look for patterns in construction and design.

- Talk to children about the function of buildings exploring both the interior and exterior.

Look, listen and note

- Look out for how children demonstrate their understanding of sophisticated scientific principles through their designs and constructions.

- Look out for how children link their first-hand experiences to their designs and constructions by naming the buildings and constructions.

Effective practice

- Children are interested in designing, making models and constructing buildings.

- Children need to have opportunities in their play and exploration to choose from a range of construction materials. They need to use developmentally appropriate tools to support them in understanding their function and purpose.

Teaching and learning

Practitioners need to create opportunities for children to use tools in their play and exploration. It is through experimenting with tools that children begin to develop an understanding, for example that a hack saw is suitable for cutting small pieces of wood but a larger saw is far more appropriate for sawing planks. Children will spend time exploring how tools work and may discover a few basic scientific principles along the way.

Planning and resourcing

- Practitioners should provide children with real tools such as:

  - hammers
  - different size screwdrivers
  - Allen keys
  - saws
  - clamps
  - spirit levels
  - string
  - tape measures
  - rulers
  - nails
  - spanners
  - screws.

- Practitioners can take small groups of children on a visit to a local timber yard to collect unwanted pieces of all types of wood, for example, ply, balsa and pine, planks and bamboo. Ask for a copy of a blank builder-supply form and add this to your role-play area.

- Organise visits to a local building site or timber workshop so that children can see machinery in action.

- Arrange to return and take photographs so that the children can see work in progress.

- Provide children with safety equipment in the role-play area – items such as a protective helmet and glasses, builders' belt, barrier tape and safety waistcoat.

- Practitioners might consider providing resources such as interlocking trains, roads and tracks for children to design layouts for a specific purpose.

- Contact the AA or RAC and ask them to visit and talk to children about roadside repairs or alternatively arrange a trip to your local garage and petrol station.

- Practitioners can contact their local town-planning offices to request old plans and drawings to display in the construction area.

- Local architects may also have a range of models made from a variety of materials and drawings to give away that will further stimulate children's interest in the construction, design and engineering processes.

- Practitioners will also need to consider providing children with a wide range of resources used in joining: for example, hinges, magnetic strips, hooks and sticking compounds.

- Practitioners should consider adding magazine pictures of waterways that feature many interesting bridges and constructions.

Home links

We are living in an age of DIY. The families that practitioners are working with may be erecting buildings with fences or brick walls and generally carrying out home improvements. Try to find out if any of the parents or members of the extended family do any of the following jobs:

- construction worker

- electrician

- mechanic

- surveyor

- planner

- architect

- engineer

- carpenter or joiner.

Use their knowledge of the industry to stimulate and enhance your learning environment. Practitioners can also talk to children about what they know about the construction tools that they see being used at home.

Additional resources

- Beswick, C. and Featherstone, S. (2003) *The Little Book of Bricks and Boxes,* illustrated by K. Ingham, Lutterworth: Featherstone Education.

- Featherstone, S. and Williams, L. (2006) *Construction Baby and Beyond,* Lutterworth: Featherstone Education.

- Hutchins, P. (2001) *Rosie's Walk,* London: Red Fox.

- Lee, V. and Lloyd-Hall, K. (1986) *My Class: Visits a Park,* London: Watts.

- Watson, C. (2002) *Building Site (Busy Places),* London: Watts.

- Community Plaything, large hollow blocks and a set of unit blocks (www.communityplaythings.com).

From 40–60 months

Development matters

- Children now construct with purpose in mind, using a variety of resources.

- Children now use simple tools and techniques competently and appropriately.

Early learning goals

- Children now build and construct a wide range of objects, selecting appropriate resources and adapting their work where necessary.

- Children now select tools and techniques they need to shape, assemble and join materials they are joining.

Key words

assemble, adaptation and modification

Learning story

Nicholas, aged fifty-four months, is described as a boy who spends a lot of time in the construction workshop area, often involved in complicated constructions using paper, tape and staplers. He has recently become interested in modelling with pieces of recycled material and sometimes uses these in conjunction with wood.

He was observed in the construction workshop area making a large crane from a wooden crate. He made parallel holes using long nails and a hammer at one end of the crate, through which he put a bamboo stick which had string wound around the middle. Nicholas attached a large paper clip to the end of the string. He manipulated the paper clip to form a hook. He tried out his crane. It did not work. He found two rectangular pieces of wood and made holes in one end of each of them. Using small nails, Nicholas hammered the two pieces of wood at an angle on to the crate from the inside. He then put another bamboo stick through the two holes. On this bamboo stick he placed an empty cotton reel. Nicholas attached the string to the reel. He tried out his crane, it worked.

Activities

Creativity and critical thinking

Practitioners can further support children's knowledge and understanding of the design and making process by providing resources and tools for children to make simple boats and paddles from balsa wood.

- Cut out a boat shape in balsa wood, ask the children to make a paddle for the boat, provide them with elastic bands, sticky tape and smaller pieces of cut balsa wood.

- Provide materials such as cut logs for children to design and construct with to add an extra bit of challenge.

- Provide construction materials that have grooves cut into the edges that enable children to design and build without permanent fixing.

- Provide children with gears, wheels, cogs and axles.

- Talk to children about the relationships between the wheel and axles, encourage them to think out aloud, and describe what they are making.

- Provide resources and materials for children to make a model with wheels such as a car.

Look, listen and note

- Look out for how children use tools and for what purpose. What sort of models or accessories are they making?

- Note down how children will use symbolic representation when they make and name their designs.

- Note down how children will use their existing knowledge of materials in a new situation.

Effective practice

Practitioners need to understand that the process of learning is important for children. Through play and exploration children will come across a range of problems that will make them have to adapt and modify their constructions and designs for their intended purpose.

Teaching and learning

Children need to see things working if they are to become interested in how they work and their purpose. Practitioners can support children by providing them with a learning environment which contains the following resources:

- interlocking trains, roads and tracks

- construction sets

- wheels and cogs

- old clocks and radios for children to take apart using real tools.

Planning and resourcing

- Practitioners should consider providing children with a construction workshop area where children are able to select tools, materials and resources for construction and design.

- Collect catalogues from building suppliers and add these to your construction area.

- Plan opportunities for children to write for purpose in the construction area.

- Ensure that the area has chipboard, pencils and blank copies of supplier order forms.

- Add old telephones, clocks, fans and radios for children to dismantle using a range of tools.

- Practitioners should use children's experiences of construction to help design and make things, for example, children may recently have had all of their windows and doors replaced at home.

- Practitioners can build on children's existing knowledge and understanding by introducing activities where they design windows and doorframes using different materials.

- Practitioners must ensure that they have sufficient materials and accessories for children to be able to design and construct a range of items.

Home links

- Practitioners need to recognise the importance of their role in planning ways in which children can extend, develop and enhance individual skills.

- It is important that practitioners try to involve and engage parents in the process of their child's development and learning.

- Practitioners can find out from parents what tools children can use and are exploring at home. This useful information can contribute to practitioners' planning as well as supporting children to make links with their different areas of knowledge.

Additional resources

Lewisham Early Years Advice and Resource Network (2005) *A Place to Learn: Developing a Stimulating Learning Environment*, Lewisham: Lewisham Early Years Advice and Resource Network.

The EYFS principles

The EYFS themes of providing an enabling environment and positive relationships are instrumental in this section 'Designing and Making'.

- Practitioners should regularly share information with parents about what motivates children to learn and their different interests.

- Practitioners must provide children with an environment in which they can explore a range of familiar and everyday things.

- Practitioners need to understand that when children are involved in construction and design they are also thinking, solving simple and sometimes more complex problems as well as making links to their learning.

- Children may learn the same thing in very different ways. What may captivate one child may not interest another. Practitioners not only need to

understand the process of learning but also need to be aware that for individual development to be enhanced, development must be understood, supported and extended by practitioners' knowledge of the children and what they know and can do.

● The learning stories and activities give practitioners a vehicle for teaching and learning through a range of practical exercises as well as opportunities to reflect on practice.

Information and Communication Technologies

From birth–11 months

> **Development matters**
>
> ● Babies now show interest in toys and resources that incorporate technology.
>
> **Key words**
>
> making connections and exploring

Learning story

Katie, aged six months, was observed looking at an interactive book. She looked at the book intently as she searched for buttons on the page. When she pressed one of the buttons, the book made animal sounds, which she mimicked by making a 'Grrr' noise in response as she waved her arms in excitement.

Activities

Active learning

One of the ways practitioners can stimulate active learning and exploration is by providing children with resources that they can explore and experiment with together with an adult, for example, providing:

- books with flaps that babies can lift

- interactive toys that they can press buttons and turn knobs on.

Look, listen and note

- Practitioners need to look out for how babies begin to show an interest in technological toys.

- Look out for how they begin to anticipate sights, sounds and actions of toys and technology resources.

- Note down the toys and resources that interest babies the most.

Effective practice

- Practitioners need to encourage babies to explore their environment and to try things out for themselves.

- Communicating with babies is important. Practitioners should talk to babies about what is under the flap or what happens when baby presses a particular button. This will help babies to make sense of the world around them.

Teaching and learning

Practitioners need to be aware that as babies begin to gain knowledge and understanding of how to operate technological toys and resources, they will apply what they have learnt to their explorations of other objects in order to discover what they can do with them.

Planning and resourcing

Practitioners should provide a range of interesting push-button resources and materials which babies can grasp and hold to explore textures, shapes and sounds.

Home links

Find out from parents what types of battery-operated toys and resources their babies are interested in at home, for example which interactive books.

Additional resources

Abbott, L. and Nutbrown, C. (eds) (2003) *Experiencing Reggio, Implications for Pre-school Provision*, Buckingham: Open University Press.

Robinson, M. (2003) *From Birth to One, The Year of Opportunity*, Buckingham: Open University Press.

From 8–20 months

Development matters

- Babies and toddlers now explore things with interest and sometimes press parts or lift flaps to achieve effects such as sound, movement or to reveal new images.

Key words

repetition of actions during explorations

Learning story

Rahim, aged nine months, was observed at his childminder's home. He was on the living-room floor, and he crawled up to the stereo and pulled himself up. He pressed buttons, turned knobs and moved dials. When the lights started to flash, he responded by shaking his whole body in excitement. The childminder moved him away from the stereo and directed him toward his baby walker. He turned the cogs and knobs and pressed buttons on the baby walker. When the music came on he bounced up and down on the floor moving his body to the music. He repeated this several times.

Activities

Learning through experience

Some ways in which practitioners can stimulate active learning:

- Make an activity board with hinges, bolts, cogs, wheels and switches.

- Make books with flaps.

- Provide babies and toddlers with simple toys that have to be programmed, for example by pressing a button to activate them.

Look, listen and note

- Look out for how babies and toddlers begin to notice the cause and effect of toys and resources that incorporate technology.

- Look out for how babies and toddlers begin to follow instructions.

Effective practice

- Practitioners need to have an understanding of the skills which the babies and toddlers need to learn.

- Practitioners can introduce activities and technology resources that will support babies' and toddlers' learning.

Teaching and learning

- Practitioners need to be mindful that babies and toddlers are unique individuals and what may work and stimulate one child may not work for another.

- It is important that practitioners provide the right amount of interest and challenge for babies and toddlers. For a baby or toddler to understand the concept of cause and effect from pressing buttons and lifting flaps, they must first have many experiences of buttons to press, flaps to lift and knobs and cogs to twist and turn. When babies and toddlers are involved in play and exploration they will press, turn and lift. It is the combination of their actions that allows them to manipulate objects and find out how they work.

Planning and resourcing

Practitioners need to provide babies with a range of stimulating resources which are appropriate for developing their emerging interest, ability and skills, such as:

- transport toys that have buttons to press and light up
- interactive steering wheels that can be pressed and operated with keys
- keyboards that light up and make sounds
- musical instruments
- toys that vibrate when pressed
- toys that when touched roll and spin
- toys that lift off such as rockets
- musical boxes
- tills
- mobiles phones
- interactive balls
- radios
- interactive clocks.

Home links

- Try to find out from parents what programmable toys and equipment babies and toddlers are exploring with at home.
- Consider how you could use this information to support the individual and make links to their learning.

Additional resources

The Early Learning Centre has a huge range of interactive toys and resources for babies and toddlers. Practitioners should consider adding resources of which children already have experience. Babies and toddlers may already have an understanding of many simple mechanisms, because they are already familiar with them.

From 16–26 months

Development matters

- Children now show interest in toys with buttons and flaps and simple mechanisms and begin to learn to operate them.

Key words

repetition, fascination and responding to outcomes

Learning story

Isobel, aged eighteen months, was seen carrying a musical shape sorter. She sat on the chair next to her childminder and gave the sorter to the childminder. The childminder lifted up the flap and began to play with Isobel at peek-a-boo with the mirror. Isobel took the sorter back from the childminder and started to press buttons and use the phone dial and beads. When the telephone rang, Isobel responded by saying hello.

Activities

Learning through experience

Practitioners can promote development and learning in this area by providing children with a range of activities that support development through their senses:

- musical instruments such as drums, guitar with strings and recorder

- picture books of domestic appliances within the home such as an oven, hoover or air freshener – ask children questions about how they sound or smell.

Look, listen and note

Look out for how fascinated children become by the mechanism of toys and equipment.

Effective practice

- Practitioners need to help children to understand simple mechanisms by talking to them about the way things work.

- Practitioners need to be aware of the ICT which children are encountering every day and to plan ways to support and extend development and learning.

Teaching and learning

Some children may have a fascination for things that fold up, particularly their buggies. Practitioners can support children by providing them with umbrellas and collapsible boxes.

Planning and resourcing

Practitioners can add simple household mechanisms to the role-play area, for example:

- garlic press

- rolling pins

- pepper grinder

- spoons

- cheese graters

- nutcrackers

- whisks.

It is important that children are able to experiment with simple machinery using real objects, for example grating a carrot or putting play-dough through the garlic press.

Home links

Find out what machines parents use at home, for example:

- hoover

- microwave oven

- toaster

- iron

- blender

- tin openers

- electric shaver.

Additional resources

- Provide simple cameras for children to take photographs by pressing a button.

- Add the following to the role-play area:
  - digital scales
  - blender
  - microwave oven
  - vacuum cleaner
  - washing machine
  - iron and board.

From 22–36 months

Development matters

- Children now show an interest in ICT.

- Children now seek to acquire basic skills in turning on and operating some basic ICT equipment.

Key words

anticipation of actions and knowledge of programmable toys and equipment

Learning story

Anna, aged thirty-six months, is interested in anything that can be pushed: for example, her buggy or things which she can carry such as bags or a shopping basket. She was observed playing with a torch, turning it on and off. Then she put it into her bag. She filled her basket with a range of different objects. She returned to the torch and went inside. She shone the light

on the ceiling then on the floor, then she moved the torch and followed the light along the wall. Anna repeated her actions for a while then approached the practitioner. She said to her, 'You put batteries in.'

Activities

Mental and physical involvement

- Practitioners can provide resources in the role-play area which will support children's sensory development and understanding of how things work.

- For activities that explore light and dark, practitioners can use battery-operated torches or solar power windup torches.

- Practitioners should talk to children about the effects of their actions; make connections with light sources such as the sun, moon, lamps and light switches.

- Encourage children to experiment with cameras that take real pictures.

Look, listen and note

- Look out for how aware children are of the purpose of equipment.

- Note down how they use equipment to sustain their play and explorations.

Effective practice

Practitioners should talk to children about the purpose of everyday items such as washing machines or television.

Teaching and learning

Practitioners need to help children to make connections by supporting them to represent their knowledge in how to control or operate programmable toys. See p. 12 for more information on making connections.

Planning and resourcing

- Practitioners need to plan for and provide children with a range of everyday technology and programmable toys to support development and learning.

- Make a list of all the ICT equipment that you have in your setting.

- How can you plan to let children use equipment such as computers, photocopiers and water coolers.

Home links

- Encourage parents to talk to children about the pelican crossing.

- Tell children that if they want the traffic to stop they have to press the button and the traffic will stop and they can cross over the road. Children will just want to press the button for effect.

Additional resources

Bee-Bot is a programmable floor robot with sounds and flashing lights which can be operated simply by young children. Contact TTS for information on Bee-Bot curriculum links (see www.tts-group.co.uk/Bee-Bot).

From 30–50 months

Development matters

- Children now know how to operate simple equipment.

Key words

interactive programs, which build on children's responses

Learning story

Alex, aged forty-nine months, is interested in exploring nature. He is often seen in the garden area erecting supports for climbing or for tall plants using a variety of wood and recycled materials. He was observed in the book area with a story sack of 'Jack and the Bean Stalk.' He took the cassette out of the pack and opened the tape recorder, pressed a button, placed the tape inside the machine and closed the lid. He checked to make sure that the head-phones were plugged in correctly. He tipped out the props on to the floor, sat down with the book and headphones on and listened to the story.

Activities

Personalised learning

Practitioners can further support children in developing an understanding of programmable equipment in their local environment. Some of the ways in which practitioners might consider stimulating children are:

- taking children out to experience ICT in their local community, for example:
    - automatic doors
    - escalators
    - the queuing system at the post office
    - parking machines

- streetlights
- neon signs

- taking photographs for discussion
- using the photocopier, scanner, or paper shredder.

Look, listen and note

Look out for how children follow a sequence of instructions such as switching the computer on and off.

Effective practice

- Practitioners should offer children opportunities to explore a range of ICT equipment based on what children already know about, such as a PSP (PlayStation Portable).

- It is essential that practitioners promote this area of children's learning through planning experiences with ICT programmes that are both challenging and achievable for children.

Teaching and learning

- Practitioners need to supervise and give children clear instructions so that they are able to operate machines for themselves.

- Practitioners must be prepared to be learners themselves in this process as children may have a great deal of knowledge and experience about a particular programme.

- Practitioners must reflect on how they talk to children as well as develop an awareness of their own ICT needs.

Planning and resourcing

- Interactive smart boards are common in early years settings. Practitioners need to ensure that the programmes they choose allow the children to work at their own pace.

- Practitioners will need to check that they have plenty of ink and paper so that children can print their drawings.

- Practitioners should also make sure that battery-operated toys have working batteries.

Home links

Find out from parents what ICT equipment children can operate independently at home.

Additional resources

Trythall, A. and Featherstone, S. (2005) *Little Books with Big Ideas of ICT*, Lutterworth: Featherstone Education.

From 40–60 months

Development matters

- Children can complete a simple program on a computer.
- Children use ICT to perform simple functions, such as selecting a channel on the TV remote control.
- Children use a mouse and keyboard to interact with age-appropriate computer software.

Early learning goals

- Children find out about and identify the uses of everyday technology and programmable toys to support their learning

Key words

ICT and its role in supporting development, learning, interest and understanding

Learning story

Emily, aged forty-eight months, is described as a little girl who loves to dress up, putting on hats, coats, dresses, necklaces, bracelets and shoes before joining in the activities at nursery. She can often be seen in the creative workshop area making lots of parcels which she fills with bits of paper.

She was observed at the computer table, operating the computer using the mouse, playing a game which involved finding cats hidden in boxes. The boxes had been camouflaged to blend in with everyday household objects. Emily displayed delight each time she found a cat in one of the many boxes on the screen. She repeatedly operated the mouse and congratulated herself for finding each cat before looking for the next box. When she had finished playing her game, she used the mouse to quit the game and switch the computer off.

Activities

Mental and physical involvement

One ways in which practitioners might support children to operate simple programmable ICT toys, is to offer them software packages that allow them to make decisions. Practitioners should consider packages which:

- support children in recognising patterns, matching shapes, colour and speed;

- allow children to match objects to different locations;

- offer children real challenge;

- children can build on gradually;

- provide opportunities for children to create their own screen saver, use a mouse, keyboard, touch screen, one or two switches and web camera;

- offer sound rewards.

Look, listen and note

Look out for how children, through their play, show knowledge and understanding of ICT toys and equipment. Do they turn the cooker or the washing machine on in their pretend play or do they like dialling numbers on the phone before speaking?

Effective practice

Children need to be offered a broad range of appropriate programs that will stimulate their interest and extend their existing knowledge and understanding of ICT.

Teaching and learning

- Practitioners will need to teach children how to operate a computer.

- Practitioners need to demonstrate and give children clear explanations, for example what happens when you press the printing icon.

- Practitioners need to have knowledge and understanding of computers if they are to support children in using programs to create pictures, using a web camera, making videos, taking pictures and printing them.

Planning and resourcing

- Practitioners need to plan time to talk to children about computers and programs.

- Children will need practitioners' support in extending their vocabulary when talking about the main parts of a computer.

- Children need practitioners to understand the basic function of computers in order to support their curiosity and interest using the computer as a tool.

Home links

Try to find out which children in your class have a computer at home and what programs they use.

Additional resources

 There is a huge range of computer software on the market. Practitioners need to consider what programs will extend children's curiosity and interest and challenge children's thinking.

See Inclusive Technology, www.inclusive.co.uk. Inclusive Technology are suppliers of hardware and software packages and equipment that supports children with special educational needs to use a computer.

The EYFS principles

The EYFS themes of creating an enabling environment and positive relationships relate directly to this section on ICT. Practitioners must support children to become confident users of mechanical and technological toys

and equipment. The learning environment should have a range of ICT programmes that encourage children to interact and build on children's responses. Practitioners often underestimate children's knowledge in this area. Parents will have information about their child's interaction and knowledge of ICT at home. This information is key as it will support and inform practitioner's planning. Children need stimulating and interesting programs to encourage learning.

As luck would have it, when children are engaged with ICT they are also engaged in decoding different signs and symbols used in communication. Practitioners have a key role to play in teaching children the necessary skills, extending vocabulary and supporting independence.

The learning stories and activities give practitioners a vehicle for teaching and learning through a range of practical activities as well as opportunities to reflect on practice and provision.

4 | Time

Development matters

- Babies anticipate repeated sounds and sights.

Key words

anticipation of sight, sounds and actions

Learning story

Rahim, aged nine months, was observed seated on his high chair. He was sliding plastic shapes around his table. He repeated the sliding action and enjoyed the sound that the plastic shapes made on the surface.

Activities

Play and exploration

- Sing songs and rhymes with babies and repeat some of the sounds that they make.

- Play peek-a-boo games.

- Make silly sounds, wiggle your tongue and make different shapes with your mouth.

- Give babies wooden spoons to bang with.

- Play games with their fingers and toes such as 'This Little Piggy'.

- Play puppet games moving them up and down or in circles.

Look, listen and note

Look out for how babies respond to everyday sights, sounds and actions. For example, how do they react when you sing their favourite nursery rhyme? How do they show anticipation of an approaching feed? What body language tells you they are expecting to be picked up?

Effective practice

It is important that practitioners sing songs and rhymes with babies. The role that practitioners play in supporting babies' play is crucial for their development.

Teaching and learning

The more opportunities that babies have to play with a range of visually stimulating objects and intriguing sounds, the more they are able to represent their experiences and to use what they have learnt in different ways.

Planning and resourcing

Practitioners need to plan opportunities for babies to explore, investigate and problem-solve within their daily routine. Practitioners also need to plan opportunities for babies to practise and try out their developing skills.

Home links

- Practitioners can encourage parents to sing songs and rhymes.

- Find out from parents if there is a particular song or rhyme that their child enjoys. If the song or rhyme is in another language, ask the parent if they mind recording it for you.

- What actions or responses do parents identify that show their baby is anticipating a routine care procedure or adult interaction?

Additional resources

Gillespie Edwards, A. (2002) *Relationships and Learning: Caring for Children from Birth to Three,* London: National Children's Bureau.

From 8–20 months

Development matters

- Babies and toddlers get to know and enjoy daily routines, such as getting-up time, mealtimes, nappy-time, bathtime and bedtime.

Key words

awareness of their personal routines

Learning story

Hugo, aged sixteen months, was observed with his key person. The key person told Hugo that it was time to change his nappy. She asked him to get her the baby wipes. He returned carrying them. The key person offered him a selection of toys and objects to choose from. He selected a bunch of keys and reached out for the key person's hand. He happily went off with her.

Activities

Active learning

- Schedules and routines are very important for babies and toddlers as they give them information as to what is going to happen next and where.

- Practitioners should provide a range of activities which relate to developing an understanding of routines.

- Practitioners should talk to babies and toddlers about what they had for breakfast, lunch and tea.

- Talk to babies and toddlers about getting dressed, ask them questions about putting clothes on and taking them off.

- Provide babies and toddlers with resources and photographs that support them in understanding the sequence of the day.

- Provide babies and toddlers with boxes and pieces of fabric so that they can put teddies and dolls to bed.

- Provide water-play activities so that babies and toddlers can explore, for example, washing dolls with sponges.

- Share a book with babies and toddlers at naptime before settling them down to sleep.

- Support babies in making connections with what is going to happen next by showing babies or toddlers their bottle or beaker.

Look, listen and note

Look out for how babies and toddlers begin to make predictions about their routine throughout the day.

Effective practice

Practitioners need to spend time talking to babies and toddlers so that they understand routines and changes in routines, for example that their grandmother will be picking them up today.

Teaching and learning

Practitioners need to understand the importance of their role in supporting babies and toddlers in learning to become independent.

Planning and resourcing

Practitioners should plan time to talk to children, for example during nappy-changing time. They should also try and ensure that there is consistency when they are changing babies' and toddlers' nappies. It is preferable that one practitioner take on this role, not several different members of the team.

Home links

Practitioners should try to find out from parents as much information as possible about individual routines at home, for example: Isobel likes to sleep with her blanket and she calls it Gee.

Additional resources

The following books are available from the Letterbox Library, 71–73 Allen Road, London, N16 8RY. Tel 0207 503 4801.

- 📖 King, K. (2006) *I Don't Eat Tooth Paste Anymore,* illustrated by L. Willey, London: Tamarind.

- 📖 Swain, G. (2006) *Get Dressed,* London: Tamarind.

- 📖 Swain, G. (2007) *Tidy Up,* London: Tamarind.

- 📖 Swain, G. (2006) *Washing Up,* London: Tamarind.

- 📖 Swain, G. (2007) *Bedtime,* London: Tamarind.

From 16–26 months

Development matters

- Children associate a sequence of actions with daily routines.

- Children begin to understand that things might happen at certain times.

Key words

making connections through spontaneous play relating to own experiences, feelings and relations

Learning story

Isobel, aged eighteen months, was observed in the kitchen with her childminder, playing on the floor with a wooden spoon and a plastic bowl. She was stirring. The childminder was chopping leeks and was talking to Isobel about chopping, telling her that when she got much older she would let her chop leeks. Isobel left the kitchen then returned carrying her bib. She had made a connection between cooking and eating.

Activities

Making connections

Practitioners should further support children to make connections by providing them with resources that allow them to imitate everyday activities:

- pots, pans and wooden spoons

- large boxes and blankets

- bottles and beakers

- buggies and car seats

- water play with buckets and dolls to bathe while talking to children about the parts of the body which they are washing.

It is essential that practitioners talk to children about what they are doing and respond supportively to their actions and words.

Look, listen and note

Look out for the connections children are making with their everyday routines. What experiences are they enacting?

Effective practice

Practitioners need to be aware that children will play with household objects and materials imaginatively.

Teaching and learning

- Practitioners have a key and important role to play in helping children understand the passage of time.

- Practitioners can sing songs or simple rhymes with children while doing everyday activities, for example 'One Two Buckle My Shoe' when children are putting on their shoes.

Planning and resourcing

- Practitioners should consider providing toddlers with everyday household objects that are familiar to children.

- Plan to make a birthday chart with the children.

Home links

- Try to find out from parents about their child's bath time and other routines.

- Practitioners could ask parents to make a growth chart.

Additional resources

- Hawkins, C. and Hawkins, J. (2004) *Sleepy Baby* London: Little Orchard.

- Hawkins, C. and Hawkins, J. (2004) *Soapy Baby,* London Little Orchard.

- Hawkins, C. and Hawkins, J. (2004) *Hungry Baby,* London: Little Orchard.

From 22–36 months

Development matters

- Children now recognise some special times in their lives and the lives of others.

- Children understand some talk about the immediate past and future, for example, 'before', 'later', or 'soon'.

- Children anticipate specific time-based events such as mealtimes or hometime.

Key words

understanding the passage of time through routines

Learning story

Michael, aged thirty-six months, attended a nursery school part-time. Wheels and things that go round fascinated him. Michael was observed at nursery talking to the practitioners about when he could go outside to play. The practitioner told Michael that as soon as it had stopped raining he could go out. Five minutes later, Michael approached the practitioner again asking her if he could go out. The practitioner told Michael that it was still raining and that he would get very wet but that as soon as the rain stopped he could go outside to play. Some fruit and water were put out for the children. Michael took a banana and some water. He approached the practitioner again, this time he had put on his coat, hat and wellington boots. 'Please can I go out?' he asked, 'its nearly home time.' Michael pointed to his coat and told the practitioner 'I won't get wet.'

Activities

Making connections

Practitioners can promote children's understanding of what happens when by providing them with familiar resources which they are able to practise activities on such as:

- boxes and blankets for putting dolls and teddies to bed;

- water play with dolls, sponges and towels;

- nappies, potties and underwear to put on and take off dolls and teddies;

- babygros, trousers and dresses for dressing.

Practitioners should talk to children about their routines.

Look, listen and note

Look out for how children show their understanding of time. Listen out for how their talk begins to reference time, for example 'It is nearly home time.'

Effective practice

Practitioners need to be aware of the importance of role-play for young children.

Teaching and learning

It is through role-play that children will act out what they know and understand. Children are interested in their routines because they experience them daily. Their play allows them to make sense of their first-hand experiences as well as enhancing their development and learning.

Planning and resourcing

Practitioners must provide resources that support children's individual routines. Practitioners can further support children's understanding by having a range of books that reflect different lifestyles and routines such as bedtime, teatime and bathtime. Practitioners should also plan to talk with children about seasonal changes and festivals.

Home links

Ask parents to take photographs of their child's individual routines, use the photographs to make a book.

Additional resources

Practitioners will need cameras to loan out to some parents, and can also consider purchasing disposable cameras.

 Cooke, T. (1996) *So Much,* illustrated by H. Oxenbury, London: Walker Books.

 Falwell, C. (1995) *Feast for Ten,* London: Houghton Mifflin.

From 30–50 months

Development matters

- Children remember and talk about significant events from their own experiences.
- Children show interest in the lives of people familiar to them.
- Children talk about the past and future events.
- Children develop an understanding of growth, decay and changes over time.

Key words

planning, predicting and speculating

Learning story

John-Paul, aged fifty months, was observed building a complex structure out of flat lolly sticks, collage and recycled household materials. He used glue to fix the lolly sticks on to the base of his structure. Once he had finished his construction, he asked the practitioner how long it would take to dry. The practitioner had a look at it and told John-Paul, 'I think it will be dry by going-home time.' It was just after lunch. John-Paul returned to the creative workshop area. He fixed lolly sticks to the base of his new construction, this time using sticky tape. John-Paul told the practitioner that he would play with the first one tomorrow.

Activities

Transforming understanding

Practitioners can support children's development of the passage of time and how things change over time by:

- growing cress and mustard seeds inside and outside (once the cress has grown the children can make cress sandwiches!);

- investigating the life of frog spawn and the sequence of growth – tadpole, two legs, four legs, frog;

- investigating their own life and growth; ask parents if they have images from their pregnancy (ultrascans and three-dimensional scans); use the images to talk to children about the growth cycle.

Look, listen and note

- Look out for how children remember significant events in their lives.

- Look out for the feelings that children show when talking about past experiences.

- Note down how children begin to link the past to their present lives.

Effective practice

Practitioners need to be mindful when growing things with children that, for the individual child, learning will be determined by the child's existing knowledge and understanding and that not all children will come from homes with gardens.

Teaching and learning

Growing vegetables with children is one of the most natural ways of illustrating growth linked to time, as they build on their knowledge and understanding of the world. Practitioners can extend children's language

by using words such as 'roots', 'stem' and 'leaf'. Extend knowledge and understanding by talking to children about the importance of light and water and different types of fruit and vegetables. Children need to learn that potatoes, carrots and parsnips, for example, are grown in the ground and not in the supermarket.

Planning and resourcing

- Practitioners need to provide children with small gardening tools such as trowels and forks.

- They should try to use seeds such as cress, mustard and other seeds, which germinate quickly to keep children interested.

- They should also plant a variety of bulbs both inside and out of doors and explain to children that they will all grow at different rates.

- Practitioners should plan to take photographs at each stage of growth. This will help to remind children of previous stages.

Home links

Encourage parents to involve children in watering the plants or garden.

Additional resources

Practitioners will need to purchase seeds and bulbs, compost, watering cans and containers.

From 40–60 months

Development matters

- Children now begin to differentiate between past and present.

- Children now use time-related words in conversation.

- Children now understand about the seasons of the year and their regularity.

- Children now make short-term plans for the future.

Early learning goals

- Children now find out about the past and present events in their own lives, and those of their families and other people they know.

Key words

developing a growing awareness of past, present and future

Learning story

Emily and Sarah, both aged forty-eight months, were seen in the role-play area engaged in an elaborate conversation about Christmas and grandmothers. They were talking on mobile phones. During their conversation, Emily told Sarah that she had not seen her grandmother since the Christmas party and that it would take three days to drive to her house. Sarah told Emily that her grandmother lived near her house and that she saw her at weekends with her cousins.

Activities

Learning through experience

- Practitioners can use old and new resources to support children's understanding of time and people of the past.

- Investigate and explore toys that practitioners, parents, grand-parents and great-grandparents played with when they were children and the toys children are playing with today.

- Add clothes to the role-play area that are modern or old fashioned.

- Talk to children about the different seasons, for example, how the weather changes in the summertime.

Look, listen and note

Practitioners need to be aware of what causes children to recall a repressed memory from their past.

Effective practice

Practitioners need to be aware of and support children to interpret information based on past events.

Teaching and learning

Children will be very knowledgeable about their families. Practitioners can talk to children about their home life and family experiences, using photographs, video recordings, pictures and familiar objects.

Planning and resourcing

- Plan a trip to the toy museum or transport museum to see how things develop and change over time.

- Visit stately homes to look at furniture, clothes and utensils.

- Plan trips to farms and allotments to see lambs and calves being born in the spring and vegetables being sown or growing – take photographs and visit again in the autumn.

Home links

Try to find out from parents what toys they played with as children. If they still have them ask them if they mind showing them to the children.

Additional resources

Practitioners need to support children by providing them with reference books of things from the past and for the present day, for example of pictures of clothes.

The EYFS principles

The EYFS principles enabling environments and positive relationships are integrated into this section on time. The learning environment is fundamental to development and learning as it can support children's exploration, particularly if there is a range of artefacts from different times to investigate. For example, when examining an old telephone with a dial, children will be able to compare similarities and differences and make predictions about how things work as well as talk about their own experiences of materials and those of others. Promoting positive relationships, parents will have key information about their children's experiences over time. Practitioners should use

this personal prior experience as a foundation upon which to develop and support children's understanding of the past and present time.

Children sometimes say the most random things which relate to events that have occurred in the past. Practitioners need to understand that it is the experience of doing that will help children to develop memories of the event. The role that the practitioner plays in supporting children to understand their own personal history is important.

5 | **Place**

Development matters

- Babies explore the space around them through movement of their hands and feet and by rolling their bodies around.

Key words

exploration through movement and senses

Learning story

Rahim, aged seven months, was observed outside on a blanket lying on his tummy. He rolled himself over on to his back and started to explore his feet; by bringing his leg up, he reached out to his feet and started to pull off his socks.

Activities

Learning through experience

Practitioners should provide opportunities for babies to explore different surroundings such as:

- outside;

- water and sand play;

- going for walks in the park enabling free movement of limbs to respond to what they see;

- exploring outside with items such as scarves and ribbons, practitioners gently caressing children's hands and faces with them ('swish swish' like the wind);

- exploring grass, leaves and different surfaces.

Look, listen and note

Look out for the deliberate movements which babies begin to make in order to aid their explorations.

Effective practice

- Practitioners need to understand that for the baby they are the primary resource.

- Practitioners should support babies' understanding of place by ensuring that they are able to see the world from different view points, for example by being held in someone's arms or being laid on their tummy or back.

Teaching and learning

Practitioners need to support babies in developing a perspective of their environment by providing activities at different levels. For example, once babies are mobile, introduce low ramps and steps. It is important that practitioners take babies outside to look at and explore their surroundings. Babies need concrete experience of place and space in order to explore.

Planning and resourcing

- Plan opportunities for babies to lie on their tummies, be held sitting up, to lie on their backs or to sit up unaided.

- Add ducks and washing toys to water play, sing songs and rhymes, add plastic and musical books.

- Practitioners might consider providing visual stimulation on different levels for babies who spend time in the prone, supine, sitting-up and standing positions.

Home links

Try to find out from parents which are babies' preferred positions to be held, fed or just to observe the world.

Additional resources

- Practitioners need to provide babies with resources that they can grasp and manipulate.

- Practitioners should consider using natural materials, such as shells.

From 8–20 months

Development matters

- Babies and toddlers now love to be outside and to closely observe what animals and people do.

Key words

active exploration

Learning story

Isobel, twenty months, was observed looking intently at a picture book with farm animals in. When she saw a picture of a cow she said 'moo' and when she saw the picture of the duck she said 'quack'. Isobel's childminder has a pond in her garden. They have been observing the frog spawn. When her mother collected her Isobel took her to the pond and pointed to the tadpole saying the words 'tadpole, one two.'

Activities

Learning through experience

Practitioners can sing songs and rhymes with children that link to people, things and animals children have seen – both in real life and in books and pictures – such as:

- The Wheels on the Bus
- Old Macdonald Had a Farm
- Roly Poly
- Sleep Bonnie Sleep
- Twinkle, Twinkle Little Star.

Also let babies explore grass and earth, give them buckets, spades and watering cans.

Look, listen and note

- Look out for babies' favourite place in the home or setting.

- Look out for what babies and toddlers are pointing at and listen to what they say.

Effective practice

Observation of babies' interest is essential for young babies as the practitioner is the richest resource for a baby's development.

Teaching and learning

Practitioners need to be aware of what interests children when they are going out for walks. Are children looking at patterns on the pavement, for example following a red or yellow line? Do they want to walk along low walls? Or are they just content standing on a drain cover?

Planning and resourcing

Practitioners should respond to children's interests they have previously identified and plan to take children out for walks and to the park. Add toys and buckets to wet or dry sand. Plan to take children on trips on a bus or train. Practitioners can arrange for different people to come into the nursery to talk to children such as a firefighter or police officer.

Home links

Ask parents to bring in a photograph of their baby's favourite place at home.

Additional resources

📖 Practitioners can also take photographs of different types of transportation and animals that they encounter and make simple books with children about the things they see on their walks.

📖 It is useful for practitioners to have resource and information books about transport, animals and different kinds of people.

From 16–26 months

Development matters

● Children are now curious about the environment.

Key words

exploration and investigation of surroundings

Learning story

Hugo, aged sixteen months, was observed in the garden. He was crawling on the grass on his hands and knees. When he reached the concrete area, he raised his bottom up so that his knees were no longer touching the concrete. Hugo crawled into the childminder's house.

Activities

Mental and physical involvement

- Going on a bug hunt in the garden or local park.

- Nature trail collecting leaves, twigs and cones.

- Digging earth and planting seeds.

Look, listen and note

- Look out for how children respond to the environment and what it is that interests them.

- Look out for how children use their knowledge of different surfaces such as soft and hard.

Effective practice

Practitioners must ensure that their outdoor environment is safe and stimulating and that children get to experience all kinds of weather.

Teaching and learning

Children need opportunities to explore different textures such as grass, earth and stone, shapes such as hills and slopes. Practitioners must ensure that they have access to natural and living things such as insects, birds and plants.

Planning and resourcing

Practitioners can support children's learning by having some natural items such as fir cones, twigs and leaves which the children can handle and explore inside.

Home links

Find out from parents what children like exploring outside, for example jumping into puddles or picking flowers.

Additional resources

Add resources books about animals, gardens and transportation.

Cousins, L. (2000) *Maisy's Bus,* London: Walker.

Crebbin, J. and Lambert, S. (1996) *The Train Ride,* London: Walker.

Hill, E. (1983) *Where's Spot,* London: Puffin.

Hindley, J. and Benedict, W. (1985) *The Big Red Bus,* London: Collins.

From 22–36 months

Development matters

- Children now enjoy playing with small-world models such as farms, toy garages, or train tracks.

Key words

re-enacting familiar situations

Learning story

Anna, aged thirty-six months, was observed assembling large groups of miniature furniture together outside of the dolls' house. Later she began to divide the furniture into much smaller groups, talking to herself continuously about what she was doing. Then she began to arrange the living-room furniture inside the house in one of the rooms upstairs.

Activities

Active learning

Practitioners can support children's understanding of their environment by:

- providing them with transportation, domestic and farm animal toys

- playing with toy cars and road layout with model traffic lights

- playing with trains, tracks and tunnels

- adding buckets and boats to water play

- taking a trip on a bus, boat or train

- playing with model rockets and spaceships

- adding domestic materials to role-play area such as dust pan and brushes, brooms, materials for delivering milk and posting letters and newspapers.

Look, listen and note

Look out for how children begin to play spontaneously with small world models such as a farm, garage or train track and use toys and animals to create their own stories. Listen out for what ideas they are exploring.

Effective practice

- Practitioners need to understand that children will invent situations in their play.

- Practitioners need to listen to the things that children say about what they are doing.

Teaching and learning

Practitioners should talk to children about their developing ideas and concepts and share stories with them that link to their play and explorations.

Planning and resourcing

Practitioners need to ensure that they have plenty of small world resources as children in this phase of development will play near other children but their play tends to be solitary.

Home links

Try to find out if parents have photographs of children from visits to places, such as the beach, farm, a trip to the zoo or photographs taken in another country.

Additional resources

Campbell, R. (1997) *Dear Zoo,* London: Puffin.

Carle, E. (1974) *The Very Hungry Caterpillar,* London: Puffin.

List of websites for nature studies

www.bbc.co.uk/springwatch (Allows you to view British wildlife using a webcam.)

www.bbc.co.uk/breathingplaces (Supports you to create and care for nature friendly green spaces where you live by typing in your post code.)

www.bat.org.uk (Provides fascinating facts about these animals, what they eat and what they do throughout the year.)

www.dragonflysoc.org.uk (Gives practitioners information about dragonflies and their natural habitats in the United Kingdom.)

www.galaxypic.com/glowworms (Information about glow-worms living in caves around the world.)

www.butterfly-conservation-org.uk (Provides you with information on wild butterflies, moths and their habitats.)

www.britishwildlife.com (Links to wildlife magazine, which looks at all aspects of British wildlife and nature conservation.)

From 30–50 months

Development matters

- Children now show interest in the world in which they live.
- Children now comment and ask questions about where they live and the natural world around them.

Key words

exploring the natural world

Learning story

John-Paul, aged fifty months, was observed during a class outing to the river Thames. He was interested in the difference between the ducks, geese, swans and baby goslings. He told the practitioners that he had photographs of ducks, geese and swans at home but he did not have any photographs of the baby ones.

Activities

Making connections

Practitioners must plan activities with children that involve them:

- visiting their local rivers, woods, farms and parks
- looking at birds' nests in trees or in picture books
- feeding the animals (chickens, ducks, ponies, etc.)
- following nature trails in the woods.

Look, listen and note

Practitioners should listen carefully to what children have to say and think about their environment.

Effective practice

Practitioners need to provide children with outdoor experiences which will enhance their understanding of the world and help them to make sense of open and built-up surroundings. Practitioners have a key role in extending children's vocabulary and understanding.

Teaching and learning

Practitioners should consider providing children with raw materials such as photographs and posters so that they can recreate their experience.

Planning and resourcing

Practitioners should plan visits to meet different people and experience new places, for example: city farms, country parks or museums.

Home links

Ask parents about children's experiences outside. Build on this as a way of increasing children's individual awareness of the environment.

Additional resources

Blackstone, S. (2002) *There's a Cow in the Cabbage Patch,* illustrated by C. Beaton, Littlehampton: Barefoot Books.

Burningham, J. (2001) *Mr Gumpy's Outing,* London: Random House.

Fraser, S. (2005) *Grandma's Saturday Soup,* illustrated by D. Brazell, London: Mantra.

From 40–60 months

Development matters

- Children notice differences between features of the local environment.

Early learning goals

- Children observe, find out about and identify features in the place they live and the natural world.

- Children find out about the environment and talk about features they like and dislike.

Learning story

Joe, aged forty-eight months, and Emma, aged forty-six months, were observed engaged in drawing their home and talking about what they were doing. Joe told Emma that he was going to live with his granny in Australia and that he would go swimming every day. Emma told Joe that she would come and live with him. Both children's drawings included a yellow sun, blue sky, green grass, brown soil, a house frame with a door and windows.

Activities

Sustained shared thinking

Practitioners can make simple maps with children to support them in developing an understanding of a different place. Also include:

- activities which involve children creating their own environment;

- activities that involve children finding out how many post boxes there are, the different names of shops and roads, etc., in their neighbourhood;

- looking at the bus, tram or train routes.

Look, listen and note

- Listen to what children are saying about what they see.

- Are they aware of patterns, shapes and sizes?

Effective practice

Practitioners need to understand that children's knowledge and understanding of place and their surroundings will be embedded in their play and explorations. Having a knowledge of place opens children up to the world.

Teaching and learning

It is the role of practitioners to identify and use this information to extend and support children's understanding of place and space.

Planning and resourcing

Practitioners need to plan meaningful experiences to introduce children to the wider world, using maps, photographs, resource books and information about where children's families may have originated.

Home links

Try to find out from parents about the different types of buildings that children live in, for example, a flat or house, caravan or skyscraper.

Add environmental resources such as small world people, transportation toys, animals and sign and play mats.

The EYFS principles

The EYFS themes enabling environment and positive relationship are at the heart of this section on place. The enabling environment is, in some respects, the starting point from which babies and young children develop their unique perception of their place and space. As babies become mobile they begin to investigate their immediate surroundings. It is this exploration that will lead babies and young children into eventually exploring the wider world. Parents will have information about how their children may associate sounds and smells with different places. This information is key to engaging and developing children's understanding of place.

Practitioners can put principles into practice when they plan trips and outings for babies and young children. Trips to the shops, park and pet shop will all support practitioners in offering children concrete first-hand experiences which will enhance their development and learning.

The learning stories and activities give practitioners a vehicle for teaching and learning through offering children meaningful learning experiences to support and extend their knowledge and understanding of the world.

6 | Communities

For children, being special to someone and well cared for is vital for their physical, social and emotional health and well-being. [...] Children learn to be strong and independent from a base of loving and secure relationships with parents and/or a key person.

(DfES 2007a: 9)

From birth–11 months

Development matters

- Babies concentrate intently on faces and enjoy interaction with those around them.
- Babies can form attachments to people who are special for them.

Key words

relationships, learning and needs

Learning story

Rahim, aged seven months, was observed looking at a mirror book called *Baby Einstein* with his childminder. He stared intently at his mirror image before he put the book into his mouth and began to suck it.

Activities

Play and exploration

Practitioners can support babies to develop their attachments by:

- making a photo album with photographs of babies and members of their family;

- singing songs and rhymes with babies, including photos as props.

Look, listen and note

Look out for how babies begin to show that they know that they are part of a family, the setting and special to someone.

Effective practice

For babies, the practitioner is their richest support resource in their learning process. Practitioners need to create a homely atmosphere in which babies feel at home and have a sense of place. Practitioners should support babies to feel comfortable in their own skin. Practitioners can do this by:

- responding to babies needs;

- following their individual interests;

- awareness of individual likes and dislikes;

- developing genuine partnerships with parents.

Teaching and learning

Practitioners need to be aware of the impact that interaction, talk and play have on development and learning. The relationships which babies have, especially with a key person, are central to development and learning. Babies are dependent on key persons to:

- provide developmentally appropriate experiences

- understand their relationships, learning and meet their developing needs.

Planning and resourcing

Practitioners must plan time to talk to parents about their observations of their children as well as to share information about what they know about the child's interests, play patterns, relationships and needs. Practitioners should also plan to involve parents in their children's early development and learning.

Training

The National Children's Bureau has developed excellent training materials to help practitioners in their work with parents. *Parents, Early Years and Learning* provides a framework in which early years practitioners can build genuine relationships with parents through involving them in their children's early learning. For more information go to www.ncb.org.uk.

Home links

There is nothing quite like the smell of home cooking. Practitioners could ask parents to bring in traditional foods from home so that the babies gain knowledge of food from different cultures.

Additional resources

Gerhardt, S. (2006) *Why Love Matters, How Affection Shapes a Baby's Brain,* London: Routledge.

Grant, T. (2007) *Baby's Day,* London: Walker.

—— (2007) *Let's Play,* London: Walker.

Whalley, M. and the Pen Green Centre Team (2001) *Involving Parents in Their Children's Learning,* London: Paul Chapman.

Whalley, M. and Bruce, T. (1994) *Learning to Be Strong, Setting Up a Neighbourhood Service for under-Fives and Their Families,* London: Hodder & Stoughton.

See www.standards.dfes.gov.uk for links to Parents as Partners in Early Learning (PPEL).

From 8–20 months

Development matters

- Babies and toddlers now recognise special people, such as family, friends or their key person.

- Babies and toddlers will now show an interest in the social life around them.

Key words

identity and self-awareness

Learning story

Isobel, aged eighteen months, was observed sharing a book with her child-minder that she had selected for herself. Isobel seemed to be involved and engaged with the meaning of the story as she responded playfully by touching the feely patches and turning over the pages.

Activities

Adult involvement

Some of the ways practitioners can support children to develop a sense of themselves are by:

- singing relevant songs and rhymes, for example, 'Ten Tiny Fingers, Ten Tiny Toes', or 'Head, Shoulders, Knees and Toes';

- sharing stories;

- offering babies and toddlers different types and patterns of fabric, boxes, shoes, hats, scarves, bags and beads to explore and to make individual choices.

Look, listen and note

Look out for how babies and toddlers communicate verbally and non-verbally.

Effective practice

An important part of the practitioner's role is to support babies and toddlers in developing a sense of identity, a sense of self. We know that babies and toddlers prefer familiar people to strangers. Practitioners have a key role to play in helping babies and toddlers to feel positive about their gender, race, culture, language and what they can do.

'Young children are vulnerable. They learn to be independent by having someone to depend upon' (Abbott et al. 2003: 9).

Babies and toddlers will grow in confidence and in their own abilities when they are in an environment where they are given time and space to do things by themselves.

Teaching and learning

Practitioners should nurture babies' and toddlers' sense of self by giving them responsibilities as individuals and as part of a group. It is important that practitioners organise routines so that babies and toddlers have opportunities to become involved and engaged with others and as part of a group.

Planning and resourcing

Practitioners should ensure that resources and experiences offered to babies and toddlers reflect the diversity of their experiences and cultures. Practitioners should pay particular attention to how they resource the role-play area. Items such as cooking utensils, Turkish coffeepots, Chinese teapots, chopsticks, woks, rice bowls, Dutch pots, and spaghetti forks will support babies and toddlers to integrate their existing knowledge and experience into new imaginative possibilities through their play and explorations.

Home links

- Ask parents to record some familiar stories and songs that the baby likes for use at the setting.

- Practitioners could also invite parents into the setting to read or tell stories.

From 16–26 months

Development matters

- Children are now curious about people and show interest in stories about themselves and their family.

- Children will enjoy hearing stories about themselves, their families and other people.

- Children now like to play alongside other children.

Key words

recalling and retelling stories and significant events

Learning story

Joshua, aged twenty-six months, was observed looking at wedding photographs in which he was a pageboy at his auntie Jackie's wedding. He playfully told the practitioner that his aunt got married and his Daddy got drunk. Joshua became quite serious and had on a stern expression. He said that his mummy was cross.

Activities

Learning through experience

Invite children to bring in objects from home to show and tell.

Look, listen and note

Look out for how children become aware that they are alike but different from others.

Effective practice

- Children need to feel accepted and valued by practitioners if they are to become independent and develop a meaningful understanding of difference in themselves and others.

- Practitioners can support children in developing an understanding of difference when they provide them with materials and resources that reflect, for example:

  - children wearing glasses;
  - children with hair, without hair, etc.;
  - children with different types of hair, clothes, skins and lifestyles.

Teaching and learning

- Practitioners have a responsibility to answer children's questions about difference.

- Practitioners need to be mindful that the child will come with knowledge and understanding of their own families.

- Practitioners have a significant and important role to play when interacting with and responding to children's questions about themselves and their families.

Planning and resourcing

- Practitioners need to plan to take children on outings in the local community.

- Practitioners could consider commissioning local theatre groups to act out stories and rhymes.

- Provide children with dressing up clothes. For example, smart Sunday clothes should be available if children have experience of going to church.

- Practitioners should consider the needs of both boys and girls.

- Cultural clothing and food, wigs and easily attachable hairpieces could be added to role-play area.

Home links

Ask parents to let children bring in an object from home to 'show and tell'.

Additional resources

Bailey, D. (1999) *Families,* photos by S. Huszar, Toronto: Annick Press.

Lee, S. and Lewis, T. (2006) *Please, Baby, Please,* illustrated by K. Nelson, New York: Simon & Schuster.

From 22–36 months

Development matters

- Children are interested in others and their families.

- Children have a sense of their own immediate family and relations.

- Children begin to make their own friends.

Key words

respecting diversity

Learning story

Kai was observed seated at the table in the role-play area, with two other children, Wesley, aged twenty-eight months, and Leah, aged thirty-one months. Kai pretended to be eating yoghurt. He asked Leah for toast, which she pretended to make for him. She then had a conversation on the telephone with the Doctor. Wesley held a doll in his arms and pretended to feed it a slice of pretend bread. As Kai left the table the other children followed him and they all hid under the large cushions in the book area.

Activities

Play and exploration

One way in which practitioners can support children to begin to under-stand their own and other people's culture is by making 'all about me' boxes. Give the children empty shoe boxes and ask them to decorate and then fill their own box, including photographs of children as babies, their families, their friends, pets, favourite foods and places, photographs of them involved in play. Let children bring in something from home. Practitioners can talk to children about the contents of their box and ask meaningful questions based on their knowledge of the child.

Look, listen and note

Look out for the many different verbal and non-verbal ways in which children express their ideas and what they know about their families and friends through their role play.

Effective practice

- Practitioners should support children in developing an under-standing of themselves and others.

- For children, being social is fundamental to development and learn-ing. Practitioners can observe children's social skills when they play and make close friendships with other children.

- Practitioners must talk to children about the differences in gender and culture, language and disability.

- At times, practitioners may need to model appropriate social beha-viours for some children, perhaps playing alongside them, helping them identify and develop the skills they need for initiating and sustaining friendships.

Teaching and learning

Practitioners can support children to take on different roles during role play by relating the activities provided for individual and group experiences. In this way, the practitioners create a learning environment in which children can practise and enjoy what they know and can do by themselves and with others. Abbott and Langston point out that 'The environment, then, is more than simply the planned space in the setting, it is everything that is encountered from the point of entry to the setting to the point of departure' (2005: 70).

Planning and resourcing

Practitioners need to ensure that the resources and materials in the role-play area connect directly to children's first-hand experiences. Practitioners must plan to support children in both sharing and celebrating their unique identities and developing an awareness and acceptance of difference.

Home links

- Try to find out from parents what their children have for breakfast, lunch and tea at home.

- Ask them to bring in the empty cereal boxes or yoghurt cartons and add these materials to your role-play area.

Additional resources

Abbott, L. and Langston, A. (2005) *Birth to Three Matters: Supporting the Framework of Effective Practice,* Maidenhead: Open University Press.

Cainizares, S. (1999) *Feelings,* New York: Scholastic.

📖 Edwards, C., Gandini, L. and Forman, G. (eds) (1998) *The Hundred Languages of Children: The Reggio Emilia Approach – Advanced Reflections,* 2nd edn, London: Ablex.

📖 Lindon, J. (2000) *Helping Babies and Toddlers to Learn: A Guide to Good Practice with under-Threes,* London: The National Early Years Network.

From 30–50 months

Development matters

- Children now express feelings about significant personal events.
- Children will describe events for family or friends.
- Children now enjoy imaginative role-play with peers.
- Children now show interest in different occupations and ways of life.

Key word

learning together

Learning story

Joe, aged forty-eight months, and Emma, aged forty-six months, were observed involved in a complex imaginative game about taking the baby to the doctor's in the role-play area. Emma played the role of the mother and Joe the doctor. Both children were dressed in dressing-up clothes. Joe was wearing a white jacket, he had his stethoscope around his neck and a case with other medical equipment in it. Emma was wearing a red dress and a straw hat. Both children seemed to be fully engaged in their roles. Emma took her baby out of the buggy; she hugged and held it whilst she told Joe that the baby kept being sick. Joe examined the baby by first putting the thermometer behind the baby's ears, using the stethoscope on the baby's chest and back. Joe told Emma that he would need to take some blood from both of

them, which he pretended to do. He then put plasters on to both Emma and the baby. Emma left the doctor's with the baby. After a little while, Joe took off his coat. Emma returned, insisting that she wanted to be the doctor. Joe agreed to change roles and be the dad.

Activities

Learning through experience

Practitioners can support children to understand and share their cultures and beliefs with others by inviting children to:

- make 'all about me' books which celebrate their cultures and beliefs, include photographs and artefacts from their home culture

- play puppet games with children to help them recreate and mentally represent the emotions of other people and themselves.

Support children to act out and express themselves through exploring feelings such as anger, sadness, happiness and fear.

Look, listen and note

Look out for how children begin to play collaboratively in role play with their peers and begin to share stories from home.

Effective practice

- Practitioners must support children in understanding how they and others might feel about different personal events such a wedding, divorce, death, birth or move.

- It is important that practitioners acknowledge children's feelings and support them by naming their feelings when they are experiencing them.

- Practitioners need to understand that children will cope with their feeling and emotions when they are in touch with them.

Teaching and learning

Practitioners can talk to children about the important events and experiences in their lives. In doing this, practitioners will need to reflect on their own attitudes, values and beliefs. This is fundamental if practitioners are to acknowledge, value and respect cultures and traditions different from their own.

Planning and resourcing

- Practitioners need to find a variety of ways of documenting children's play and explorations in the setting.

- Practitioners should add role-play clothes of male nurses, nurse, medical kits, surgeon gowns, doctor's coat, paramedic and ambulance technician coats, police officers and fire fighters.

Home links

Practitioners need to try to find out information about the children's cultures and traditions at home so that they can accurately reflect everyone's culture within the setting.

Additional resources

- Hutchins, P. (1997) *Titch,* London: Red Fox.
- Brownjohn, E. (2007) *All Kinds of Feelings,* London: Tango.

From 40–60 months

Development matters

- Children gain awareness of the cultures and beliefs of others.

- Children feel a sense of belonging to their own community and place.

Early learning goals

- Children begin to know about their own cultures and beliefs and those of other people.

Key words

culture, practices and beliefs

Learning story

Hannah, aged forty-two months, and Nathaniel, aged fifty-eight months, were observed at the lunch table having a discussion about how to make the sign of the cross. Nathaniel demonstrated to Hannah. He used the correct words that reflected the significance of his actions. Hannah insisted that Nathaniel was doing it wrong. She said, 'It is like this', using words and actions to demonstrate: 'It is from my head to my heart, from my shoulder to my shoulder.' 'No, no, no,' Nathaniel insisted, repeating his demonstration.

Activities

Learning through experience

Practitioners need to plan activities in which children can talk about and handle religious and cultural artefacts. They can also provide:

- music and movement sessions both inside and outside where children can express themselves through dance and movements – to, for example, Irish, Caribbean and Scottish music;

- cooking activities that reflect the cultures and traditions in the setting.

Look, listen and note

Look out for how children demonstrate their developing knowledge and understanding of religious practices.

Effective practice

Practitioners must support and extend children's learning about themselves and other people in ways that are supportive to their individual development and understanding.

Teaching and learning

Practitioners need to find out about and develop an understanding of the significance and importance of religion for children and their families.

Planning and resourcing

- Practitioners must provide children with resources and materials that support their understanding of religious practices and beliefs. Resources such as the Bible, the Holy Cross, the Virgin Mary, plaques, the Qur'an, prayer mats, Ganesh, Buddha, Greek Orthodox religious symbols and Jewish candelabra will support practitioners in introducing children to different cultures and religions.

- Practitioners should also add clothing and accessories that reflect the diversity of cultures within the setting. For example, costume jewellery or Henna for Eid.

- Practitioners must provide children with resource books which look at religious places of worship as well as resource books which look at tradition and ritual.

- Practitioners need to consider providing children with books, foods for role play, wigs and other play equipment.

- Practitioners may want to consider commissioning a theatre to perform stories and songs from other cultures.

- Practitioners may also want to consider getting involved in community events such as carnivals and fêtes.

Home links

Ask parent to tape some traditional music from their culture to use in music sessions with children.

Additional resources

- Ashley, B. and Thompson, C. (2003) *Double the Love,* London: Orchard.

- Buckley, H. (1997) *Grandfather and I,* illustrated by J. Ormerod, London: Puffin.

- Davis, M. (2003) *Movement and Dance in Early Years,* 2nd edn, London: Paul Chapman.

- Lindon, J. (2005) *Understanding World Religions in Early Years Practice,* London: Hodder & Stoughton.

- Role-play clothes are available from East–West (www.eastwestedu cation.org).

The EYFS principles

The EYFS themes of 'positive relationships' and 'enabling environments' are intrinsic in this section on communities. Positive relationships with parents enable practitioners to extend children's experiences and understanding of the world. Enabling environments should support children to learn through play and relationships with other children. Ultimately, play allows children to recreate their experiences imaginatively. Children are unique and will use various different ways to communicate meaning through the process of their play.

When children are encouraged to ask the right questions, they begin to discover solutions for themselves actively and independently. All aspects of knowledge and understanding of the world are used by children when they begin to make connections about their community. Positive relationships with parents can be used as part of how practitioners create a powerful enabling learning environment.

The learning stories and activities give practitioners a vehicle for teaching and learning through a range of practical activities as well as opportunities to reflect on practice, resources and provision. Practitioners need to understand that children must go beyond their perceived limits when acquiring the knowledge to connect ideas and understanding of the world.

Bibliography

Arnold, C. (2003) *Observing Harry: Child Development and Learning 0–5,* Maidenhead: Open University Press; McGraw-Hill Education.

—— (2005) *Child Development and Learning 2–5 Years: Georgia's Story,* Hodder & Stoughton. London.

Athey, C. (1990) *Extending Thoughts in Young Children: a Parent-Teacher Partnership,* London: Paul Chapman.

Brainerd, C. (1978) *Piaget's Theory of Intelligence,* Englewood Cliffs, NJ: Prentice-Hall.

Bruce, T. (1987) *Early Childhood Education,* London: Hodder & Stoughton.

—— (1991) *Time to Play in Early Childhood Education and Care,* London: Hodder & Stoughton.

—— (1996) *Helping Young Children to Play,* London: Hodder & Stoughton.

—— (1997) *Early Childhood Education,* London: Hodder & Stoughton.

—— (2001) *Learning through Play: Babies, Toddlers and the Foundation Years,* London: Hodder & Stoughton.

—— (2005) *Early Childhood Education,* 3rd edn, London: Hodder Arnold.

Bruce, T. and Meggitt, C. (2002) *Child Care & Education,* 3rd edn, London: Hodder & Stoughton.

—— (2005) *Child Care and Education,* 2nd edn, London: Hodder & Stoughton.

Bruner, J. (1967) *Towards a Theory of Instruction,* Cambridge, Mass.: Harvard University Press.

Catherwood, D. (1999) 'New Views on the Young Brain', *Contemporary Issues in Early Childhood,* 1 (1): 23–35.

Davis, M. (2003) *Movement and Dance in Early Childhood,* 2nd edn, London: Paul Chapman.

Department for Education and Skills (2000) *The Curriculum Guidance for the Foundation Stage,* Nottingham: DfES Publications.

—— (2002) *Birth to Three Matters Framework,* London: DfES Publications.

—— (2004a) *Every Child Matters: Change for Children,* London: DfES Publications.

—— (2004b) *Choice for Parents, the Best Start for Children: A Ten Year Strategy for Childcare,* Norwich: Department for Education and Skills.

—— (2006) *The Childcare Act 2006: (Provision of Information to Parents (England) Regulations 2007),* London: HMSO.

—— (2007a) *Early Years Foundation Stage,* Nottingham: Department for Education and Skills Publications.

—— (2007b) *Statutory Framework for the Early Years Foundation Stage,* Nottingham: DfES.

—— (2007c) *Every Parent Matters: Helping You Help Your Child,* Nottingham: Department for Education and Skills Publications.

—— (2007d) *Practice Guidance for the Early Years Foundation Stage: Setting the Standards for Learning Development and Care for Children from Birth to Five,* Nottingham: Department for Education and Skills Publications.

Department of Education and Employment (DfEE) (2000) *QCA/DfES Curriculum Guidance for the Foundation Stage,* Nottingham: Department of Education and Employment.

Duffy, B. (1998) *Supporting Creativity and Imagination in the Early Years,* Buckingham: Open University Press.

—— (2002) *Supporting Creativity and Imagination in the Early Years,* Buckingham: Open University Press.

—— (2005) 'Creativity Matters', in L. Abbott and A. Langston, *Birth to Three Matters: Supporting the Framework of Effective Practice*, Maidenhead: Open University Press.

Easen, P., Kendall, P. and Shaw, J. (1992) 'Parents and Educators: Dialogue and Developing through Partnership', *Children and Society,* 6: 288.

Edgington, M. (2003) *The Great Outdoors: Developing Children's Learning Through Outdoor Provision,* 2nd edn, London: British Association for Early Childhood Education.

Gopnik, A., Meltzoff, A. and Kuhl, P. (1999) *How Babies Think: The Science of Childhood,* London: Weidenfeld & Nicolson.

Gross, R. (2005) *Psychology: The Science of Mind and Behaviour,* 5th edn, London: Hodder & Stoughton.

Gura, P. and Bruce, T. (1992) *Exploring Learning: Young Children and Blockplay,* London: Paul Chapman.

Harner, L. (1981) 'Children Talk About the Time and Aspect of Action', *Child Development,* 52 (2): 498–506.

Hohmann, M. and Weikart, D. (2002) *Educating Young Children,* 2nd edn, Ypsilanti, Mich.: High/Scope Press.

Holt, J. (1989) *Learning All the Time,* Ticknall: Education Now.

Isaacs, S. (1968) *The Nursery Years,* London: Routledge & Kegan Paul.

—— (1981) *The Educational Value of the Nursery School,* London: The British Association for Early Childhood Education.

Johnston, J. (2005) *Early Exploration in Science: Exploring Primary Science and Technology,* Maidenhead: Open University Press.

Katz, L. and Chard, S. C. (1989) *Engaging Children's Minds: A Project Approach,* Norwood, NJ: Ablex Publishing Corporation.

Kilton, N. (1994) *The Excellence of Play,* Buckingham: Open University Press.

Laevers, F. (1994) *The Leuven Involvement Scale for Young Children,* Leuven: Centre for Experiential Education.

Laevers, F., Vandenbussche, E., Kog, M. and Depondt, L. (1997) *A Process Oriented Child Monitoring System for Young Children,* Leuven: Centre for Experiential Education.

Leach, P. (1977) *Baby and Child: From Birth to Age Five,* Harmondsworth: Penguin.

Lindon, J. (2001) *Understanding Children's Play,* Cheltenham: Nelson Thornes.

—— (2003) *What Does It Mean to Be Three?* Leamington Spa: Step Forward Publishing.

Lloyd, P. and Fernyhough, C. (1999) *Critical Assessment of Leading Psychologists,* London: Taylor & Francis.

Malaguzzi, L. (1996) 'History, Ideas and Basic Philosophy', in C. Nutbrown (ed.), *Respectful Educators, Capable Learners: Children's Rights and Early Education,* London: Paul Chapman, p. 61.

Manning-Morton, J. and Thorp, M. (2003) *Key Times for Play; The First Three Years,* Maidenhead: Open University Press.

Matthews, J. (2003) *Drawing and Painting: Children and Visual Representation,* London: Paul Chapman.

McMillan, M. (1930) *The Nursery School,* London: Dent.

Meade, A. and Cubey, P. (1995) *Thinking Children: Learning About Schemas,* Wellington: New Zealand Council for Educational Research and Institute for Early Childhood Studies, Wellington College of Education/Victoria University of Wellington.

Meek, M. (1985) 'Play and Paradoxes: Some Considerations of Imagination and Language', in G. Wells and J. Nicholls (eds), *Language and Learning: An Interactional Perspective,* Buckingham: Open University Press.

Minett, P. (1985) *Child Care & Development,* London: John Murray.

Montessori, M. (1912) *The Montessori Method,* London: Heinemann.

Moyles, J. (ed.) (2005) *The Excellence of Play,* Buckingham: Open University Press.

Newton, D. P. and Newton, L. D. (2000) 'Do Teachers Support Causal Understanding Through Their Discourse When Teaching Primary Science?' *British Educational Research Journal,* 26 (5): 559–613.

—— (2000) 'Do Teachers Support Causal Understanding Through Their Discourse When Teaching Primary Science?', *British Educational Research Journal,* 26 (5): 559–613.

Nutbrown, C. (1999) *Threads of Thinking,* London: Paul Chapman.

Ouvry, M. (2005) *Exercising Muscles and Minds: Outdoor Play and the Early Years Curriculum,* London: National Children's Bureau.

Phillips, J. (1969) *The Origins of Intellect: Piaget's Theory,* San Francisco, Calif.: W. H. Freeman and Company.

Piaget, J. (1927) *The Child's Concept of Time*, London: Routledge & Kegan Paul.

—— (1932) *The Moral Judgement of the Child,* London: Routledge & Kegan Paul.

—— (1955) *The Language and Thought of the Child,* London: Routledge & Kegan Paul.

—— (1962) *Play, Dreams and Imitation in Childhood,* New York: Norton.

Post, J. and Hohmann, M. (2000) *Tender Care and Early Learning, Supporting Families and Toddlers in Childcare Settings,* Ypsilanti, Mich.: High/Scope Press.

Rinaldi, C. (2005) 'Dialogue on Education', Lecture, 3 May, The Preschool and Infant Toddler Centre of Reggio Emilia.

Selleck, D. and Griffin, S. (2001) 'Quality for the Under Threes', in G. Pugh (ed.), *Contemporary Issues in the Early Years,* 2nd edn, London: Paul Chapman.

Sheridan, M. (1975) *Children's Developmental Progress from Birth to Five Years: Stycar Sequences,* Slough: NFER Publishing.

Shonkoff, J. and Phillips, D. (2000) *From Neurons to Neighbourhoods: The Science of Early Childhood Development,* Washington, DC: National Academy Press.

Shore, R. (1997) *Rethinking the Brain: New Insights into Early Development,* New York: Families and Work Institute.

Singer, D. and Singer, J. (1990) *The House of Make Believe,* Cambridge, Mass.: Harvard University Press.

Siraj-Blatchford, I. (2000) 'Early Childhood Pedagoy: Practice, Principles and Research', in P. Mortimore (ed.), *Understanding Pedagogy and its Impact on Learning,* London: Paul Chapman.

Siraj-Blatchford, I. and Clarke, P. (2000) *Supporting Identity, Diversity and Language in Early Years,* Buckingham: Open University Press.

Smilansky, S. (1968) *The Effects of Socio-Dramatic Play on Disadvantaged Pre-school Children,* New York: John Wiley.

Solomon, J. (1994) 'Towards a Notion of Home Culture: Science Education in the Home', *British Educational Research Journal,* 20 (5): 565–77.

Steiner, R. (1996) *The Education of the Child,* New York: Anthroposophical Press.

Sylvia, K., Melhuish, E., Sammons, P., Siraj-Blatchford, I., Taggart, B. and Elliot, K. (2003) *Effective Provision of Pre-school Education (EPPE) Project,* London: Institute of Education, University of London.

Vygotsky, L. S. (1967) 'Play and Its Role in the Mental Development of the Child', *Soviet Psychology,* 5 (3): 6–18.

—— (1978) *Mind in Society: The Development of Higher Psychological Processes,* Cambridge Mass.: MIT Press.

—— (1986) *Thought and Language*, Cambridge, Mass.: MIT Press.

—— (1962) *Thought and Language*, Cambridge, Mass.: MIT Press.

Whitehead, M. (2002) *Developing Language and Literacy with Young Children*, 2nd edn, London: Paul Chapman.

Wood, E. and Bennett, E. (1997) 'The Rhetoric and Reality of Play', *Early Years*, 17: 22–7.